Prehistoric
Mining and
Allied Industries

Studies in Archaeological Science

Consulting editor G. W. DIMBLEBY

Prehistoric Mining and Allied Industries

R. SHEPHERD

1980

ACADEMIC PRESS

A Subsidiary of Harcourt Brace Jovanovich, Publishers
LONDON   NEW YORK   TORONTO   SYDNEY   SAN FRANCISCO

ACADEMIC PRESS INC. (LONDON) LTD
24/28 Oval Road,
London NW1 7DX

United States Edition published by
ACADEMIC PRESS INC.
111 Fifth Avenue
New York, New York 10003

Copyright © 1980 by
ACADEMIC PRESS INC. (LONDON) LTD.

British Library Cataloguing in Publication Data

Shepherd, R
    Prehistoric mining and allied industries. – (Studies in archaeological science).
    1. Mineral industries, Prehistoric – Europe
    I. Title   II. Series
    622'.0936   GN803   80–41228

    ISBN 0–12–639480–6

G N
8 0 3
S 4 8

Filmset by Willmer Bros. Ltd., Birkenhead
Printed in Great Britain by
Fletcher & Son Ltd., Norwich

Contents

568478

Preface

I suppose the decision to become involved in the writing of this book was made a few years ago when I was asked for information concerning prehistoric mining. It was presumably expected that I, as a mining engineer, would have a broad knowledge of the subject, i.e. mining before the dawn of history. The prehistory of mining and indeed the more recent history of the industry is not taught in schools of mining and the romance of the past can be regarded as an interest outside the formal curriculum. I knew that some of the desired information was available, even if far from complete, in archaeological journals dating back to the middle of the last century, but there was no standard textbook on the subject and even the works by eminent prehistorians devote scarcely more than a single page to mining and mostly an odd sentence at appropriate stages in the discourse. When we look at ancient history as written by classical authors we have a wealth of detail at our disposal, for writers such as Pliny with his *Natural History*, Strabo, Tacitus and many others cover the subject of ancient mining to various degrees even if not always with the greatest accuracy. Later books, devoted essentially to ancient mining, tend to dismiss, like those of present day prehistorians, the earliest aspects of mining in a few pages.

I have had an interest in prehistory for many years and I understand from professional archaeologists, with whom I have come into contact, that a book on prehistoric mining would fulfil a need and they have given me every encouragement to write this work which, by a mining engineer, might give a new dimension to this aspect of archaeology and mining.

This then constitutes the reason for attempting to write this book, the absence of a specialized survey of prehistoric mining. I suppose it is customary for an author to say at the outset that the implication of such a decision presents a forbidding picture. Usual reasons are given and one of these is that the number of books on the market on a particular subject is great hence the appropriate apologies are offered for inflicting yet another on the reader. In my case the problem is exactly the reverse of this, as I have indicated, for all or most of the available information is disseminated in journals and transactions of learned societies throughout the world, and is often not readily available for reference.

An undertaking of this nature is in certain respects unique. Originality is a very difficult objective to achieve. Very few sites are available for inspection or photography and most, in fact nearly all, are backfilled and nothing remains of the original excavation to be seen. So in most cases we must depend on old reports, papers and articles. All that is possible is interpretation on the basis of facts as presented by the original workers, the inspection of museum exhibits and discussions with the original investigators whenever possible. To a certain extent this is valid also for most archaeological projects, but habitation sites, etc. are being discovered at a far greater rate than are mines, new information is forthcoming and new theories evolved so the problems are not so significant.

O. Davies, in his *Roman Mines in Europe* (1935), refers to the problem of poor evidence for ancient mines and suggests that archaeologists must not demand so strict a standard as in other branches of their disciplines. If this is true for ancient Greek and Roman mines it is still more valid for prehistoric workings. Another problem might be that prehistoric mining has been within the scope of the archaeologist and it is only within recent times that mining engineers have been consulted, i.e. on the Continent of Europe and been invited to take an interest in the interpretation of finds from relevant mining sites. There does appear to be a need for the involvement of mining engineers in the specialist fields of prehistoric and ancient mining if the maximum possible useful information is to be obtained from excavation.

The aim of the work is to describe and discuss prehistoric mines and to consider the areas from which early man obtained his supplies of raw materials. However, to confine the book to these aspects would result in a very narrow coverage and many no less important facts would have to be ignored. The scope is therefore widened to cover the relevant cultural features, way of life of prehistoric miners, types and treatment of materials and problems of recognition and dating. The relevant chapters or appendices are not intended to be exhaustive and indeed can be omitted by the appropriate specialist. I hope, however, that the general reader or student, who is not conversant with such aspects of the subject will find them useful.

Scope of treatment in terms of chronology and geography was somewhat more difficult to define. Prehistory ended when writing appeared on the scene, but when did this occur? In Britain it might be said that the Romans, following the invasions of Caesar in 55 and 54 BC, and the conquest by Claudius in AD 43 brought in literacy. History probably began in Britain in AD 45, in Gaul 58 BC and in southern France in 121 BC. But the classical world knew something about prehistoric peoples in Britain as long ago as 325 BC. It is said that a Greek merchant, Pytheus, in that year travelled to Britain, returned home and wrote on the mode of living, housing, etc. of the Iron Age peoples in these islands. Late classical writers were sceptical of Pytheus, but archaeological excavations have verified many of the facts as set down by the early traveller.

The geographical boundaries were considered later and it was soon realized that the scope of the book must be limited to the West, chiefly owing to the lack of published material in English, French or German in eastern Europe and Asia. The general boundaries are therefore: in the North, Britain and Scandinavia, in the South, the Mediterranean, in the East, Poland and West Russia and in the West, Spain and Portugal. There has been occasional departure across these boundaries when it has appeared to be necessary to illustrate a particular point.

Mining, with all its variations, is probably the oldest industry and commenced when prehistoric man first "grubbed" in hillsides and at outcrops for his supplies of rough stone and flint to make rudimentary tools and weapons. As Bartholomew and Birdsell (1953, American Anthropologist 55) succintly write, "man is the only mammal which is constantly dependent on tools for survival". Furthermore mining is basic to human survival and its culture and has been so since man first appeared on the earth.

This consideration of the background and scope of the book will I trust provide the justification for the content and treatment and it is hoped will fill some gap in archaeological publications if not in those of mining.

May 1980   Robert Shepherd
The Paddock
Coldharbour Lane
Thorpe
Egham, Surrey

Acknowledgements

Before and during the process of writing this book I had discussions with many well-known workers in allied fields. It would be impossible to mention all by name and if I have inadvertently omitted any I hope they will accept my sincere apologies. I would like to express my appreciation of the help I received from many institutions both in London and abroad especially the Library of the University of London and that of the Institute of Archaeology. Dr I. A. Kinnes and Dr de G. G. Sieveking of the Department of Prehistoric and Romano-British Antiquities at the British Museum kindly read through two of the chapters in their early draft form and I appreciate the advice I had from these gentlemen. My thanks are also due to Professor Colin Renfrew of the University of Southampton who suggested contacts abroad. I also had invaluable discussions with Dr Peter Northover of the Department of Metallurgy and Science of Materials of the University of Oxford on the source of Bronze Age metals. Mr Alan Tyler also helped me with his views on the copper mines of Gt Ormes Head in North Wales. I would also like to thank the many archaeologists overseas who have helped by showing me their collections, answering my queries and providing me with up to date material. These are especially Dr J. Neustupny of the National Museum in Prague, Dr Gerd Weisgerber of the Deutsches Bergbau-Museum in Bochum, West Germany, Professor J. C. Becker of the University of Copenhagen and M. le Roux of the Ministry of Culture and Communications, Rennes, France. The last two gentlemen also provided me with recent reports on their work and illustrated by Figs 60 and 65 respectively. Professor Beno Rothenberg, Director of the Institute of Archaeo-Metallurgical Studies also kindly supplied up to date material. I am also grateful to Professor B. Jovanovic of the Institute of Archaeology, Belgrade and Professor Elisabeth Schmid of the University of Basel for permission to publish Figs 89 and 55 respectively.

For permission to reproduce other drawings, photographs, etc. acknowledgements are made to the following: Acta Archaeologia, Budapest, Fig. 96; Anthropologische Gesellschaft, Vienna, Fig. 102; Archäologia Austriaca, Franz Deuticke, Vienna, Figs 62, 63, 91; Antiquaries Journal, Fig. 95; Associated Book Publishers (Archaeology of

Sussex—E. C. Curwen), Figs 27, 30; British Museum, Department of Prehistoric and Romano-British Antiquities, Figs 25, 39; British Museum, Natural History, Fig. 24; Cork Historical and Archaeological Society, Fig. 77; Department of the Environment, Figs 36, 37, 38; Economic Geology Publishing Company, Minnesota, USA, Fig. 93; German Mining Museum, Bochum, West Germany, Figs 19, 20, 42, 46, 52, 55, 56, 57, 81; Institute of Archaeology, University of London, Figs 82, 83, 87; Journal of Field Archaeology, Boston, USA Fig. 64; Museum of History, Cologne, West Germany, Fig. 69; Museo de Prehistoria, de la Excma, Valencia, Spain, Fig. 92; Prehistoric Society, Cambridge, Fig. 40; Römisch-Germanisches Commission, Frankfurt, West Germany, (Germania), Figs 68, 98; Society of Antiquaries, London, (Antiquaries Journal), Figs 97, 99; Sussex Archaeological Society, Sussex Archaeological Collections, Figs 28, 73; Wiltshire Archaeological Society, Figs 34, 72; Worthing Archaeological Society, Fig. 23; Universa, Wetteren, Belgium, (Helinium), Fig. 47.

1
Scope of Prehistory
with Reference to Mining

There is an element of mystery about old abandoned mines, something ghostlike whether they were worked 100, 2000 or even 5000 years ago. The stillness and peace is in stark contrast to the noise and industry which must have been paramount in more active days. Some remnant remains of what was hacked out of nature by human hands, but what kind of man created these relics? What sort of existence had he and what was his life style? Why did he subject himself to arduous physical labour with crude tools and to dangers to health and life, and hence what were his necessities? To try and answer these questions it is necessary to study prehistory, but at the same time to avoid giving general reasons in the context of our modern way of life; for we have to endeavour to understand conditions in those far off days by making every possible use of the flimsy evidence from pottery fragments, skeletons, burials, dwelling foundations, stratification, artefacts and pollen analysis.

No attempt is made here to consider prehistory in depth for reasons of relevance and space, but what is more important is that the author does not consider himself competent to do so. On the other hand no book which deals with one specialized aspect of prehistory would be complete without some general survey, however brief, of relevant elements of the subject especially for the benefit of the general reader.

Prehistory is concerned with man's remote past before the advent of written records. This fact alone presents a challenge to the investigator for the obvious difficulties are immense. The term "prehistory" is comparatively new for it appeared in *The Times* for the first time in 1888 and it was not until the turn of the century that it began to be used freely by scientific journals. Prehistory is a relative term, however, in one particular sense as it is based specifically on locality rather than on chronology. What were prehistorical times in Europe in the fourth millennium BC were actually years of the development of civilization and

1

history in the Near East so it would be incorrect on a world basis to say that prehistory ended on an absolute date. On the other hand, in Europe at least, it is now known fairly reliably that mining extraction was often more advanced in prehistorical times than it was in the early historical epoch of the Near East. So at least as far as mining is concerned, unlike pottery manufacture and agriculture, a more generalized treatment is possible.

It was not until the nineteenth century that the concept of man appearing on the earth millions of years ago was accepted. The issue had been clouded by religious dogma such as the declaration by Dr Lightfoot of Cambridge University in the seventeenth century that the heavens and earth were created in 4004 BC on October 23 at precisely 9 a.m. Even Dr Johnson said that all history of man is contained in a few pages and that nothing new could be determined. The history of the development of archaeology as a discipline in the early years concerns that of a conflict between geologists, who were the early archaeologists, and the so-called Diluvial Catastrophists who supported the flood theory. One problem which provided heated discussion was that of the origin of the sedimentary rocks. Charles Lyell, the first of the Fluvialists, postulated an order of succession determined by river and marine deposition, i.e. the new strata on top and the older below involving a laying down of sediments which constituted the future strata. From this concept geological time could be evaluated, the various epochs from the Pre-Cambrian to the recent, over hundreds of millions of years, being marked by either upheaval of the earth, recession of the oceans or deposition under marine conditions. Lyell's "Principles of Geology" (1833) and Darwin's "Origin of Species" (1859) finally convinced sceptics despite views of eminent geologists of the calibre of Dean Buckland, who earnestly advocated the comparative newness of the earth. By now the stage had been set for a more scientific approach to prehistory.

As long ago as 1807 the Danish Government set up a Classification Committee for antiquities and in 1819 the Danish Museum of Antiquities under C. Johannsen Thomsen created the Three Age System, i.e. stone, bronze and iron. He became known as the Father of Prehistory.

It would indeed be an advantage if the original simple concept of the Three Age System could have been retained, but results from extensive archaeological research have necessitated the introduction of many subdivisions. Thus the Stone Age is divided into the Palaeolithic (Old Stone Age), the Mesolithic (Middle Stone Age) and the Neolithic (New Stone Age). In western Europe the Palaeolithic is thought to have ended c. 8000 BC, the Mesolithic c. 3000 BC and the Neolithic c. 1800 BC.

Geologists term the period of the Old Stone Age the "Pleistocene" which, extending over two million years at least, is marked by the occurrence of four main glaciations or ice ages; the Lower Pleistocene having the Günz and Mindel glaciations, the Middle Pleistocene, the Riss and the Upper Pleistocene, the Würm or last glaciation. The periods between the main glaciations are termed interglacial phases. Thus between the Günz and the Mindel glaciations is the Cromerian interglacial, between the Riss and Würm glaciations the Hornian and between the Mindel and Riss glaciations the Ipswichian interglacial. No detailed consideration of conditions in the Palaeolithic age need concern us from the point of view of mining. It is sufficient to remember that Palaeolithic man, developing from the homonids, used at first pebbles and boulders for his tools, grubbed out of hillsides and from river beds, later using roughly shaped flints, hand axes and finally in the Upper Palaeolithic and in the post glacial period, more expertly shaped knives, arrowheads etc. of flint, chert or bone. However, Palaeolithic man exercised a great amount of discretion in choosing materials for his tools

TABLE 1: Late glacial and post-glacial epochs in Northern Europe

			Vegetation
Upper palaeolithic — Late glacial			
IA	Oldest Dryas	*c.* 14 000–11 000 BC	Arctic flora
IB	Bølling Oscillation	*c.* 11 500–10 500 BC	More temperate
IC	Older or Middle Dryas	*c.* 10 500–10 000 BC	Alpine-less Arctic
II	Allerød Oscillation	*c.* 10 000–8800 BC	Tundra in NW. Europe Forest pine in S. France and Germany
III	Younger or late Dryas	*c.* 8800–8300 BC	Return to colder conditions
Mesolithic — Holocene			
IV	Pre-Boreal	*c.* 8300–7500 BC	Trees and forest advent of pine
V⎫ VI⎭	Boreal	*c.* 7500–5600 BC	Warmer—pine, hazel and oak in northern zone
VII	Atlantic	*c.* 5600–3000 BC	Oak and elm forest, 4000 BC was the warmest period
Neolithic			
VIII	Sub-Boreal	*c.* 3000 BC–	Agriculture

and weapons. He recognized the properties of hardness and abrasion. Man, for example, of the Solutrean culture, 17 000–20 000 years ago, was able to fashion exquisite blades to the shape and design of laurel and willow leaves. The material used, flint, when weathered absorbs water rapidly and becomes brittle. He could have had great difficulty in tooling if weathered varieties had been used. Two problems emerge, therefore, one being whether Palaeolithic man did actually dig deep for unweathered varieties of flint and rock, and if so has all evidence of such excavation been irreparably destroyed? It is quite possible that early Neolithic workings were merely extensions of Palaeolithic or Mesolithic excavations. On the other hand why was there a need to mine if such excellent materials were available on the surface, and hence why did later Neolithic man go to the trouble of digging narrow and relatively deep and dangerous mines? There is, however, little evidence yet that Palaeolithic man carried out any form of mining apart from the digging of holes at outcrops for his flint. This is indeed surprising in view of the duration of the Palaeolithic. All progress was made from about 3000 BC onwards, a mere 5000 years compared to the pre-Neolithic period of at least two and a half million years. Palaeolithic man lived mainly by hunting whereas his successors in Mesolithic times were hunters, gatherers and fishermen.

Much work has been done on post glacial flora of the period from c 14 000 BC onwards after the retreat of the ice sheets. Table 1 shows the types of vegetational changes and chronology of the period from 14 000 BC to the present day in Europe based on pollen analyses.

We are chiefly concerned in this book with Zone IV onwards, following the appearance of forests, the rising of the sea levels and the land after the weight of ice had gone. Around 8000 BC the land bridge between the British Isles and the Continent of Europe finally disappeared. Conditions farther south in the Middle East, especially in Mesopotamia, were far different as there were no ice ages and so the chronology is not relative. Agriculture did not appear on the scene in southern Europe until the sixth millennium BC whereas in Mesopotamia and Anatolia early farming dates back to c 8000 BC.

Prehistory of the Palaeolithic is concerned chiefly with tool types of flint and bone, development of man, cave art (i.e. Magdalenian of the Upper Palaeolithic) and the type of animal hunted. Flint tools became more specialized in the Mesolithic as a greater diversity of functions were performed. At that time the interest was in the mode of dwelling, fishing, type of food etc. The Neolithic era was essentially marked by the introduction of farming, both arable and the herding of animals.

Neolithic man became more settled and his increased activities demanded better types of tools. Consequently it is in the Neolithic era that we find the first attempts at the mining of flint and chert by underground methods.

At one time the Bronze Age, which is divided into Early, Middle and Late, was thought to follow on directly after the Neolithic, but now the intervention of what is termed the Copper Age (Eneolithic or Chalcolithic) is considered to be desirable. Although it is possible that Neolithic man first used native copper, and copper mines dating back at least to the Eneolithic period have been found in the Balkans during the last ten years, it was not until the Bronze Age that intensive underground copper mining using shafts and adits was undertaken. In fact copper sulphide ores were not worked until late in the Bronze Age. Tin bronzes were not made until very late in that period, although tin bronze had been discovered accidentally by the use of copper containing tin. What is certain, however, is that tin in prehistoric times, especially in Cornwall, was only worked from alluvial or stream deposits.

Although iron is plentiful throughout the world it was not until around 750 BC, the date which is supposed to mark the commencement of the Iron Age in Europe, that actual iron metalurgy came on the scene. The Hittites, however, whose empire lasted from 1800 to 1200 BC, are known to have used iron for tools and weaponry, although this is in the early historical period in the Near East.

Finally Table 2 (overleaf) shows in diagrammatic form the approximate periods of development of mining in prehistoric times in Europe. The dates given can only be very approximate since advances in archaeological excavation are continually changing the picture. What must be remembered is that progress travelled north from the Near East and the Balkans in early Neolithic times so that, for example, a date for the introduction of copper mining in southern Europe will be much earlier than one for similar development in Ireland.

TABLE 2: Development of mining in northern Europe in prehistory

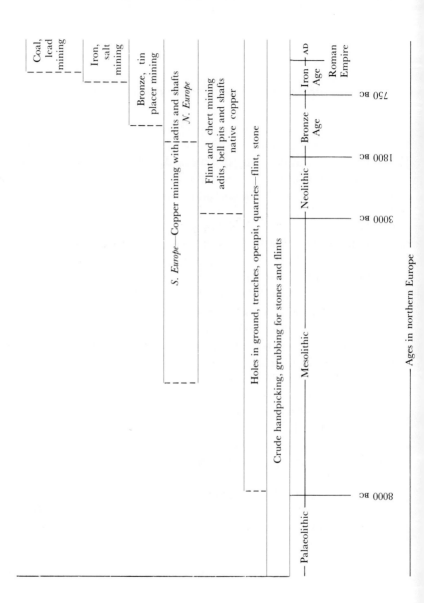

2
Elements of Early Mining

Before the dawn of history man found it necessary to extract rock, minerals and metallic ores from deposits. Long before he embarked on cultivation of plants for food, or on animals domestication, as a hunter and gatherer he required tools and weapons. When did mining actually start? Long ago when man first appeared on the earth he practised a basic form of mining. When he scratched away loose rock from a scree or hillside, often only with his bare hands, he originated one of the oldest trades or professions, for he was only performing the same task as the early underground miner did somewhat later, but without crude hand-held tools.

Prehistoric man dug, mined or quarried flint, chert, copper, tin, gold, silver, lead, salt, coal and other rocks representing the more important useful materials. In doing so he originated methods of extraction which were the forerunners from which modern mining has slowly evolved throughout the millennia.

Occurrence of Deposits

Materials such as flint, the sedimentary rocks, iron and coal occur in seams and although sometimes located in a contorted or disturbed state are usually bedded in conformity with the containing strata. Conversely mineral ores are not always bedded, but often occur in veins or lodes running through massive igneous rocks and sometimes sedimentary rocks, and vary appreciably in thickness and quality. Iron, a constituent of many rock types, can appear in the bedded form or in metallic ore veins.

A seam may vary in thickness from a few centimetres to many metres and may be almost level to nearly vertical depending on the mode of sedimentation and the degree of earth movement after being deposited.

7

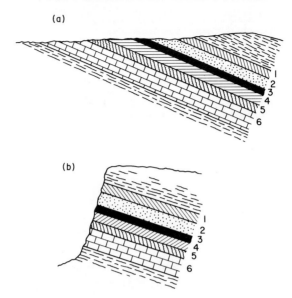

Fig. 1. Outcrops of seams or beds. (a) Level surface, (b) steeply dipping terrain or cliff face.

All seams outcrop at the surface unless laid down in a basin and/or covered by newer or unconformable strata.

In Fig. 1(a), seam 3 outcrops at a level surface and in Fig. 1(b), on a hillside or cliff face. In both these simple cases the seam is said to be conformable with the strata, i.e. it has the same dip and direction as the containing rocks. Also the upper beds are newer than those lower down, i.e. 1 is newer or more recent that 2, likewise 2 was laid down later than 3 and so on. If a bed or seam is regarded as a dipping surface or plane, then the maximum inclination measured on that plane is known as the full or true dip, any other being the apparent dip on a given line or in a given direction. Any line drawn at right angles to the full dip is known as the direction of strike or level surface of the bed or seam as shown in Fig. 2.

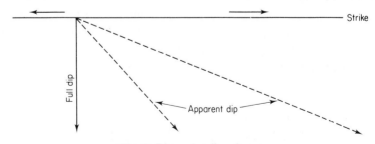

Fig. 2. Dip and strike of seam.

(a)

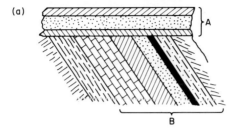

(b)

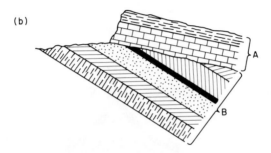

Fig. 3. Unconformities in strata.

Thus if a deposit has a full dip to the north or south the strike is in a direction east–west. Any reference later to dip refers to the full or true dip.

Such examples represent the simplest cases, but where the beds are overlain by others not having the same dip they are said to be mutually unconformable For example in Fig. 3 beds A have been deposited at a later date on top of the outcrops of the beds B after these had been tilted by earth movements. Figure 3(b) could represent the Permian beds A of the Midlands of England resting unconformably on the Carboniferous Coal Measure Series B.

Excessive movements of the earths crust such as uplift or major subsidence can result in beds being folded as in Fig. 4. A is known as an overthrust fold, B is a syncline and C an anticline.

Appreciable lateral tensile stress, or pulling apart, and compressive lateral stress may produce what are termed faults or dislocations. The simplest of these is the normal or tensile fault. As a result of the occurrence of this type of fault, shown in Fig. 5, the seam at A is displaced to a new position B on the downthrow side of the fault. Any borehole put down at C would not intercept the seam. D is known as the displacement and the angle α, the hade of the fault.

Another type of fault which is not so common as the normal fault, is the reverse or compression fault. The reverse fault is often found in strata

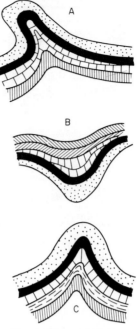

Fig. 4. Types of folds.

which have been subjected to heavy stressing and is shown in Fig. 6. A borehole put down at C would pass through the same seam twice as would one drilled through an overthrust fold and give an erroneous impression of the presence of two seams.

There are several other dislocations in the continuity of bedded deposits, such as washouts, igneous intrusions etc. but these need not concern the student of prehistoric mining.

Ores unlike bedded deposits are sporadic and often scarce. In comparison with the enclosing rock mass they are often small and difficult to recognize. Consequently more expertise in prospecting techniques is

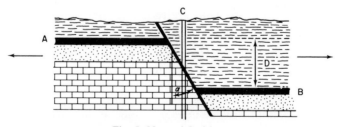

Fig. 5. Normal faulting.

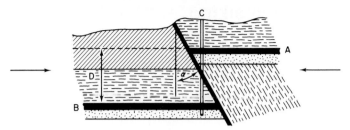

Fig. 6. Reverse faulting.

necessary than in the case of bedded deposits. Major ore deposits in hilly countries have been found as a result of what is termed "panning" of the streams running across lower alluvial terrain. In fact this could well have been one of the earliest methods used by prehistoric man to obtain gold and tin. With hand panning it is possible to deal with 1 m³ of gravel in about 10 h. The method consists of placing gravel in a circular dish 25·5–40·5 cm in diameter and 5–55 cm deep with sides sloping at 35–40°. Water is added and the contents stirred by hand to break up any lumps of clay. A circular motion is then performed, the pan or dish being tilted from time to time to wash off the surface layer. The heavy minerals of gold or tin remain at the bottom after each panning procedure. The mineral which is recovered has probably been washed down by the stream from a lode in the hillside and maybe the prospector would trace the stream to its source.

The surrounding rock in metal mining terminology is known as the country rock or bedrock. In its simplest condition a metalliferous lode is a vein traversing the bedrock. Figure 7 shows a simplified sketch of a lode. In this sketch AB is known as the dip angle and α, the hade. What is known as the "roof" in the mining of bedded deposits is referred to as the "hanging wall" in steep metalliferous mining and correspondingly the floor as the "footwall". Normally lodes are very much steeper than bedded deposits.

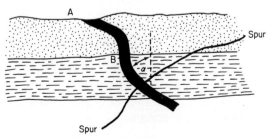

Fig. 7. A metalliferous load.

Methods of Working

All methods of prehistoric mining are confined to very shallow deposits and are therefore very simple. Nevertheless they are basic to modern mining which differs only from its ancestors by virtue of depth and development of improved methods of extraction, ventilation and transport which have been made possible by advances in technology and science not available to prehistoric man.

The earliest tools consisted of pebbles picked up from rivers and streams and small pieces of suitably shaped rock scratched out by hand from weathered exposures. When prehistoric man realized the potential use of flint he began by utilizing pieces of this material broken from exposed outcrops and later he soon learned to ease out pieces from the solid. As he extracted flint from the outcrop it was probably not long before he realized that the thickness of chalk overlying the deposit increased as he tried to free the flint further and further from the outcrop. He must also have noticed that as the depth increased so did the quality of the flint improve. The very first mining venture was the digging of crude shallow holes or pits through the overburden to a depth of only a metre or so. In some cases outcrops are often defined by undulations in the ground which also indicate former old workings spread across the countryside. Such methods were not confined to flint workings and there is some evidence of shallow extraction of coal from outcrops as, for example, in the vicinity of Nostell Priory in Yorkshire, by monks, in medieval times.

Trenches were later used as a means of mining by prehistoric man as at Obourg and other sites in Belgium. These were dug to a depth of 3–4 m to the flint and had a length of up to 10 m. They were tapered to give support to the sides and sometimes made in pairs, these being connected by a crosscut as shown in Fig. 8. This method was the forerunner of the first shaft or bellpit.

Bellpits were dug up to 2 m in diameter at the surface and narrowed towards the middle as in Fig. 9. The depth was up to 10 m, the seam being dug away in all directions at the base, i.e. undercutting until the working

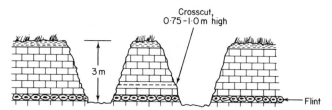

Fig. 8. Early trenching method.

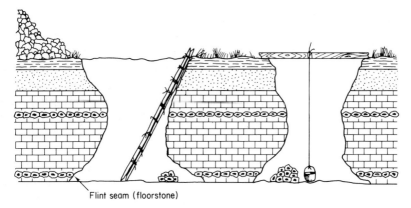

Flint seam (floorstone)

Fig. 9. Bell pits.

was no longer safe. The pit was then abandoned and another similar pit dug several metres away. As a new pit was dug the debris from it was used to backfill the old one. This method was used for working coal and ironstone in Britain until as late as the nineteenth century. As can be imagined the making of such bellpits in weak strata was a very hazardous undertaking.

It seems strange that prehistoric man embarked on the digging of shafts to exploit seams of flint which, by his standards and with his facilities, were too deep to work by opencast methods. Probably he did not drive adits from the outcrop owing to problems of supporting roof and sides. In fact the early workings at Grimes Graves in Norfolk were simple shallow shafts with no connections or underground galleries, but only with some degree of undercutting at the base.

The real ancestor to modern methods of mining was the rudimentary system employed later at Grimes Graves, at Cissbury and other mines in Sussex, at Spiennes in Belgium and at many others. The basic concept was to sink a shaft down to the seam to be extracted and then to work radially from the shaft bottom with a network of galleries or tunnels leaving pillars of chalk, in the case of flint mining, for support. The shafts were either rectangular or more commonly circular. When the distance from the shaft became too great for ease of transport another was sunk and the process repeated. Often there was access between shafts underground through the galleries. As with the bellpit method disused shafts were stowed with debris from the next one being made.

A first glance at a plan of such prehistoric flint mines will inevitably give the impression of casual layout and haphazard exploitation. There is, however, an underlying attempt to layout systematic workings and it is possible to schematize the result to produce a tidier or idealized version. The difference between the two does not necessarily signify unsatisfactory planning, but reflects the absence of today's surveying facilities. Anyone experienced in mining practice is aware of the departures from a planned layout which can be inadvertently made when checks are not carried out frequently enough by surveyors. The old story, true in a great many cases, of two apparently straight tunnels which have "passed in the night" is very apt in this context. In no case has any evidence of measuring or checking procedure been found in a flint mine and in the systems used would have been necessary.

Another factor which is probably as significant as the absence of surveying checks is the nature of the labour employed. It does seem highly likely that labour used in flint mining was both casual and seasonal. This aspect is considered in Ch. 6, but it is possible that mines remained idle for long periods between visits by wandering tribes from distant farmlands who encamped with their cattle, took what flint they had extracted and then went back to their habitation sites often trading some flint for other necessities. There would probably have been some understanding between flint miners visiting the sites concerned regarding the general layout of working to be used. The ideal representation of the apparent planned method of exploitation at Grimes Graves from one of the main shafts is shown in Fig. 10, but the actual working, however, is of

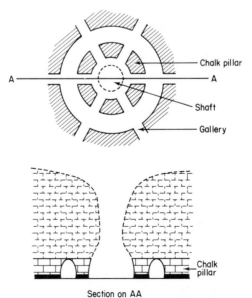

Section on AA

Fig. 10. Idealized representation of an underground flint mine. Not to scale.

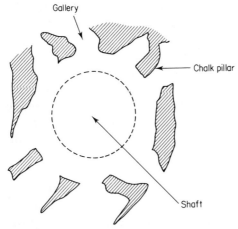

Fig. 11. Generalized actual layout of a flint mine.

the form shown in Fig. 11. The layout at Cissbury, consisting of a group of circular and rectangular shafts and galleries, is as shown in Fig. 12, whereas schematized it is as shown at Fig. 13.

Further details of prehistoric sites so far mentioned and of others are given in Chs 3 and 4, but it is worth noting the layout at Spiennes in

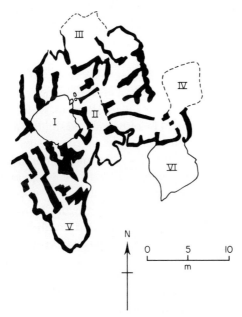

Fig. 12. A group of shafts and galleries at Cissbury. I–VI = shafts.

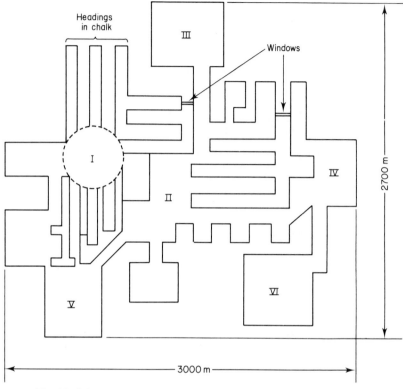

Fig. 13. Schematic layout at Cissbury. I–VI = shafts (after Willert).

Belgium. Unfortunately this site has been badly disturbed and almost obliterated by wanton exploitation of limestone for cement manufacture. Whereas shafts in Britain were up to 10 m in width, in Europe they seldom exceeded 0·5–1·0 m. The only inclined shaft or adit in a flint mine was located at Spiennes, but the shafts there were mostly vertical. The layout at this site appears to have been more systematic than at most British flint mines. Shafts were up to 16 m deep and the workings consisted of galleries with rectangular pillars for support, the system of working almost resembling board and pillar working used in coal mining. Figure 14 shows the schematic layout based on an illustration made by Willert (1951). The prehistoric shafts passed through several seams of flint which were considered to be of inferior quality, before intersecting the working seam at the base of the shaft.

The fascinating conclusions to be drawn from a study of layouts of prehistoric flint mines are: (a) miners were capable of recognizing the better types of flint even if these were deeper and did not outcrop and (b)

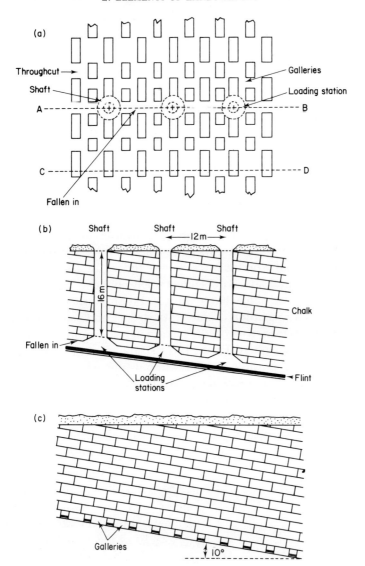

Fig. 14. Schematic layout at Spiennes flint mine with vertical shafts and working places. (a) Plan, (b) section on AB, (c) section on CD.

the miners realized the benefits to be gained by leaving chalk pillars unworked as a means of support.

Although inclined shafts are rare in prehistoric flint mining, copper ore was worked by adits as at Mitterberg, Austria, whereas older mines used shafts as at Rudna Glava in Yugoslavia. The Hallstatt salt mines in

Austria also used adits. Unfortunately there are no records available concerning the methods used to excavate such shafts.

Support

Pillars were used for support, but there is little evidence to date of timber having been used to hold the roof in prehistoric flint mines. Notches have been noticed in shafts and galleries which might have been recesses for roof beams, but any timber left would have decayed without trace. Timber was however used for roof and side support in both copper and salt mines in Austria and there is much evidence for this.

A layman, so far as mining is concerned, is often under the impression that it is more necessary to use supports in deep mining than in shallow workings. Although primitive stresses, i.e. the stress inherent in the strata, are a function of depth and so increase with the vertical distance from the surface, the actual working stresses may indeed be less. The ability to support the roof and sides is dependent solely on the strength of the nether strata or that directly adjacent to the excavation. As soon as an opening is made there is a relaxation of the strata stresses and redistribution takes place, any increase in stress occurring on a new solid abutment away from the excavation (Shepherd 1970). If the strata are strong and reasonably homogeneous it is possible to mine without supports at any depth, as in many metalliferous mines, whereas at a depth of only a few metres below the surface in weak strata strong support may be needed.

The flint bearing chalk at Spiennes lies under weak Tertiary sands and clays and there is evidence in both the inclined shaft and vertical shafts of timber having been used where such shafts passed through such beds, as in Fig. 15.

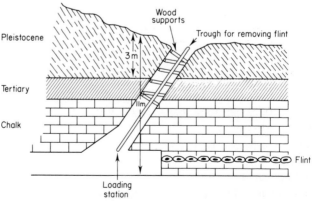

Fig. 15. Inclined shaft at Spiennes with wood supports (after Willert).

It is known from pollen analysis at Grimes Graves that in Neolithic times there was extensive forest. There would then have been ample timber for support and it would be surprising if none was used in the flint mines there. Mining in chalk can be a very hazardous undertaking and the accident rate was probably very high. The chief danger arose from the working of flint at a shallow depth when blocks or pieces of chalk would fall out from between breaks or joint planes. Sides of shafts would tend to flake and it would be most unusual today to sink shafts in weak sedimentary strata without the use of artificial support.

Tools

The implements and methods used to work the flint, chert, copper ore or other materials are described in later chapters, but for the sake of completeness are mentioned here. They vary from flint hand axes which, apart from hammers made from igneous rocks such as basalt, granite or greenstone, are the oldest, to picks made from the tines of deer horns. Later flint axes were mounted in deer horns or wooden handles and fastened with leather thongs.

These tools, when used in soft chalk to make galleries and shafts and to ease out flint nodules from the seam, were quite adequate. When hard limestone had to be worked to obtain chert or even tougher materials to get copper, deer horn picks at least would not have been effective. Explosives were of course not available so a procedure called "fire setting" was used to break out hard rock in some countries, as recently as in the last century. The method consists first in making a fire of dry brushwood or wood sticks close up to the face of the rock to be broken. When the rock has become heated sufficiently water is rapidly applied to achieve rapid cooling. It is only really successful in heterogeneous rocks for it makes use of the property of differential rates of thermal expansion or contraction of the constituent minerals. Although hard rock can be cracked into a state for extraction there are some serious disadvantages. A ventilated circuit must be maintained so that men do not have to work in the smoke or steam produced by the process. An adequate and ready to hand supply of water is also necessary and this results in problems of disposal. Paradoxically the use of fire setting assists the ventilation as warm air is less dense and tends to rise, providing there is a suitable air circuit from intake to return. Fire setting was used at the Rammelsberg mines in Germany, according to Collins (1893), up to 1878, about 250 years after the introduction of gunpowder there for blasting. So firesetting was not discontinued in the mines solely because gunpowder was available, but only as a result of the increasing cost of firewood and labour and a growing regard for the health of the workpeople.

Pliny mentions the use of vinegar to soften heated rocks and states that when vinegar was poured on such rocks in large quantities they were split. He refers to the use of this method in the Roman gold mines of Spain.

Haulage and Transport

There is very little evidence concerning the method of transportation of material from the working face to the surface in flint mines. It is usually accepted that the flint was put into leather bags. A tree trunk was probably placed across the mouth of the shaft around which was passed a rope. Miners standing at the foot of the shaft pulled on the rope on the end of which was attached the loaded bag or sack thereby raising it to the surface where it was emptied. Chalk debris from the workings was stored as far as possible in the worked out galleries. Access to the shaft especially if it was wide, such as at Cissbury, was probably by ladders which were made from tree branches; the treads being bound to them by leather thongs. Entry by miners into the narrow European shafts would be by climbing up and down wooden struts set across the sides and these might also have served as supports for the shaft. Willert (1951) mentions the use of wooden troughs in the inclined shaft at Spiennes along which bags of flint were hauled.

In Austria Bronze Age copper mines were worked with slightly dipping adits from the hillside and followed the lode and this also applies to the Iron Age salt mines in the same country. The copper ore or rock salt was loaded into leather sacks which were hauled or dragged along the floor by leather ropes. Baskets of leather were also used in the salt mines, but windlasses were not used before Roman times.

Ventilation

Some workers mention the use of fires for ventilation at Grimes Graves, Champignolles in France and Mur de Barrez also in France and quote the finding of soot marks on the roof as evidence of this practice. Fires could have been made underground for the purpose of cooking and maybe to provide warmth, but the use of fires for ventilation is extremely unlikely. Furnace ventilation with the aid of fires made at the base of an upcast shaft was introduced much later than prehistoric times and was still in use in Britain in early Victorian times. As mentioned already the use of fire setting inadvertently assisted natural ventilation, but normally natural ventilation sufficed especially in the shallow flint mines.

Lighting

Chalk lamps, based on the burning of animal fats, were used in most flint mines and in the salt mines of Austria there is evidence of the use of wooden spells. The discovery that a wick, soaked in and fed by fat or oil, will provide a lasting light goes back at least to the Palaeolithic age according to Forbes (1955). One of the very early lamps was found at La Mouthe in France; a Magdelinian lamp cut in a piece of reddish sandstone, the hollow of which contained bear fat. It is possible also that twisted hair, moss, dried weed etc. was used as a wick. It is probable, however, that the miners used daylight as far as practicable for illumination. Old drawings of flint mines often show "windows" in chalk pillars between two galleries or working places. These were small orifices and were probably made to permit the penetration of daylight. In a discussion on Cissbury at a meeting of the Royal Anthropological Institute in 1878 a speaker suggested that such "windows" were made to determine the thickness of pillar for safety purposes. This is unlikely as it would not have been an easy task to break through up to 1 m of solid chalk, especially if this was hard, merely to justify curiosity. A form of measuring by straight lines and right angles constituting a rudimentary form of surveying would not have been beyond the capabilities of the Neolithic miner, as there are indications that he had to estimate distances both in laying out his workings and during his operations.

This somewhat brief outline of the basic elements of prehistoric mining only covers those aspects which are strictly relevant to the subject. It would be outside the scope of the present study to cover wider ground. As far as bedded deposits are concerned development continued through the ages as mines became deeper. This necessitated greater attention being paid to planning and surveying. Systematic layout of protective shaft and working pillars and partial or full extraction either in concert with advancing methods from the shaft bottom or in retreat, were developed in the nineteenth century. The advent of gunpowder or blackpowder facilitated extraction procedures followed by high explosives until quite recently fully mechanized extraction methods for tunnel and working drivages and for pillar working were introduced on a large scale. Metalliferous mining became more systematic with overhand and underhand stoping, shrinkage stoping etc. depending on the type of deposit.

Quarrying and a crude form of opencast mining were used in prehistoric times for surface outcropping deposits, but evidence for these is rare although the Romans and medieval miners have left such workings, which could probably have been a continuation of earlier operations.

This, it is hoped, gives some background to the study which has been undertaken and is described in the following chapters.

3
Flint Mining in the British Isles

The first materials to be used in prehistorical times for the manufacture of tools and weapons were flint, chert, igneous rocks and obsidian. A broad outline of the general methods employed in early mining has been given in Ch. 2 and the nature and origin of flint will be considered in Ch. 9. Since stone and flint were used very early in prehistory it is logical that the oldest type of excavation should be associated with the extraction of flint and similar materials.

Consideration is given later in this chapter to British sites which have been discovered and explored. These are numerous and it would serve no useful purpose to give a detailed description of all of them. However, typical examples are discussed in so far as these show relevant features.

Generally, with minor exceptions, most of the actual mining of flint, i.e. by underground excavation, took place in the Neolithic period, extending in some cases into the Bronze and Iron Ages although Schild (1976) reports on a Polish mine dating from the Upper Palaeolithic and Schmid (1972) a possible Mousterian mine. At present pre-Neolithic mines are rare, but future excavations might yield a more extensive network of such mines. Indeed this is extremely feasible if cognisance is taken of the pronounced workmanlike and often artistic flint artifacts found on Palaeolithic sites and which must have required the utilization of less weathered raw materials. In Britain most Neolithic mines are found in the chalk beds of the Cretaceous and they often were commenced in areas where there had been a strong Mesolithic flint industry, according to Hawkes (1973), who cites North and West France and southern Britain as typical examples. Workable chert is mostly found in many other West European countries and Poland, Russia, the Far East etc.

The prior need for better types of flint taxed the ingenuity of Neolithic man. In that period in Britain over 5000 years ago, wheat, barley,

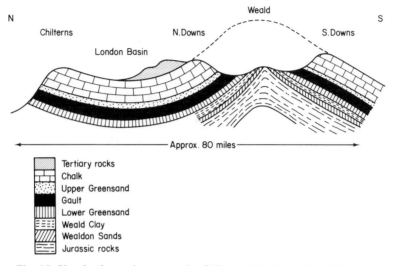

Fig. 16. Sketch of a section across the Chilterns, North and South Downs.

legumes and flax were planted, sheep, pigs and cattle bred and dogs kept as domestic animals. Earlier man had been content to dig flint or chert from seam outcrops, but he soon realized that, despite the parent rock of hard chalk or limestone and unconformable loam overlying the beds, by digging deeper through the pits or shafts he could reach supplies of better quality material. Thus the prehistoric miner was the forerunner of today's prospector or geologist. Were the miners specialist or had they time to tend their herds and cultivate plots? Childe (1963) was of the opinion that mining was seasonable. This aspect is discussed later, but the high degree of skill which went into the mining and preparation of the flint would lend direct support to the view that mining was highly specialized. There is also an opinion that extensive trade patterns emerged and modern petrographical methods of rock analysis reinforce this theory. Joan Oates states that flint and obsidian tools found at Tepe Guran in the Zagros Mountains had originated 800 km away at Lake Van in 6500 ± 200–5810 ± 150 bc.*

The largest number of ancient British flint mining sites are found in the chalklands of southern England, although the most famous example is Grimes Graves in Norfolk. Flint is normally found in the thick chalk deposits of the Cretaceous period which stretches across eastern and south-eastern England. A typical cross section of the stratification of the London Basin and the Weald is shown in Fig. 16.

*For an explanation of these see Appendix II.

The deposit of chalk as represented today in the Chilterns section of the London Basin, the North Downs and the South Downs was much more extensive in Cretaceous times, i.e. 136 million years ago, than at the present time. It probably occupied a large part of the west, even covering the Pennine Chain and mountains still farther over into Wales. Mesolithic man camped on the sands and clay surfaces in the Weald, whereas his successor of Neolithic times lived on the North and South Downs.

Being rich in flint of good quality the chalk uplands of the south of England and East Anglia attracts Neolithic settlers although possibly Mesolithic man had dug out surface flint when he required it. Evidence for the industry of the Neolithic period abounds in the relics of prehistoric abandoned mines and surface workings in Norfolk such as at Massingham and Grimes Graves near Brandon and in Wiltshire and Sussex there are mines of Easton Down, Martins Clump, Blackpatch, Bow Hill, Church Hill, Cissbury, Harrow Hill, Lavant, Peppard, Stoke Down, Tolmere and Windover. There may be many more still unrecognized and therefore not yet excavated, but although the ones mentioned have been explored to various degrees, there still remains much more to be done. The tendency today has been to open up many pits and after exploration carefully refill and so preserve the relics for posterity. However, one shaft and radiating galleries have been kept open at Grimes Graves for inspection by visitors.

Shaft depths in Britain varied from a mere few centimetres to over 10 m and from 3 to 10 m in diameter. At many sites there are the remains of over 100 shafts and this would have involved the moving of up to 5000 t of chalk to gain access to the seams.

The location of present known flint mines in Britain is shown in the map in Fig. 17.

Age of British Flint Mines

When flint mines were first recognized as such they were mostly classed as pre-Neolithic. This is not surprising since early workers, prior to the nineteenth century, had no knowledge of the Neolithic. Now it is generally agreed that flint mines, i.e. those having shafts and galleries, did not exist prior to the Neolithic, at least in England, and some were in fact worked into the Early, Middle and Late Bronze Ages. Only 50 years ago a mine existed near Brandon, in Norfolk, solely for the purpose of extracting flint for the manufacture of gun flints.

In the past there have been many conflicting statements made

Fig. 17. Location of prehistoric flint mines and stone quarries in the British Isles. Flint mines and openpits; confirmed (●), unconfirmed (O): hard rock quarries; confirmed (■), unconfirmed (□). 1 Buchan Ness, 2 Balleygalley Hill, 3 Massingham, 4 Ringland, 5 Grimes Graves, 6 Pitstone Hill, 7 Liddington, 8 Peppard, 9 Findsbury, 10 East Horsley, 11 Windover Hill, 12 Cissbury, 13 Church Hill, 14 Blackpatch, 15 Harrow Hill, 16 Tolmere Pond, 17 Stoke Down, 18 Lavant Caves, 19 Bow Hill, 20 Martins Clump, 21 Easton Down, 22 Durrington, 23 Beer Head, 24 Trevebulliagh, 25 Great Langdale, 26 Graig Lwydd, 27 M ynydd Rhiw, 28 Prescelly, 29 Cwm Mawr, 30 Rum, 31 Arran, 32 Craig na Cailloch, 33 Purbeck.

regarding the actual age of flint mining in Britain. For example Julius Andrée (1922) quotes a date of 8000–4000 BC for Cissbury and 8000–3000 BC for Grimes Graves, i.e. in the Mesolithic era. Cissbury was regarded by Pitt-Rivers, however, 100 years ago as Neolithic whereas R. A. Smith (1912) estimated the workings to be within the age of the Aurignacians of the Upper Palaeolithic and he bases his theories on the type of primitive chipped flint found in refuse on the site. L'Abbé Breuil thought that the workings were pre-Aurignacian as he did for the workings at Grimes Graves and likened the latter to Abri Audi in France. He postulated that evidence of red deer dated the mines as Mousterian and he mentioned, as an example, floor 85c at Grimes Graves where antler picks had been found and and Boyd Hawkins agreed with this hypothesis. Armstrong also dated Grimes Graves as Upper Paleolithic.

Toms considers the dating of the British flint mines in some detail (1928). He observed that there was only 1 ft of mould over the depressed centres of the shafts at Grimes Graves, Cissbury, Blackpatch and Stoke Down and said that they were all of the same period. Toms quoted Kennard and Woodward, who, reporting on the Grimes Graves molluscs, said that the species found were living today and required moisture and shade. Wisely they said that the mines were worked between the end of the Pleistocene and the beginning of the Roman period in Britain, i.e. of the order of 8000 years! Toms concludes that the mines at Cissbury represented a transition from the Neolithic to the Bronze Age, a theory accepted today on the basis of new evidence.

Estimates of the ages of the major British flint mines have been derived from a study of the pottery sherds found on the sites, i.e. in or near the workings, and from the more recent radiocarbon dates, which for Grimes Graves lie between 2400 BC and 1600 BC. Some of the other British flint mines can be dated before 3000 BC. The associated pottery at flint mine sites is generally of the Neolithic "A" type although that from Grimes Graves is Grooved Ware, an example being shown in Fig. 18. Hawkes (1940) states that Peterborough peoples seem to have reached Wessex not long before the Beaker immigration in Wiltshire. They had a site at Winterbourne Dauntsey and like the Beaker folk they are in evidence at the nearby site of Easton Down. A rim of Grooved Ware was found at Grimes Graves in Pit 12. From Cissbury there are three examples of bowls in the Pitt-Rivers Museum at Oxford and one in the British Museum, all similar to the Windmill Hill class of pottery. West Kennet longbarrow had pottery similar to that found at Grimes Graves. Clark and Piggott state that three types of mining succeeded one another at Grimes Graves: (1) primitive bell shaped pits, 3 and 4; (2) intermediate or masked pits,

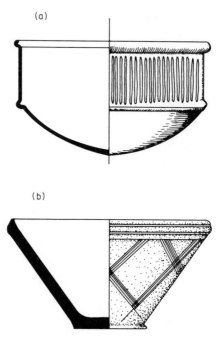

Fig. 18. Types of Neolithic pottery found in flint mines. (a) Neolithic A pottery, (b) Grooved ware (Rinyo-Clacton). Approx. x 0·2.

8–12; and (3) galleried pits, 1 and 2 (1933). All three types are said to be Neolithic. They reason that the pottery found has cord, birdbone-twisted cord and whipped impressions, and that a chalk cup apparently used for lighting is the same as in galleried mines in Neolithic camps and nowhere else. L'Abbé Breuil, however, instances the engraving found on bone which he claims to be that of red deer so he claims that the pits were earlier than Neolithic. At Easton Down there are primitive bell pits with no galleries, but Windmill-type sherds have been found. Modern methods of radiocarbon dating have since resolved most of the problems which have existed with regard to dating.

Tools for Excavation

The typical type of tool used for levering out blocks of chalk was made from the antlers of red deer. This was obtained by removing all the tines except one which represented the blade. Every part of the antler appeared to have an economic use. The tines which were removed were used as gouges, punches, hand levers and piercing instruments. The beam was deprived of its tines and cut into sections to make adzes, cutting implements and even hammers. The combination of beam and tines produced a tool which has a dual purpose of pick and rake. The most common tool was the pick and, according to Sanders (1910), by severing the cup end and removing the bez and trez tines, a beam was left to form the haft and brow tine thereby giving a pick, while the burr was retained in position to give strength to the weakest part, i.e. the angle of intersection between the handle and the blade, and to add weight to the blow. Antlers from fully grown animals appear to have been preferred. At the Beauvais flint mines in France all the picks were double handled. A typical pick is shown in Fig. 19.

It has been reported that marks made by flint tools during tine removal have been identified. In many mines holes have been found in the chalk *in*

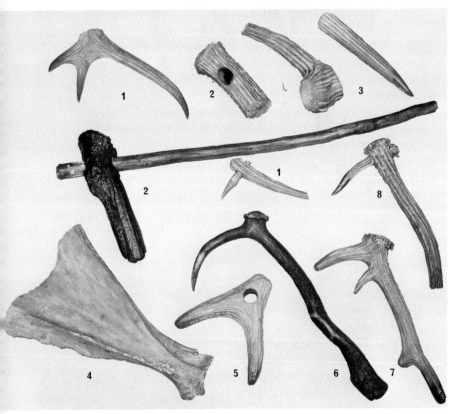

Fig. 19. Prehistoric flint mining tools. 1 Mattock and 2 hammer, deer horn tools from Mur de Barrez, France; 4 scapula shovel from Cissbury; 5 two edged rake of deer horn; 6 pick; 7 two edged mattock from Obourg; 8 pick in deer horn Bergbau-Museum, Bochum.

situ, strategically located as to represent an anchorage for levering out the blocks. This appears to have been the common method of excavation, the fire setting method not having been used in British flint mines and in Europe until later. Clark and Piggott (1933) refer to a method of extraction used at Flint Ridge in the USA. The overlying limestone (probably chalk) was cut away by the use of fire and water to free the underlying flint, the latter being protected with clay during the process. From this mine the raw material was traded as far afield as New York, Illinois and East Virginia. Schmid (1952) also reports on the use of fire setting in jasper workings at Isteiner Klotz in the Rhineland (see Ch. 4). The mode of operation has been mentioned in Ch. 2, but made use of differential contraction by rapid cooling with cold water. Antler picks could then be used to lever out the blocks of limestone.

Typical antler picks have been found in England at Blackpatch, Cissbury, Grimes Graves and Harrow Hill. Another form of tool was the hammer, also made from antlers. The handle was formed from the massive frontal tine and the head was the crown from which the beam had been cut off. Simplified forms of antler hammer are shown in Fig. 19 and 20.

Curwen and Curwen (1923) report on an experiment carried out by Pitt-Rivers. He made a pair of picks, a mandril, two wedges and five tine punches out of a pair of red deer antlers and found that by working turn about with one of his men he was able to make an excavation approximately one metre square in a face of hard smooth chalk in 1·5 h. He concluded that 12 h would be ample for a gallery 9 m long which represents the longest at Cissbury and Blackpatch. The rate would be

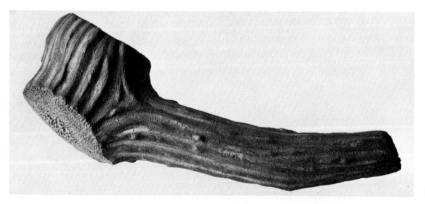

Fig. 20. Deer horn hammer from Spiennes. Bergbau-Museum, Bochum.

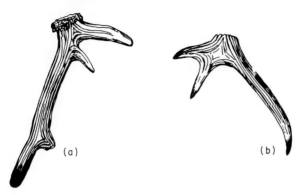

(a)   (b)

Fig. 21. Similarity of (a) two handled deer horn pick (Grimes Graves) and (b) combined rake and lever (Mur de Barrez).

faster still if the blocks were loosened and levered out, punches being used to make the holes.

Andrée (1922) refers to axes made from deer horn and picks at Grimes Graves and Champignolles in France, the former had a single handle while the latter had two handles. He is probably referring to a pick at Grimes Graves and a rake at Champignolles as in Fig. 21.

Greenwell when digging the first pit at Grimes Graves in 1869, found a

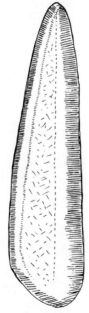

Fig. 22. Ground basalt pick from Grimes Graves.

ground basalt pick of the type shown in Fig. 22. It has been assumed that prehistoric man transported rocks many hundreds of miles, as for example the huge blocks of dolerite which were possibly taken from South Wales to Salisbury Plain for the erection of Stonehenge (see Chap. 5).

There has been considerable controversy over the use of the scapula shovel five of which were found at Cissbury. They were probably made from the shoulder blade of the so-called Celtic ox. A worn one was found at Avebury and was probably Neolithic, and Wade (1922) found one at Stoke Down. Curwen became interested in the possible use of these so-called shovels and wrote to Egypt, Palestine, France, Belgium, Austria, Italy, Greece, Norway, Sweden and Ireland. None had been found in these countries, but Reinerth of Tübingen had written a reference to the use of scapula shovels, i.e. scapulae with resected spines, in the Neolithic villages of Riedschachen and Aichbühl and in the Early Iron Age settlement at Wasserburg, Buchau. Curwen presumed that scapula shovels as found in Swiss lake dwellings as at Robenhausen were used only for the moving of material such as grain. He shows skethes of scapula shovels and these are reproduced in Fig. 23. At Harrow Hill a shovel was

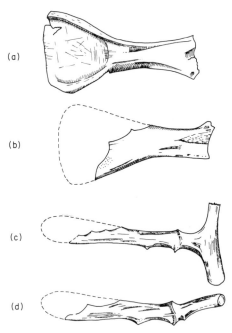

(a)

(b)

(c)

(d)

Fig. 23. Shoulder blade or scapula shovels; (c) has antler handle. Acknowledgements to Worthing Archaeological Society.

found which had apparently a socket for a handle extension. Curwen carried out some experiments with three different methods of filling a basket with chalk rubble. If x min represented the time to fill the basket with a pointed army spade, it took $3x$ min by hand grubbing and as long as $4x$ min using the scapula of a modern ox. He concluded that the scapula shovel was inefficient and this was the result of there being little available room for the left hand on the neck of the bone. This probably also explains the relative scarcity of the shovel as compared to that of the antler pick.

Antler picks and shoulder blade shovels were also tested in connection with an experimental earthwork at Overton Down in Wiltshire by the British Association in 1960. Part of the work was done with only antler picks and shoulder blade shovels as in Neolithic times. The picks proved to be very resilient and could be used either with a swinging blow or by battering the tine into the chalk with a wooden mallet or large stone. None of the picks broke although one of the points became splintered and all became shorter with use. The shoulder blade shovels, on the other hand, were found to be inefficient and were best used to scrape the broken chalk for carrying from the ditch to the bank.

Flint Processing

Neolithic man perfected the finish of his flint tools to an extent unknown to his predecessors. Often the rough flints were broken up at the base of the shaft before being raised to the surface. In many of the prehistoric pits excavated debris has been found and indeed in the rubble used for the final infilling of the shafts when a pit was abandoned. Mostly the pits were filled in very soon after their use was exhausted.

The most common method was to transport the flint nodules to a flint knapping floor or factory central to the site of the shaft area on the surface. Flint axes chiefly for use in agriculture and forest clearance were manufactured here and might have been traded far afield. Flint knapping floors have been identified from the multiplicity of flint fragments struck off during processing. The chief characteristics of the Neolithic axe is the fine polishing all over the surface. The axe head was first shaped by flaking and then the surface ground down by rubbing on a whetted stone slab known as a "sarsen" which was made from rock foreign to the locality in which it was found, e.g. in Wiltshire at Avebury, Stonehenge and in the numerous barrows. The sarsen stones used in flint processing were especially chosen for their abrasive properties and one such sarsen is shown in Fig. 24. Two unpolished Neolithic axes are shown

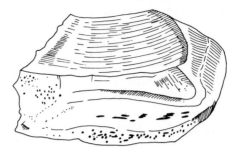

Fig. 24. Sarsen stone used for polishing axe heads. Reproduced by permission of the Trustees of the British Museum, Natural History.

in Fig. 25a and polished ones in Fig. 25b. Recent work, however, at Grimes Graves has led to the conclusion that only rough shaping of the flint nodules was carried out on this mining site. They could then be transported easily to the habitation sites or workshops for local finishing. The evidence for this is that few finished axes have been found at Grimes Graves although scrapers, knives etc. exist and these were probably used

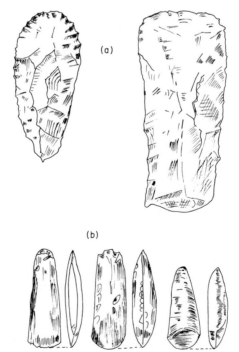

Fig. 25. Unpolished and polished Neolithic tools; (a) celts, (b) axe heads. Reproduced by permission of the Trustees of the British Museum.

by the miners and their families on site for food and skin preparation.

There was a great demand for axes and these constituted the main final product of the flint mines. Although in later times copper and tin were available such materials were costly and scarce, at least in England, so flint and hard rocks were used and axes often made to a shape corresponding to that of a metal axe.

The seeds of the old controversy regarding the dating of flint mines were also planted as regards tool types found on the sites. For example Smith (1912) based his opinion that Grimes Graves and Cissbury were of Palaeolithic age also on the types of tools found there. Although his theories are now quite unacceptable, chiefly as a result of the availability of modern dating methods, it is probably worthwhile to state some of the bases from which he drew his conclusions and even in 1912 he said that these were revolutionary. An ovate hand axe, found at Grimes Graves, with primary flaking was said to be Acheulian and a flint chopper Mousterian, likewise a steep edged scraper was attributed to Mousterian. Even the chalk lamps were thought to be of Palaeolithic origin. It has been stated already that the hand axes polished with basalt are now attributable to Neolithic man. Smith accepted that they were basalt polished, but remarked that there was nothing to prevent pre-Neolithic man from polishing axes in this manner. Earlier in his paper he rules out the polishing theory by quoting the finds of hammers made from quartzite pebbles which had produced no evident traces of grinding on the flint axes. Smith also states that out of 600 flint tools found by Pitt-Rivers at Cissbury only one was of the polished variety. Whether or not the polishing of flints was prima facie evidence of Neolithic culture is not really basic to the old problem of dating for radiocarbon dating has now put the existence of Neolithic flint mines beyond any shadow of doubt.

Some Confirmed British Flint Mines

The two chief areas of prehistoric flint mining are Sussex and Norfolk, but there are also several isolated sites outside these two counties and brief mention is made of these later. The most developed of the Sussex mines is Cissbury and the only one worthy of much consideration in Norfolk is the famous one of Grimes Graves. A map showing the approximate locations of the principal mines is given in Fig. 17.

Cissbury

This site, which lies roughly a mile to the east of the village of Findon, and

4 miles due north of Worthing, is archaeologically famous both for its Iron Age fort and the contained remnants of flint mines. It is one of the more important Iron Age forts in Britain and about 60 acres are enclosed by a ditch and stout bank.

As in the cases of many other flint mines there was intense speculation and argument amongst amateur archaeologists in the nineteenth century concerning the nature of the pits and the use to which they were put. It was an obvious conclusion in those days, over 120 years ago, that they were part of the hill fort. In 1850 Turner interpreted them as of religious significance, e.g., barrows or consecrated places for religious worship. Irving, in 1857, dug down a metre or so into a few of the pits, was in a quandary over what he found and merely called them cattle enclosures.

Pitt-Rivers, about 100 years ago, was attracted by the numerous bumps and depressions which are present in the west part of the earthworks. These represent about 200 shafts. Outside the earthworks there can be seen a line of 39 shafts lying at the hill fort south entrance. Pitt-Rivers found that some of the pits had no radiating galleries, but others joined up with intricate patterns of tunnels. The deepest shaft was over 13 m and cut through six seams of flint. During the early excavations two burials were found. One was a skeleton of a young woman who had apparently fallen into the pit. The other was that of a young man in a crouching position at a depth of 4·9 m in a shaft containing 9 m of debris. Around the skeleton was a series of chalk blocks to make a simple grave. At a depth of 10 m Pitt-Rivers found charcoal which later proved to be from willow, gorse and beech. A plan of the Cissbury flint mine is shown in Fig. 12 and a section through one of the circular shafts in Fig. 26. Most authorities agree that the age of Cissbury is early Neolithic and dating, according to Thomas (1976), to between 2900 BC and 2500 BC. A more up-to-date radiocarbon date is 2770 ± 150 for an antler pick.

A vast selection of flint tools manufactured on the site were found and is shown in the paper by R. A. Smith (1911). These were specially given in the paper to illustrate their suspected Mousterian–Aurignacian connection to which reference has already been made. In addition five scapula shovels were found on the site.

At a depth of 4 m a fragment of the side of a shouldered pot of the Neolithic A type similar to one found at Whitehawk Camp, which is situated on the racecourse at Brighton. This find gave an early clue to the Neolithic origin of the mine.

Scratch marks were found on the blocks of chalk left behind and on the walls, the meaning of which as with those found on other sites is still problematical.

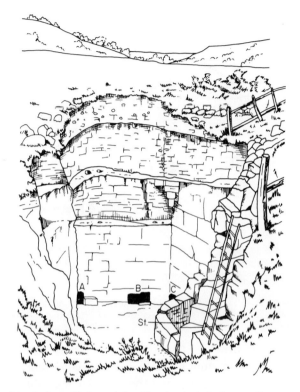

Fig. 26. One of the shafts at Cissbury (after Harrison). A, B, C, = gallery entrances, St = fireplace constructed from chalk blocks.

Harrow Hill

The site of this prehistoric mine should not be confused with a similar place name in Middlesex. It is situated $2\frac{3}{4}$ miles north-west of Findon and 4 miles west-by-north of Cissbury. The site has a large group of mine shafts and Thomas (1976) gives a figure of 100 whereas Dyer (1973) estimates as many as 160. So far one large shaft and three smaller ones have been opened. There are three seams, the upper one outcropping on the north side of the hill and this has been worked opencast. The second one has a depth of 2·4 m and the bottom one which is of the best quality forms the floor at about 6 m from the surface. Evidence for the presence of old flint workings lies in the numerous depressions which average 4 m in diameter. Early in the Iron Age a small sub-rectangular enclosure 59·4 m × 51·8 m, with rounded corners, was built over the filled-in mine shafts.

Pit 21 shown in Fig. 27 is 6 m deep and 7 m diameter and has seven

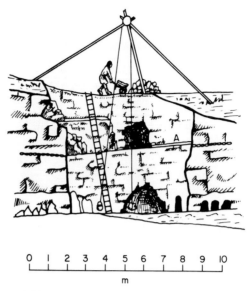

0 1 2 3 4 5 6 7 8 9 10
m

Fig. 27. Section through Pit 21 at Harrow Hill. Acknowledgements to Methuen and Co. Ltd.

galleries radiating from its base into the solid chalk. This pit was excavated by Curwen and Curwen (1923), who report extensively on the work carried out on the site when they and their fellow workers dug out 350 tons of chalk on Saturday afternoons during one month! The finds from this excavation were interesting as they confirmed a working contemporary with that of Cissbury and suggested a date of c3000. Curwen (1954) states that only pottery was lacking. However, in 1933, Worthing Archaeological Society was excavating at New Barn Down half a mile south of Harrow Hill mines and came unexpectedly on a Neolithic dwelling pit which contained two flint axes similar to those produced at the mine although one was polished, and several Neolithic vessels of both the A1 and A2 types. At Harrow Hill Curwen and Curwen (1923) found nests of flint flakes and charcoal together with evidence possibly for artificial lighting, i.e. soot on the roof from miners' lamps. In addition there were abundant animal bones, picks, hammers, red deer antlers and ox shoulder blades, probably used as shovels as they had a socket for a handle extension. One gallery was supported by chalk blocks the removal of which resulted in a considerable roof fall. The projecting angles of the walls were often found to be rubbed, i.e. rounded, according to Curwen, by the passage of men into and out of the mine. A hammer was found which apparently had a handle formed from the massive frontal tine of an antler and the head was the crown from which the beam had been cut off. It was noted that there was a tiny specule of flint embedded in the hock marks at the cut end of an antler and this was attributed to the fact that the antlers were cut by a flint tool. Another interesting fact was the unexplicable series of complicated designs consisting of scratch marks forming an irregular chess board pattern on the wall and west side of Gallery VI. Were these tallies or were they some form of doodling by prehistoric man?

Curwen was of the opinion that only one culture was involved in the Harrow Hill mines, i.e. that of the Middle or Late Neolithic. Patination on flint varies inversely with depth and patination at this site indicated one culture, i.e. depth was the same. The same worker says that the oyster shells found were not Roman as these were not eaten in the Harrow Hill area. The climate was damp as was evidenced by the existence of the mollusc *Hortensus* which does not now live on the chalk downs. The charcoal was from ash and willow both of which thrive under damp conditions.

Holleyman (1937a,b) carried out excavations on the site in 1936. His objective was to find the date and purpose of the small rectangular earthwork on the summit of the hill and to attempt to discover the hut of the Neolithic folk who worked the mines. He failed to find the hut site, but during the trenching of the earthworks he located several more mine shafts. Shaft I was circular, 1·5 m in diameter and 3 m deep with a single gallery 3 m long and about 1 m wide and which curved slightly to the left, as shown in Fig. 28. Three axes were found, one being partly polished,

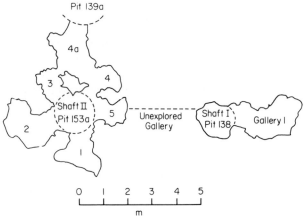

Fig. 28. Plan of shafts 1 and 11 with galleries at Harrow Hill. Acknowledgements to Methuen.

and some fragments of antler tools. The gallery was stowed with chalk rubble. About 5 m from Shaft I a second shaft (Shaft II), circular in shape and 2 m in diameter was located beneath the ramparts of the hill fort on the site. Six short galleries radiated from the base. Just below the turf line there was a filling of clay and fine chalk merging lower down into small chalk rubble and at the bottom large chalk blocks. The third shaft, i.e. Shaft III contained 33 axes and was 2·5 m in diameter and just under 3 m deep to a solid chalk floor. The walls were in a process of disintegration probably resulting from the shallow depth of the mine. Consequently only one gallery was excavated and it was entered on the north-east side 24 cm above the floor. It was 4 m long and at 3 m it turned sharply to the right. There was only one perfect specimen of an antler tool found which was of a mallet made from a red deer antler. Charcoal found came from elm, hawthorn and hazel and was confirmed to be Neolithic. The excavations were interesting, but nothing new or original was found. The general opinion was that Harrow Hill was a Neolithic working with an overlap into the Bronze Age. A more recent radiocarbon date for one antler pick from a gallery was 2980 ± 150 BC.

Church Hill, Findon

A third group of mines in the Findon area is situated at the top of Church Hill about 300 m south-west of Findon Church and $1\frac{1}{2}$ miles west of Cissbury. It is not a large group compared to that of Cissbury or Harrow Hill and was first recognized by Willett in 1868 (Law 1927). Since then Toms (1928) has investigated the site and J. H. Pull (1933, 1953) later cleared several shafts and flaking floors, which were 10–20 m square and contemporary with the mining industry. They sometimes overlie the dumps and filled in shafts and are occasionally partly covered by the debris thrown from other shafts. Both core and flake industries are well represented by scrapers, knives and saws as well as the debris from manufacture. In the early excavations no galleries were found probably as a result of the very friable nature of the chalk. A plan of the galleries, from Shafts 4, 5 and 5a found later is shown in Fig. 29.

In the upper part of the shaft excavated west of the centre of the area, 4·9 m deep and 5·5 m wide, a beaker was found containing a cremation together with two local flint axes, see Fig. 30. It was at the time assigned to the Early Bronze Age and Curwen (1954) quoted a date of c. 1500 and considered the beaker to be a late arrival from Holland. At the same level in the soil, fragments of another vessel were found with a flat out-turned lip and a decoration consisting of vertical rows of punches. It was similar

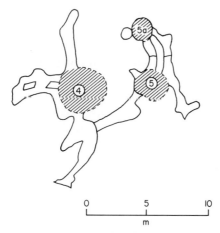

Fig. 29. Plan of shafts and galleries at Church Hill.

to one found at an Early Bronze Age site overlying a Neolithic camp at Whitehawk near Brighton.

Pull (1953) resumed his work in November 1945, assisted by helpers from the Worthing and Brighton Archaeological Society. Mine Shaft 4 was excavated first of all (see Fig. 29). Roman pottery and a shell of a Roman snail, *Helix asperse*, were found and the pit had been filled in with chalk rubble. Fifteen layers were removed over a period of two years. Pull suggested that a partly filled-in pit had been used as a shelter for flint workers. Before the soil could form, the surface was covered by a great flint workshop extending well beyond the area of the mouth of the pit.

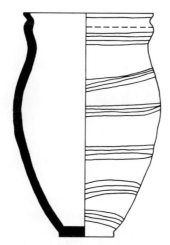

Fig. 30. Beaker from Church Hill. Acknowledgements to Methuen.

There were interesting finds in the various layers excavated. A heavy mallet was found which was formed from a red deer antler and used for flint knapping and this is shown in Fig. 31. Neolithic A pottery was present as well as the carbonized remains of a wooden bowl formed from black poplar. In the base of the layer of silt and sealed beneath the large undisturbed floor which lay above it, were fragments of three Middle Bronze Age urns with overhanging rims (*c.* 1400), a Neolithic type bowl, an Early Bronze Age beaker (*c.* 1800) and two celts which had been sharpened by the "tranchet" technique.

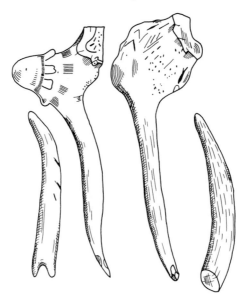

Fig. 31. Antler mallets and punches from Church Hill.

Altogether three shafts were excavated and all were roughly circular and slightly tapering from 5 m diameter at the surface to 4 m at the base and were 5 m deep. They all passed through four seams of nodular flint. The third seam was hardly worked, but the fourth had galleries driven in it as shown in the plan in Fig. 29. The galleries were about 1 m high and one or 2 m wide and nearly 10 m long. All the work had been done by picks, levers and punches cut from red deer antlers and shovels from the shoulder blades of oxen.

Pull also found evidence for the use of a wooden ladder in a shaft and also for the use of wooden bars with rounded ends to lever out blocks of chalk. There were no similar finds in Sussex in other flint mines up to that time.

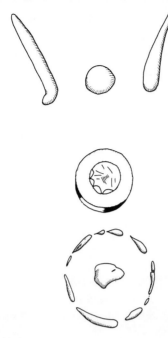

Fig. 32. Symbols above entrances to galleries at Shaft 4, Church Hill.

Some incomprehensible symbols had been cut into the roof at galleries presumably with the aid of antler picks. These are shown in Fig. 32 taken from the sketches made by Pull. These also had not been found previously in any other Sussex flint mines. The symbols at (A) might be interpreted as representing some prehistoric ball game, but no trace of what could be evidence of this has yet come to light, i.e. at habitation sites.

A hut site was found to the south east of the shafts and was just under 4 m in width with a shallow containing ditch. To the west there was a circular depression 3 m in diameter with flint instruments, a small hearth with burnt out flint, bones and teeth of oxen and pigs. Pottery fragments were dated as Middle Bronze Age *c.* 1400 BC. Two other shafts were excavated, i.e. Shafts 6 and 7. Shaft 6 was 6 m deep and passed through five seams of inferior flint to reach the sixth in which five short headings had been driven. Shaft 7 was sunk later and very close to Shaft 6 and nearly 6 m × 5 m in plan and nearly 6 m deep. An attempt had been made to work the fifth seam from this shaft and it was here that the evidence for the use of a ladder had been found.

Church Hill represents one of the few British flint mines that are at present known to have been worked from the Neolithic into the Bronze

Age. The site although small must have been worked over a long period with intermissions as a radiocarbon date for an antler pick found in one of the galleries gave an early date of *c.* 3390 ± 150 BC according to Burleigh (1975).

Blackpatch

This flint mining site is the fourth of the block, including the ones already described, in the Findon area. It is located on a spur of Blackpatch Hill 1¾ miles west of Findon and a ¼ mile north-east of Myrtlegrove Farm. Today, as with many of the prehistoric mining sites not much of the actual site is visible as it has been levelled and ploughed over. The chief items of interest recorded from excavations made from 1922 until 1930 are (a) the burials, cremations and barrows and (b) the miners' dwelling site.

There were about 100 shafts and seven of these were excavated during the period mentioned. The first shaft was dug out in 1922 (Pull 1932a) and found to have seven radiating galleries at the base. The shaft was 5 m in diameter 3·4 m deep down to the seam worked and had vertical sides. As the walls showed no signs of weathering it was assumed that the shaft had not been in use for very long. In fact the galleries appeared to radiate out only so far as natural illumination by daylight permitted. To reduce labour apparently each gallery was filled in with debris from the next one being dug. Dyer (1973) is of the opinion that a new shaft dug every five years would certainly supply the needs of a small community. In addition to the seven shafts four flaking floors were cleared.

The positions of the galleries radiating out from the shaft excavated in 1922 are shown in Fig. 33 taken from the report prepared by the Worthing Archaeological Society (Goodman *et al.* 1922). Only one gallery, i.e. Gallery V forms a thoroughfare to a neighbouring Shaft 3. Galleries II and VII communicate with galleries of other shafts by means of small apertures. Only Galleries IV and V communicate with one another. The actual excavation of the shafts and galleries yielded little knowledge of a general nature additional to that already determined for other flint mines in the neighbourhood. For example there was no sign of access to the shaft in the form of ledges or holes to which a beam might have been fixed and no grooves which might have been made by ropes or thongs. There were no shovels or scapulae as found at Cissbury and merely a few fragmentary antlers and tines of red deer, but on the other hand seven antler picks were found in one gallery alone.

A feature not found at many other flint mines was the arrangement of

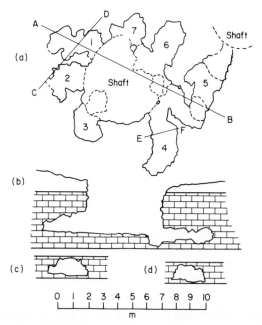

Fig. 33. Plan of first shaft excavated at Blackpatch in 1922. (a) Plan, (b) section on AB, (c) section on CD, (d) section on EF.

seven pick holes in the wall of Gallery I arranged in two approximately parallel rows to take advantage of the breaks to lever out intervening blocks of chalk.

At one point a beautiful celt had been made, but had broken and the two halves, which fitted perfectly, were 3 m apart. The writers of the report suggested that they were thrown away by disgruntled knappers. A similar instance has been reported from Grimes Graves.

It was at Blackpatch that some early doubt was cast on the dating. The celts appeared to be Neolithic, but side scrapers, similar to those of Le Moustier were found and these are not common to later cultures. The ovate hand axe appeared to resemble those associated with the Acheulian culture.

Some charcoal was found and might have been the remains of a torch. The charcoal came from willow and so moister conditions than are existent today might have been prevalent. North-east of the mining area, dwelling sites were found. These are seen today as shallow depressions 2–7 m wide and 23–46 cm into the chalk. They were found to contain pottery, flint flakes, axes and scrapers, animal bones and burnt flints. Unfortunately the pottery fragments are scanty.

The most important finds are the burial sites which are contemporaneous with the mines. Altogether four cremations and four inhumations were found. One cremated burial was discovered under a flaking floor and a burial mound consisted of a barrow over a filled-in shaft (Shaft 3). Cremated human bones were found one third of the way down Shaft 7. One striking feature was that the surrounding chalk was not burnt so the cremation must have been carried out elsewhere. In a barrow overlying Shaft 5 two contracted skeletons were found which were in a position typical of Neolithic or Early Bronze Age burials, one was a male and the other a female burial.

Cremation itself was not common until the late part of the Early Bronze Age, and a collared urn found was typical of the Middle Bronze Age. The excavators (Curwen 1954) note this as evidence that mining at Blackpatch also continued through the Early Bronze Age into the Middle Bronze Age. Although this is highly likely it would appear that the evidence is too slender to allow such supposition. Moreover the flint instruments are unmistakably typical Neolithic. Thomas (1976) gives c. 3200 BC as the date for starting the mines and this is very much in line with an actual radiocarbon date later quoted by Burleigh (1975) for an antler pick found in one of the galleries of 3140 ± 150 BC.

Pull (1932b) gives an interesting account of his work at Blackpatch in a book devoted entirely to the site.

Stoke Down

The four mining sites already considered are in the Findon area of Sussex. Stoke Down lies about 16 miles west of Findon, $3\frac{1}{2}$ miles north-west of Chichester and half a mile north-east of Stoke Down Church. The site is marked chiefly by a series of 21 surface depressions along the brow of a hill. Wade (1922) who excavated three shafts from 1910 to 1913, says that the Lavant Caves which are about half a mile away to the south-east, could probably have been miners' homes, but this has never been established.

The shafts were found to be 3–4 m wide and 3–5 m deep. In Shaft 1 Wade found 2000 flakes resembling "a pile of oyster shells" to a depth of 35 cm and then chalk rubble to 50 cm No galleries were found. Some undercutting was evident at the base and Wade likened the pit to a Wellington boot, although the diameter was unchanged to a depth of 5 m. A flint adze was found, but no metal, pottery or polished implements, either on top or below the flakes. Some wood charcoal was present, but no chalk lamps and indeed these would have been thought to be unnecessary with non-gallery working. Shaft 2 was only 3 m in diameter and 3 m deep with no undercutting or step at the base. However, in this shaft some excellent implements were found including the top stone of a greensand saddle quern, which showed marks of use. Curwen (1954) associates this find with an indication of the miners' familiarity with agriculture. In this context Pitt-Rivers found a flint sickle at Cissbury.

Shaft 3 bore a resemblance to Shaft 1 except that a step was used by the miners as shovelling point for the chalk on its way to ground level. The shape of this shaft was slightly oval 3–4 m across the width and 4 m deep and as in Shaft 1 there was definite evidence of undercutting at the base. The implements included a double ended flint celt and Gorham, a co-worker of Wade's, reported a roebuck antler 2 m down and two very fine implements. A shoulder blade shovel was also present.

There seems to be no doubt that, despite the absence of pottery, the site is Neolithic. There are also some traces of a village dating back to the Iron Age at least the early part, but this has no association with the mines.

No radiocarbon dates are at present available, but as the mining method involving shallow shafts and no galleries is not as advanced as at the other proved Sussex flint mines, it is quite possible that the workings commenced fairly early in the Neolithic.

Lavant Caves

These are located 3 miles north of Chichester and, according to Allcroft (1916), were found in 1890 by a shepherd when he was making holes for his hurdles. His bar slipped from his hands and vanished into the ground. He then lost a second tool. The site is marked by a group of crude depressions close to Hayes Down. Later investigations showed a set of underground galleries quite near the surface and occupying almost an acre. The exploration was carried out by Charles Dawson and John Lewis in 1893 and they found a series of domed chambers of irregular size and plan and connected by passages of height of from 1 to 1·5 m. The Duke of Richmond, the landowner, built a stairway down to the caves, but this is no longer in existence. Dawson and Lewis managed to explore for a distance of 30 m from the foot of the stairs.

The chief interest in the site lies in the finds which when considered together, complicate any possible logical interpretation of the purpose of the site. An antler pick, i.e. the lower tine, a miner's chalk lamp, a small number of worked flints and some small bronze objects were found. The objects of bronze consisted of rings and pins. In addition there was a diamond shaped enamel pendant and a small mask of 3·4 cm diameter showing a female face having Roman features. Some charcoal was also found.

The theories relating to the layout and use of the pits put forward by various interested parties were inclusive of the following:

(1) They were flint mines of pre-Roman age and analogous to Cissbury and Grimes Graves. There were, however, no flint chips and no flint seams in the native chalk.

(2) It was an underground quarry for working chalk. Against this is the obvious fact that an open quarry would have been cheaper, more expedient and safer than underground mining.

(3) The storage of grain in what are called "dene holes". Allcroft (1916) refutes this by saying that they were not dene holes.

(4) They were havens of retreat from invaders or other dangers. This is difficult to believe.

(5) The lamp and antler picks would appear to have been used during excavation. This would not necessarily have been so for flint mining.

(6) They were discovered by the Romans and used for storage. A seal of wool packs dated to the sixteenth century which either proves rediscovery or a continuity of use until at least Roman times.

(7) They could have been dwelling places, but evidence is lacking.

Unfortunately subsidence of the surface as marked by the depressions have destroyed the caves and made further exploration impossible. Furthermore radiocarbon dates, as with many old excavated sites which have been destroyed, are not available.

Bow Hill

Four miles north of Chichester there is a series of pits and mounds which resemble those of extinct and proved flint mines. They are on the south east end of Bow Hill and according to Allcroft (1916) are "strewn thickly with vestiges of human occupation which may antedate the Romans". In addition there is an ancient road running through the pits and mounds and also through some prehistoric earthworks to quote Curwen (1954). A small pit was excavated by Hamilton in 1933, but nothing positive was reported. It is possible that the features do not represent old flint mines, but future excavations might give some more conclusive results.

Windover Hill

There is a small group of pits and mounds on the north side of Windover

Hill and 200 m east of the figure of Long Man carved on the steep north face. The site lies roughly 5 miles north-west of Eastbourne. Between the "flint mines" and the Long Man is a Roman road of the well known design. Another Roman road of similar type passes SW.–NE. on the west side of Wilmington Hill. In the vicinity are modern chalk quarries and prehistoric barrows. Curwen (1928) is of the opinion that the pits and mounds are probably flint mines and resemble those of Harrow Hill. Thomas (1976) refers to them as specifically flint mines and even quotes a date of *c.* 3500–2500 BC and contemporary with the 60 m long and 15 m wide barrow.

Easton Down

The flint mines at this Wiltshire site lie approximately three-quarters of a mile north-west of Lapscombe Corner on the Salisbury to Andover road. Stone (1934) gives a comprehensive account of his excavations in 1930. He discovered many depressions from 16 cm to 1 m deep and having diameters varying from 3 to 10 m. The surface was strewn with massive flint flakes, broken celts and other implements.

To assist his description Stone divides the area covered into four zones, A–D, over the large site dipping from roughly 145 m in the north-east to 115 m in the south-west. A is the north-east sector occupying 40 acres and is adjacent to a Beaker folk site with the ground strewn with beaker fragments and allied pottery, burnt flints and bones of animals. B, in the central north-west area, contains up to 90 or so silted up mine shafts which are mostly visible from the ground. Sector C, at the date of the report had not been excavated and D was cleared as another habitation site possibly being an extension of the settlement in A. The whole area, including habitation sites and mine shafts occupies about 100 acres.

One shaft and three flaking floors were investigated. The shaft designated as B1 was found to be 3·5 m deep and 4 m in diameter, although in plan was 5 m × 4 m and oval in shape.

A celt like tool and other implements were found in Layer 1 including a rough chopper or hand axe. Thousands of shells of land molluscs were found in the loose packing of Layer 2 as shown in Fig. 34 and as at Grimes Graves and Cissbury. There were, in addition to flint implements, a few broken tines of antlers. Blocks in Layer 4 contained marks of antler picks in the form of compressed clay impressions probably indicating very wet conditions and antler picks in dry conditions make very sharp clean holes. A rake was found at 2 m depth in Layer 4, and at 2·5 m a beam with signs of having been cut by a very sharp flint. Compared with Grimes Graves

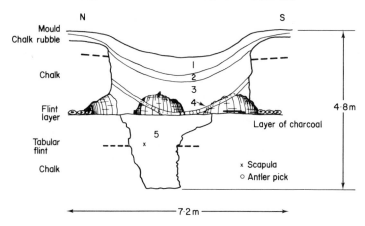

Fig. 34. Section through a shaft at Easton Down. Reproduced by permission of Wiltshire Archaeological Society.

and Cissbury there was, as at Blackpatch, a scarcity of antler tools at Easton Down.

Although there was an undercut under the south-west wall, no tunnelling was attempted, probably owing to the weak nature of the chalk as compared to the Sussex flint mines. There were some burnt pieces of flint, but no hearths. The miners here must have been a hardy race as no evidence of post holes was found.

Stone (1933, 1934) gives a full account of the various flint tools found especially on the flaking floors B2, B3 and B4. He also mentions the discovery of 45 grey, yellow and red Eocene pebbles and suggests that they were possibly collected together by miners' children in connection with a primitive game of marbles.

There was some doubt at the time concerning the age of Easton Down site as apparently Palaeolithic types of tools have been found lying side by side with Neolithic celts as they have at other British sites. There is not what might be called a typical tool at Easton Down comparable with the celt of Cissbury. However, Burleigh (1975) quotes radiocarbon dates of 2530 ± 150 for an antler pick found in a gallery.

There is also some controversy concerning the implication of the presence or otherwise of galleries. Depth is not a real criterion as shallow pits at Blackpatch had galleries whereas similar ones at Grimes Graves had none. It appears reasonable to presume that the character of the chalk decided whether galleries were feasible, e.g. the weak chalk at Easton Down prevented the miners tunnelling from the base of the shaft. On the other hand it is curious to understand why relatively advanced peoples such as those of Neolithic stock, who had already gained a knowledge of agriculture and pottery manufacture, did not use wooden roof supports.

Stone states (1934) that the conifer charcoal found at the site was unique in southern England, but was similar to that noted at Woodhenge, near Amesbury. Woodhenge represents one of the few Neolithic wooden buildings so far found in Britain and might have been a temple. It formed part of the Durrington Wells hinge monument and flint mining site complex around 2000–1500 BC.

The Easton Down flint mines are also reported to have temporary dwellings for the miners and their families. They are represented by stake holes and sherds of both necked and bell type pottery. According to Stone (1937) a skeleton of presumably a pet dog was found buried at the bottom of a bone ash filled pit.

Mention has been made of the thousands of land molluscs found by Stone in his excavations. He is of the opinion that the molluscs produced evidence of heavier rainfall than today with a good amount of sun and winters very much as at present in southern England.

Peppard

Two flint mines which were excavated first over 60 years ago have little mention in archaeological proceedings or in text books. They lie at the small Oxfordshire village of Peppard in the Chiltern Hills being four miles from Henley on Thames and six miles from the Oxfordshire boundary. They were excavated by Peake (1913a) and later by R. Smith according to Peake (1913b).

Peake noticed saucerlike depressions in the grass growing in a ploughed field and below these a large quantity of roughly shaped flints suggesting a factory site in the neighbourhood of the two sites later excavated and shown in the sketch produced from the article by Peake (see Fig. 35).

Site 1 was a deep hollow cup in the grass in the Upper Chalk on sloping ground with dimensions of 20 m by 16 m. Peake excavated down to 4 m over a space of 8 m by 10 m and defined upper and lower sharp margins. The section opened up revealed surface soil and loam, reddish sandy gravel with small flint and quartz pebbles, the first band of flint, an upper clay layer and then the workshop floor. This was followed by a second band of flints with a few fragments of coarse pottery and traces of charcoal, a lower clay layer, in which was embedded an iron knife, a third band of flint with a few cores and flakes and finally what appeared to be a floor of solid chalk.

Site 2 was shallower than Site 1 being only 1–1·5 m down to the solid chalk with again a workshop floor under yellow clay.

The evidence from both sites is scanty and Peake raises the question concerning the possibility of a deeper shaft with galleries. As for many other flint mines the question of age based on the finds is indefinite. Unfortunately no radiocarbon dates are available. Hand axes were found

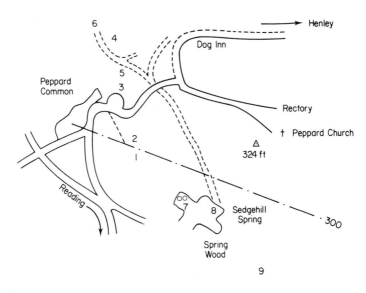

Fig. 35. Location of Peppard flint mines. 1, Site 1; 2, Site 2; 3 and 4, large chalk pits; 5 and 6, layers of flint 3 ft apart; 5–10, circular cup-shaped depressions in grass, probably old mines or chalk pits; 7 and 8, 3 pits arranged around a vallum and ditch (Grims Ditch).

and also large choppers and a round-nosed implement of Aurignacian form. Even a broken leaf shaped blade of Proto-Solutrean type was found in addition to a Cissbury type celt. None of the implements is polished or ice-scratched. Peake says that the two sites bore resemblance to an Aurignacian site such as Brassempony.

R. Smith opened up Site 1 again in October 1913 and found it to be an open pit. Apparently the miners at Peppard had discovered an outcrop of a horizontal layer of flint in the hillside and had quarried it for a distance of 12 m. There was no trace of a horizontal tunnel being made when the overburden became too great for removal.

Grimes Graves

About $5\frac{1}{4}$ miles north-west of Thetford in Norfolk lies the extensive prehistoric mining site of Grimes Graves. It is second only in size to the famous site of Spiennes in Belgium. Colin Renfrew (1973) states that the site almost rivals Rudna Glava the prehistoric copper mine in Yugoslavia. A view of the site is shown in Fig. 36.

The site contains over 366 mine shafts and shallower workings spread over 34 acres. There may even be more shafts, but a portion of the site outside the defined area has been levelled and ploughed over. The plan at Fig. 37 shows the configuration of the site with the excavated pits clearly marked. There are two types of workings at Grimes Graves. In the north of the site the flint may have been worked opencast or by shallow bell pits down to a depth of 3·7 m whereas later workings were by shafts and radiating galleries with a maximum cover of 12·2 m.

The known history of the site is not without interest, indeed the existence of the strange depressions and mounds was known and recognized in the historical records in fact before the Norman Conquest. Camden in 1586 (Norfolk Archaeology 1946) referred to "certain small

Fig. 36. Air view of Grimes Graves. Crown copyright—reproduced with permission of HMSO.

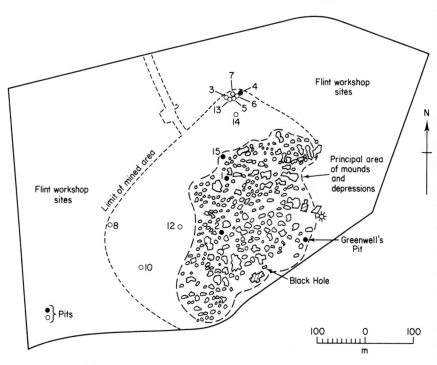

Fig. 37. General layout of Grimes Graves. Shapes, sites and numbers of depressions and mounds in the principal area are only diagrammatically represented. Crown copyright— reproduced with permission of HMSO.

fortifications called Grimes Graves". Later still Blomefield described the site as a "very curious Danish encampment in semi-circular form". Much later at a meeting of the Norfolk and Norwich Archaeological Society on 4 March 1852 the Rev. C. R. Manning (1855) reported the result of an examination he had made of the large collection of pits commonly known as "Grimmers" or "Grimes Graves" on the heath at Weeting near Brandon. This examination, according to Manning, appeared to confirm that they were the remains of a British village. Manning later (1872), in fact July 1866, said that the site represented a British town in the form of a fortified settlement of the Iceni, probably predating the arrival of the Romans. In February 1853 Manning had dug a trench through several pits and found a small oval of flints which he described as a fireplace.

It is interesting at this stage to consider the derivation of the site name. "Grims" is known to be a Norse name meaning witch or watersprite. "Grave" did not imply a burial place, but simply a pit dug out. In fact the usual implication of the term "grave" has rarely been used although it was once thought to have been used as a Viking cemetery. Place names beginning with "Grim" are not uncommon in Britain for there are Grimsdykes or Grimsditches in Berkshire, Essex, Hertfordshire, Oxfordshire and the Antonine Wall between the Firths of Clyde and Forth is known as "Graemes Dyke".

Since controversy appears to have been prevalent over at least 300 years it is difficult to understand why no earlier concerted effort was made to excavate fully at least one pit down to the solid chalk. An early reference to depressions being actual flint mines is noted as having been made when G. L. Gomme (1884) reported on "Open Air Hundreds Courts in Norfolk" said

> ... about the centre of the hundred of Grimeshaw, two miles from Weeting, on the road from Brandon to Norwich, is a very curious Danish encampment in a semi circular form. At the east end of this entrenchment is a tumulus pointing towards Thetford and here the hundred court used to be held. This remarkable place retains the name of Grimes Graves.

A footnote to this statement points out that the site is now known to be a collection of pits for mining flint and refers to Norfolk Archaeology (1872, p. 359).

It was on 3 May 1870 that Canon Greenwell first mentioned his famous excavations. This was at a meeting of the Norfolk and Norwich Archaeologial Society. He along with assistants opened up a pit shown in Fig. 37 as Canon Greenwell's pit. The pit was marked by a hollow on the surface and on digging through 4 m of yellow sand, boulder clay and chalk, which constituted the infilling he found it to be a shaft 8·5 m in diameter at the top, 3·75 m at the bottom and 12 m deep. About a quarter of the way down there was a seam of irregular shaped nodules of flint of coarse texture and reported to be "not well fitted for implement production". Another seam, designated as "wallstone" at 6 m depth, was of better quality, but not for implements. It is significant that the prehistoric miner knew much about flint qualities, for they, as at many other mines, often ignored the higher and poorer seams of flint and suspected often quite correctly that better quality flint lay still deeper. Greenwell's pit contained infilling of chalk between the two lower seams of flint and this was apparently brought from another pit. It seems therefore that after a pit ceased production it was infilled with rubble from a nearby pit. The worked flint at Grimes Graves is known as "floorstone". The rubble in Greenwell's pit seems to have been made up of chalk, charcoal, burnt sand, wood ashes, cores of flint and dear horn tools. There was, therefore, apparently some evidence of a fire having been made.

At the base of the shaft on solid chalk radiating galleries had been driven 1·25–2·0 m wide and 1·0–1·5 m high. Greenwell removed the chalk blocking the galleries and commented on the impressive site in one of them 6·5 m from the base of the shaft, for what the excavators witnessed was a working place with antler picks left behind by workmen when they departed after a roof fall. Greenwell and his co-workers were the first humans to see the place after it was abandoned 3000 years earlier. There were even imprints of miners' fingers in the chalk on the picks. Four cup lamps were found during the excavations, a multiplicity of deer picks, i.e. 79 in total and a hatchet made from basalt. There were also numerous water-rolled quartzite and other pebbles, and the bones of a small ox, *Bos longifroms*.

Since Canon Greenwell carried out his work at Grimes Graves which proved once and for all that it was a flint mining site, many other excavations, mostly during the present century have been made. These have added considerably to the body of knowledge now available.

In 1914 Peake supervised the clearing of two pits, i.e. Pits 1 and 2. Both were 9·5 m deep. Pit 1 was estimated to have involved the removal of nearly 200 m³ of chalk during excavation by the miners. The infilling took three men (two digging and one barrowing) 20 days to clear. The shaft pillar at the bottom was pierced by six galleries which led into an irregular series of chambers and pillars were left as in the pillar and stall system of coal mining. The flint deposit consisted of a seam of nodules which covered the floor of the galleries. Apparently rope haulage was used in the shaft as there were marks where a rope could have possibly made grooves in the chalk. The disused galleries were packed with debris from new excavations. Most of the tools used were deer antlers, but some polished and ground flint axes were used to a limited extent. Figure 38 shows the bottom of Pit 1 and entrances to the radiating galleries.

Armstrong (1936) reported the complete excavation of Pit 14 which contained an elaborate system of galleries and was slightly earlier in age than Pit 12, i.e. pre 2340 BC.

Pit 15, cleared in 1939, was originally open to the public, but is now closed owing to dangers of falls of rock. This pit contained an interesting find in the form of an altar of flint lumps surrounded by a pile of seven deer antlers and at the base a chalk lamp. In front of the altar was an offering of chalk balls and a phallus calved out of chalk, a fertility symbol and a chalk figurine of a fat woman, Fig. 39, Apparently according to some theories, the miners were unsuccessful in locating the floorstone in Pit 15 and made an offering to the gods in order to be successful in future ventures. The genuine nature of the find is open very much to question.

Fig. 38. Shaft bottom and gallery entrances at Pit I Grimes Graves. Crown copyright—reproduced with permission of HMSO.

This aspect is quoted in many guide books and publications and yet from another source (Lease *et al.* 1938) comes the statement that Pits 15 and 16 contained a series of galleries and were circular and, although no pottery was found, they were the first pits to yield evidence of the mining of the wallstone layer in deep caves around the shaft. There were two chipping floors, one technique being Clactonian or Mousterian and the other Levalloisian. Other finished products of fine workmanship were found including discoidal flake tools, other flake tools and celts. The picks used were exclusively from red deer antlers.

It was in 1923 that Armstrong noticed on the valley slopes to the north a group of shallow pits without galleries and in 1926 he classified a series of pits on the western boundary as intermediate. Thus there are three types of pits at Grimes Graves: (1) shallow pits which are primitive 2·1 m × 1·9 m in size and of depth 3·5–4 m. Examples are Pits 3, 4, 5, 6, 7 and 13. (2) Intermediate pits which are 2·1–4·2 m in depth. They are larger in size than the shallower pits being up to 6·3 m in width. There are no galleries, but a small degree of undercutting. Examples are Pits 8, 9, 10 and 11. (3) Deep pits having galleries and from 6 to 12·2 m in depth.

Fig. 39. Chalk figurine of goddess from Grimes Graves. Reproduced by permission of the Trustees of the British Museum.

There are at least 360 of these and they have galleries 2·1 m wide and up to 1·5 m high. Some of the excavated pits include Pits 1, 2, 12, 14 and 15. In some guide books and reports ungalleried pits are often referred to as "opencast". This is incorrect usage since opencast is reserved, in mining terminology, for a form of openpit mining or quarrying with advancing faces.

The products from Grimes Graves were mainly axe blades, which were roughly chipped to shape and then taken away or traded, the customer probably providing his own finish to his own taste.

In addition to Pit 15 one other pit was kept open for public inspection. This pit, Pit 1, is 9·5 m deep and is entered by an iron ladder through a trap door in a modern concrete roof. A section through Pit 1 is approximately:

Silt	0·0–0·92 m
Sand	0·92–1·84 m
Boulder clay	1·84–3·08 m
TOPSTONE (flint)	3·08–3·22 m
Upper crust of soft chalk	3·22–5·51 m
Hard chalk	5·51–6·93 m
WALLSTONE (flint)	6·93–7·06 m
Hard chalk	7·06–8·90 m
FLOORSTONE (flint)	8·90–9·20 m

Greenwell's pit is at the time of writing being re-excavated for use by the public for inspection purposes.

Burleigh (1975) gives a range of 14 radiocarbon dates for various shafts and galleries. Some of these are quoted later in this chapter. The range extends from 2500 ± 150 to 1400 ± 150 BC. The mines at Grimes Graves, according to these dates, started somewhat later than those in Sussex. The recently published radiocarbon dates confirmed many old theories regarding the age and duration of flint mine workings.

It has been estimated that 7 tons of flint were taken from a single shaft. Furthermore it is also assumed that seven miners worked at a time on flint extraction and five men carried the flint nodules to the surface. The work lasted over a period of several months. Ladders set at 45° to the vertical appear to have been used in the shaft to a ledge half way up. In recent excavations traces of these ledges have been found by Mercer (1976). Markings on shaft walls, crudely scratched, could well have been tally markings used for recording the basket loads of flint hauled or carried up the shaft. It is probable, if the work was continuous and not seasonal, that a shaft would be worked out every 2–3 years.

Pottery found at Grimes Graves is purported to be of the Neolithic A

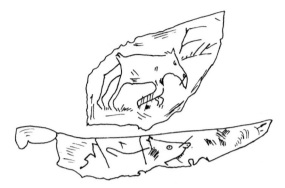

Fig. 40. Flint crust engravings at Grimes Graves. Acknowledgements to the Prehistoric Society.

culture, but was said at one time to have been left there by traders coming up the Icknield Way in search of flint axes from the mines.

In addition to the tally marks there were found crude drawings of animals scratched on flints the most famous being that of a red deer shown reproduced in Fig. 40.

A report published by Mercer (1976) describes an excavation made at Grimes Graves in 1971–72. In it the work of Greenwell in 1870 at Grimes Graves and by Lane-Fox (Pitt-Rivers) in 1875 at Cissbury is criticized as not having been done very well and that the dating and context were enveloped in controversy. It must be remembered, however, that in the nineteenth century very little was known about the Neolithic and of course modern methods of dating, identification and sampling were not at that time available. Conversely today the archaeologist can avail himself of the services of all types of specialists. Despite the non-availability of modern methods it is certain that many of the conclusions put forward in the 1870s by the main investigators can be accepted.

Mercer and his colleagues stripped 400 m² of an extensive chalk dump and found antler pick tines. The internal bands of weathering in the dumps were thought to indicate intermittent working of the shaft. A shaft was next cleared and in the uppermost layers were found a number of bones of horse and other large mammals, several molluscs and highly patinated flint instruments. Two early Iron Age burials were found, one being a woman who had a plaque of chalk on her hip and was about 20–25 years of age. There were also the remains of a man in a crouching position with two iron ring beads close by the neck. The date for these inhumations was mid sixth century BC. Lower down a Middle Bronze Age collared urn was found and at the base charcoal of radiocarbon date *c.* 1820 BC. It was here that the evidence for the use of a wooden platform was found. The platform is said to have served the double purpose to protect the miners working underneath and to provide a stage for the ladder system. The pit excavated was apparently active around *c.* 1800 BC and associated at that time with grooved ware. In *c.* 1130 BC it was probably resettled by Bronze Age farmers using cordoned pottery and finally in *c.* 600 BC used as an Iron Age burial place.

An investigation which included geophysical and chemical surveys and aerial photography was carried out by Sieveking *et al.* (1973). Excavations were made to test the validity of the scientific surveys. The authors of the paper referred to are also critical of the early work and state that in their opinion the site of Easton Down with 253 shafts and Grimes Graves having 93 acres were too large for the methods used. It is somewhat difficult to visualize the alternatives in those days unless it was mass digging. Again it should be stated that few alternatives were available to the nineteenth century archaeologist. A preliminary investigation using phosphate surveys was made. Core samples were taken over a pit and at the ground levels alongside. The principle of the method is based on the fact that an absolute concentration of phosphate can be taken as evidence of human activity.

It has always been assumed that the older workings at any prehistoric mining site were shallower than the newer ones. According to Sieveking *et al.* (1973) at Grimes Graves the reverse is the case as shown by the relevant radiocarbon datings:

$$\text{Pit} \quad 8 \ c. \ 1340 \pm 150 \text{ BC}$$
$$10 \ c. \ 1920 \pm 150 \text{ BC}$$
$$11 \ c. \ 1750 \pm 150 \text{ BC}$$
$$12 \ c. \ 2340 \pm 150 \text{ BC}$$
$$15 \ c. \ 2320 \pm 150 \text{ BC}$$

At the same time the authors give a date of *c.* 1430 ± 55 BC for an antler pick, *c.* 1657 ± 300 BC for some charcoal and *c.* 2340–1340 BC for the working of Pit 12. An antler pick from Gallery III of Greenwell's pit gave a radiocarbon date of *c.* 1860 ± 130 BC.

Concerning the environmental aspect of the workings at Grimes Graves an interesting comment is made by J. G. Evans (1975). Chalk waste spread over 35 acres or more at Grimes Graves had resulted in the destruction of valuable pasture or grazing land. However, in the long term at any rate at Grimes Graves, results may have been of soil improvement for, whereas the original soil was sandy and susceptible to wind erosion the soil today, where developed on the chalk upcast is calcareous and fertile. The side effects of industrial processes are therefore not always detrimental.

Clarke (1935) mentions that recently flint knapping was in operation at Brandon. Clarke (1935) refers to the nearby Linghearth mines where flint was fashioned into gun flints and exported abroad.

Grimes Graves will probably continue to be one of the more important flint mines to be excavated for many years to come. There are still many shafts remaining uninvestigated scientifically and many questions still to be answered. Maybe there still remains some valuable piece of evidence awaiting discovery which may assist in the confirmation or refutation of present day theories.

Other Flint Mines in the British Isles

Massingham is the only other recognized flint mining site in Norfolk and lies roughly 21 miles due north of Grimes Graves. Excavation at this site was reported in 1891 and was accredited in Norfolk Archaeology Society Transactions to Plowright and Wade (1859). The pits here averaged 11·5 m × 9·25 m in plan and 1·5–1·75 m in depth and were filled with masses of flint lumps and chalk rubble, the deepest and largest pit being 22 m × 18·5 m in size and 7·75 m deep. There were no galleries and the excavations were cup shaped. It appears that Massingham represents an early attempt at flint mining. The pits could have been filled in and left undisturbed, but if the flint had been of good quality later generations of miners might have reopened the pits to drive galleries and exploit the apparently shallow deposits.

About 2 miles north of Easton Down and just over the West Hampshire border, on the same downland ridge, lies Martin's Clump. Like its better known neighbour it is now not easily accessible. There are the remains of possibly 100 shafts and was first discovered in 1932.

Durrington flint mines, which are situated in the village of that name near Amesbury, constitutes an interesting site since trial pits were dug here by Neolithic miners apparently to prove the quality of the flint. They also demonstrated that it was possible to cut galleries in relatively weak chalk only 1·25 m below the surface. They were discovered quite accidentally during the making of trenches for pipes in connection with a new drainage project. The flint was first excavated with three pits 3 m apart and were roughly 60 cm deep. Later a fourth pit 60 cm wide and 1 m deep was undercut and the fifth, 60 cm wide and 1·5 m deep had short galleries at its base. Petit tranchet arrowheads as at Grimes Graves, in addition to antler picks and the nearby Woodhenge were found. J. D. G. Clark (1934) states that tranverse arrowheads are firmly fixed in the Late Neolithic/Early Bronze Age and overlap especially on sites connected with Grooved Ware and are not characteristic of the Western Neolithic. The Grooved Ware people were responsible for the nearby Woodhenge monument in Late Neolithic times. The Woodhenge Durrington Walls–Durrington flint mines thereby constitute an important complex in Late Neolithic times overlooking the River Avon according to Wainwright and Longworth (1971).

There has inevitably been some controversy over the relative lack of known flint mines in Wiltshire. Booth and Stone (1951) attribute it possibly to later cultivation in the Early Iron Age and the Romano-British type of top soil which would have attracted Neolithic and Early Bronze Age miners. Flint mines were generally filled in and later obliterated by ploughing so discovery must be fortuitous.

A short note in the journal of the Wiltshire Archaeological Society (Passmore 1942) from a Mr Passmore concerned pits worth investigating half a mile north-east of Liddington Castle on high ground in a small clump of trees. Below these to the south are a series of pits extending around the east flank of Liddington Hill. Passmore suspected deep shafts with galleries along beds of fine flint.

On the south side of the main road opposite Tolmere Pond and three quarters of a mile west of Gun Inn at Findon in Sussex lie a series of scoops or depressions on the west face of Church Hill all on the contour. They appeared to Curwen and Curwen (1927) to be mines sunk on the outcrop of a seam of flint. It is pointed out that the depressions appear to interrupt an ancient cart track so the latter would be very old in comparison, or the tracks might have been made to the mines. Some excavation was made into one of the mines and an early Romano-British vessel was found lying on the chalk filling. A rough flint implement had been buried along with the chalk.

Two further sites in Norfolk have been thought to represent flint mines and are Markshall and Great Malton. Kingland which is also in Norfolk, was excavated by W. G. Clarke (1915). He found 900 implements and several thousand flakes. The site lies midway between Beehive Lodge at Castessy and the Ringland Hills and constitutes a low chalk spur running about 25 m from the foot of Cobbs Hole. Axes were found of the Cissbury type, but no bones, charcoal or molluscs. It was estimated that 970 m³ of chalk have been removed by prehistoric workers. Other possible flint mines in Norfolk are Buckenham Eaton and Whitlingham.

Surrey is not recognized, unlike Sussex, Wiltshire and Norfolk, as a flint mining area primarily because the chalk formations are not so vast. However, Todd (1949) found a Neolithic flint mine at East Horsley in this county. This was located on the edge of a narrow strip of woodland to the west of a dry tributary valley of the River Mole at a height of 400 ft OD. There were two saucer-like depressions with flint flakes scattered on the surface. One depression was excavated and found to be a 6 m diameter shaft having a stairway cut into the chalk down to a depth of 3 m. Three seams of flint were passed through before a thick floor of good flint was found at 4 m. In addition trial trenches 10 m away from the shaft uncovered an occupation floor on the chalk at a depth of roughly 6 cm from the surface. The flint assemblies found included 715 complete flakes, 14 scrapers, six rough choppers, 40 cores, an adze, a backed knife, two fabricators, a flake from a polished axe, two polishers, a pick and a Campigny-type flake axe. There were remnants of a possible house, but no signs of postholes. Todd presumed that the mine was not regularly worked, but only visited by workers from time to time as and when flint was required. The evidence for this is the high proportion of roughly dressed flint amongst the flakes.

In Scotland the only important source of flint is, according to Scott (1950), several acres of quarries in a thick bed of flint on a low ridge from Buchan Ness to Dudswick Hill north of Ellon at the head of the estuary of the Ytham. Apart from this and the flint found on raised beaches in various parts of Scotland the only abundant deposits are in Aberdeenshire, and so according to Callandar (see Scott 1951), flint must have been a very valuable commodity as very poor flints were often worked. Flakes have been found a very great distance from the actual deposits and were remains of, or half finished attempts at making saws, borers, scrapers and knives. Hammer stones of quartz and quartzite and sandstone rubbing stones have also been found. It appears to be quite evident that no shafts were made and the flint is not deep; and in the Neolithic and Early Bronze Ages was probably quarried.

A flint mine was discovered at Balleygalley Hill in County Antrim in 1957 during the making of a golf course, according to a report in the Prehistoric Society Proceedings (1958). In addition Neolithic flint debris and some sherds was found in addition to evidence of flint flaking and Neolithic occupation levels amongst uneven outcrops. Opencast mining had taken place as the stepped solid chalk indicated and the dipping flint beds had been extracted deep into the hillside. Mining was carried out on a broad front the chalk rubble and knapping debris being deposited behind the miners as they worked forward.

Clark and Piggott (1937) list the more important flint sites in Britain and Europe and mention a few which are deemed to be of a debatable character.

High Wycombe which is mentioned in the Museums Journal for 1902–3, has also been suggested as a possible prehistoric flint mining site.

Cook and Killick (1922) wrote an account concerning their finds of thousands of flint artifacts of Palaeolithic age, the flint axes of which were said to be of Acheulian type. The site of the finds was near the church of All Saints at Findsbury on the left bank of the River Medway within the boundaries of the city of Rochester. A quarry had been made in the chalk which had been deposited in Pleistocene times by the Medway which was then 28 m higher. Flint working floors were discovered in shallow depressions in the calcareous loam which had been deposited on the chalk. This find lends validity to the theory that Palaeolithic man did find flint if only by shallow diggings into superficial chalk beds. Similar excavations were made by Palaeolithic man contemporaneously in the Somme Terraces in France (see p. 87).

Beer Head in South East Devon has long been reputed to be a prehistoric flint mining site. It is situated about 4 km south-west of Seaton and the chief interest in the area is in the Beer flint found in the chalk cliffs. This is black and shiny with a relatively brown cortex. This represents, according to MacAlpine Woods (1929), who investigated the site and workshop floors in the vicinity from 1929 to 1952, the most westerly source of flint in England. Tools made from the flint were in the earliest levels at Hembury. No pottery has come to light, but thousands of flint implements including Neolithic celts and Mesolithic microliths. Tardnoisian and early Neolithic dating has been suggested. North and west of Beer at Bovey, according to MacAlpine Woods and McAlpine Woods (1933, 1948), a workshop of Upper Palaeolithic date is possible as parts of Solutrean leaf-like blades have been found. Although there are no traces of flint mines, there are numerous filled in and grass green hollows 3–10 m in diameter with large refuse heaps alongside. It has been suggested that the depression represents old flint mines enlarged for agricultural purposes, i.e. lime storage.

Dyer and Hales (1961) found three flint mines on the Chiltern escarpment at Pitstone Hill near Aldbury. These were reported to be the first to be found in the Chilterns. Two pits had been dug and one left incomplete. Also there was evidence of an attempt having been made to tunnel into the hillside before the shafts were sunk. The two completed pits were 16 m in diameter and 3–4 m deep, the other being only 3 m in diameter and just under 2 m deep.

4
Silex Mining in Europe

As in Britain, Neolithic miners on the Continent of Europe were extracting flint and similar materials in prehistoric times. Workings are spread over practically every important country in both western and eastern Europe, including Belgium, Holland, Germany, France, Switzerland, Denmark, Sweden, Spain, Portugal, Sicily and Poland, the most important sites being shown in Fig. 41. There is now evidence that, in certain localities, flint mining was carried out even in Palaeolithic times and further investigations might demonstrate wider and earlier activity than at present believed. What is known, however, is that Neolithic settlers on their arrival in the north sought out suitable plateaux for their habitation. Following the Mesolithic tradition in some countries, such as in northern France and Belgium, they soon discovered that the best flints originated in the chalk uplands so they settled near the outcrops. They required good tools for deforestation and agricultural projects and it was not long before Neolithic man began to dig pits or make openpits to locate possible flint beds followed by shaft sinking to exploit the better qualities. Whereas many prehistoric miners in Britain sank trial pits to locate possible seams of flint, thus exercising a degree of prospecting, often the European miner had the advantage of outcrops to guide him. For example there is no outcrop of the worked floorstone at Grimes Graves whereas at Spiennes in Belgium, the flint beds outcrop, although of the six seams, according to the early investigators only the sixth from the surface was worked. This again demonstrates the discerning ability of the prehistoric miner to recognize the best flint *in situ*. In fact greater selection was made at Spiennes from 12 seams at the later and deeper pits.

When perusing literature concerning European sites the term "silex" is frequently encountered. The author has at times adopted this term for general usage, i.e. when not referring specifically to actual flint, and *silex*

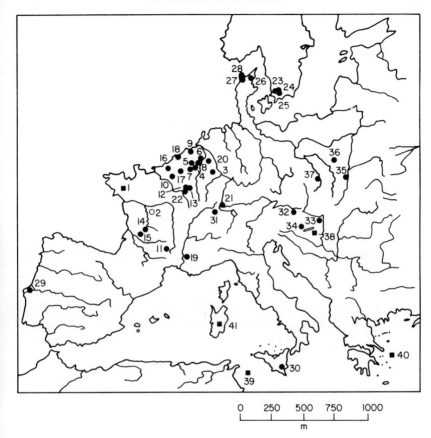

Fig. 41. Silex and rock workings in prehistoric Europe. Silex mines (●), silex openpits (○), rock quarries (■). 1 Selédin, 2 Grand Pressigny, 3 Mayen, 4 Spiennes, 5 Meefe, 6 Braives, 7 La Flénu and Strépy, 8 Avenues, 9 Obourg, 10 Champignolles, 11 Mur de Barrez, 12 Petit Marin, 13 Vert la Gravelle, 14 Petite Garenne, 15 Les Martins, 16 Nointel, 17 Fricourt, 18 Lumbres, 19 Malaucène, 20 St Gertrude, 21 Kleinkems, 22 Bas Meudon, 23, Kvarnby, 24 Gallerup, 25 Tullstorp, 26 Aalborg, 27 Hov, 28 Bjerre, 29 Rocio-Lisbon, 30 Monte Tabuto, 31 Lowenburg, 32 Mauer, 33 Tata, 34 Magyorósdomb, 35 Krzemiouki, 36 Orousko, 37 Saspow, 38 Tokaj, 39 Pautellaria, 40 Milos, 41 Sardinia.

is a French word, but is especially found in German papers and reports. For example, silex in German usage includes actual flint (*feuerstein*), chert (*hornstein*) and jasper (*jaspis*). Jasper is often referred to in Britain as "bloodstone" and is an opaque red quartz containing much iron oxide. It occurs in very hard limestone as, for example, in the Jura Mountains at Kleinkems in West Germany.

Western Europe

It is probably justified to consider first the flint mines of Belgium as here is sited the most famous prehistoric mine, probably in the whole world, even more so than Grimes Graves, this being Spiennes.

The recognized Belgium flint mines, lying in the Cretaceous chalk belt, are located in a line running approximately north-east to south-west across the central part of the country north of the River Meuse from near Liege to Mons. The principal sites are Braives, Avennes and Meefe located north of the Meuse valley and then the group near Mons consisting of Ciply, La Flénu, Obourg, Spiennes and Strépy. In the neighbourhood of Liège and near Mons flint mining flourished and the product was possibly distributed and traded all over the Low Countries and used for the manufacture of urgently needed tools.

Spiennes

This important site, consisting of a chalk plateau covered with loess, is located in the province of Hainaut about 5 km south-east of the city of Mons. The actual site is marked on many maps as Camp à Cailloux or Camp à Cayaux which means a field of stones or a flint field. As long ago as 1860 Albert Toilliez identified the area as a Neolithic workshop for the processing of very good flint according to de Loë (1928). In fact Spiennes was reputed for massive deposits of flint cuttings lying often to a depth of nearly 1 m in cultivated fields.

Scollar (1959) makes the significant point that this important and famous flint mine, and indeed Obourg and Avennes and Rijckholt St Gertrude in Holland, were certainly exploited by the Michelsberg culture, the Belgian tools being an almost exact parallel with the British forms. There were two types of axe of the trapezoidal type and with a butt nearly as wide as the cutting edge. It could be possible that Belgian and French travellers to Britain brought with them an expert knowledge of flint tools and mining know how.

The actual mining site is bounded on the west and south by the river Trouille and, on the eastern slopes of the Trouille, flint bearing layers in the chalk come to the surface. Rutot (1921) is of the opinion that the banks of the Trouille valley were inhabited almost continuously since man first appeared on the earth, i.e. since the beginning of quaternary times. There are four successive river terraces. The second at 75 m represents Eolithic, a transition from primitive to Palaeolithic. The third at 30 m contains a seam of flint at the base of the early alluvium and relics

Fig. 42. Adits exposed at Spiennes (Bergbau-Museum, Bochum).

of the first palaeolithic industry. This is stated to correspond with the Swanscombe site in Kent and with Galley Hill, also Le Moustier and St Acheuel. Aurignacian, Solutrean and Magdalenian are not represented. The site of mining was discovered by Malaise in 1866 when he was working a bank of flint for pottery manufacture and noticed galleries exposed by landslips (see Fig. 42). Less than a year later a large trench was cut during the making of the Mons to Charleroi railway. Fortunately the work laid bare 25 vertical shafts sunk through 6–10 m of tertiary and quaternary deposits to reach the beds of chalk, see Fig. 43. These deposits

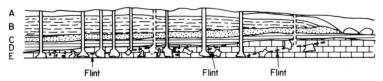

Fig. 43. Profile of eastern part of railway cutting at Spiennes showing shafts and galleries (after Andrée). A soil, B gravels, C water-borne deposits, D Tertiary greensand, E chalk with flint. Scale 1:560.

consisted of upper brown clay, yellow clay or *l'ergaron*, pebbly deposits, greensand, gravel and then the chalk. Immediately Briart *et al.* (1868) set to work to excavate further and their findings are reported at length. After that date many excavations have been carried out such as those of de Loë and de Munck (1887), de Paaw (1889), Stevens (1911), de Loë (1912, 1913, 1914, 1928), de Laet (1966) and Verheyleweghen (1966).

There were two methods of flint extraction at Spiennes, the earliest being the driving of galleries or adits from the outcrop of the flint on the valley sides of the River Trouille and the later method of sinking deep shafts on the higher plateau. The shafts first excavated were found to cut five seams of flint before reaching the sixth which was worked. The method appears to have been the sinking of a shaft of Roman glass shape (unquentorium), i.e. belling out the sides of the shaft at the fifth seam to provide room for working the sixth. There are over 50 ha of such shafts on the site. These shafts averaged 9·25 m in depth. Antler picks were found similar to some found at Furfooz in the province of Namur, which were used to work two veins of calcium carbonate to extract calcite for mixing with clay in connection with the manufacture of pottery. The shafts of the antler picks were generally larger than those commonly found on British sites and unlike them were mostly used to trim sides of shafts and galleries. Sometimes antler picks were hafted with deer horn handles, see Fig. 19. There seems to be no logical explanation of the fact that British flint miners evidently did not adopt the method of fitting flints to available antler handles.

Clarke (1915a) also states that the first workings were adits and when these proved to be dangerous, 1 m diameter pits 10–11 m deep were cut through 4–5 m of quaternary beds. This, however, is pure supposition and it is extremely unlikely that shafts of only 1 m in diameter in loose clays and pebbly gravel beds, were any less dangerous than adits. Short adits can indeed be as dangerous as long adits without artificial support. It is incredible to believe that these intelligent miners, who could recognize the best flint *in situ* and obviously knew something about the basic principles of geological stratification, did not apparently use wood sawn directly from trees for support. With this facility adit walls and roofs in solid chalk, particularly if similar in physical hardness to those examined by the author at Grimes·Graves, would have been safer if they had been supported with wood than vertical shafts of small diameter in crumbly pre-Cretaceous strata.

In 1911 some shallow depressions were examined by C. Stevens and he found a kind of a vault supposed to be the base of a dwelling with two hearths with wood charcoal and a fine arrowhead of Spiennes flint of

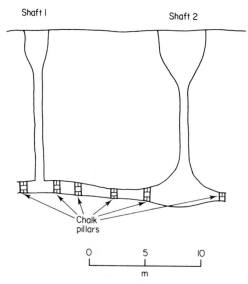

Fig. 44. Deeper shafts discovered at Spiennes by de Loë.

elongated triangular type, a bone piercer, some coarse pottery and undisturbed clay below round hearths.

Important excavations subsidized by the Comte Louis Cavens were carried out on the upper plateau in 1912, 1913 and 1914 by de Loë (1928) and co-workers. The area was ground being recovered for communal development. Two very deep shafts were discovered which led to underground galleries as shown in Fig. 44. Shaft 1 was 16 m deep and 1 m in diameter and enlarged at the base to form a vaulted chamber "arched" or "corbelled' by the natural disposition of the beds of chalk overlying the seam of flint. This provision was evidently to facilitate the drivage of several galleries and separated by chalk pillars similar to the pillars of coal left in bord and pillar workings in later coal mining practice. Shaft 2 was 15 m from Shaft 1 and was a short distance up the rise towards the outcrop so was slightly less deep. Shaft 1, although 1 m in diameter in the actual shaft, was 3·5 m at the collar, whereas Shaft 2 measured 2 m. The second shaft also had radiating galleries.

Unlike the shafts excavated in the nineteenth century the deeper shafts crossed 12 seams of flint in order to reach the thirteenth which was of very good quality. This would appear to indicate once again that given unfaulted stratification the previously worked sixth seam was passed through without development, thereby demonstrating the knowledge and ingenuity of miners of over 5000 years ago. The galleries were stowed with debris from the worked out beds. Notches had been cut in the walls of the shafts probably indicating the use of beams for staircases a practice not normally adopted in the larger diameter British shafts. If this is reliable evidence it would probably indicate the use of wood and it would have only been a short step to adoption of the material for support.

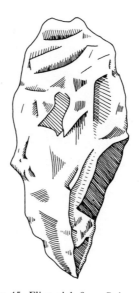

Fig. 45. Flint pick from Spiennes

In the galleries explored over 1500 miners' flint picks of the type shown in Fig. 45 were found, these probably having been used to cut the chalk containing the flint nodules (see Fig. 46). The Spiennes flint is very homogeneous varying from light, clear grey to bluish grey or dark and in some cases light brown. De Loë quotes the composition of the flint as analysed by Henri Boissant as follows:

Silica (by difference)	94·94%
Alumina Al_2O_3	0·64%
Ferric oxide Fe_2O_3	0·06%
Limestone Ca O	2·25%
Magnesia Mg O	0·10%
Anhydrite Carbonic CO_2 Combined Water H_2O	2·01%

The triangular flint tools were slim and varied from 15–23 cm in length. Some percussion discs of imported stones were found probably for

Fig. 46. Block of chalk from Spiennes showing the impressions made by flint pick shown in Fig. 45 (Bergbau-Museum, Bochum).

tool manufacture. Important fragments of pottery were found and it was possible to reconstruct a brownish red vase of this construction from material containing flint. There were marks on roofs and walls of the galleries made by tools. These excavations, reported fully by de Loë (1928), had to end in 1914 and were not resumed until 1924–1925 when the Royal Museums of Cinquanternaire took over the work. The later investigations revealed extensive burial sites possibly of miners, workshops and huts made in depressions as discovered earlier by Stevens. Bones were well preserved and came from sheep, goat, red stag, dog, pig and wild boar, mostly from skulls and paws. They had been badly bruised by blows and there was evidence of burning. Agriculture was evident from the grain imprints on the pottery.

De Loë points to Spiennes as a major industrial centre 4000–5000 years ago and a habitation site of a cultural and expert mining community. He is also of the opinion that flint was exported over enormous distances by the River Trouille, the marshes of Haine and Escaut. Products received in exchange for the flint doubtless included wheat, cattle, game, skins or hides, deer horn and salt.

Clason (1971) gives an up to date account of later investigations at Spiennes and at Rijckholt St Gertrude in the Netherlands and deals particularly with the work of Verheyleweghen (1966) who postulates four phases for Spiennes and gives actual radiocarbon dates. The object was to determine by what group or groups the Spiennes mines at Camp à Cayaux were occupied. Phase I is denoted as an archaic phase during which the site was visited by Michelsberg people to obtain good tools. The miners restricted themselves to mining on the eastern slopes of the River Trouille in the west part of Camp à Cayaux, but no bones or pottery have been found. Vogeland and Waterbolk in 1967 gave a radiocarbon date as 3470 ± 75 BC. South of Camp à Cayaux is Bosca d'el Tombe which is also Neolithic and has a date of c. 3360 BC. Phase II marks the first appearance of arrowheads and axes replacing knives. The mines both in this phase and in the other two phases III and IV were worked more to the east. The cow in this phase is beginning to show increased dominance over the pig, sheep and goat. In Phase III the axe continued to replace the knife and the first separate burials of skulls was noticed. The cow now commenced to diminish at the expense of the sheep and goat. There appeared to be two cultures, i.e., Michelsberg and Somme-Oise-Marne (SOM), the latter being recognized by the appearance of antlers with lateral perforations. The dating of the SOM culture is given by Verheyleweghen as c. 1850 BC. Two fragments of local later Neolithic or domestic Beaker ware were found buried in Iron Age detritus. Phase IV marks an industrial decline and the disappearance of Neolithic pottery. The author concluded that Camp à Cayaux had been mainly occupied by a single and the same group of people. The period lasted from ± 2400 BC to ± 1700 BC as confirmed by radiocarbon dates. The material from the paper referred to has been summarized in some detail as it probably represents the first real attempt to consider the culture and way of life of the inhabitants of a Neolithic mining site. Although Verheyleweghen gives no dates for all the phases which he postulated, there is a small mine near Mesvin, where the finds are similar. For this mine Clason quotes de Laet's radiocarbon dates as 3270 ± 170 BC and 3390 ± 150 BC, these apparently corresponding to Phase I at Spiennes.

The phases postulated by Verheyleweghen are shown in Fig. 47 which has been reproduced from the paper by Clason (1971). In the same paper is a detailed analysis of the remains of the animals found at Spiennes a topic which is somewhat outside the scope of the present study.

Most investigators accept that houses must have been built in the vicinity as a mining area alone would not have held the large stock of

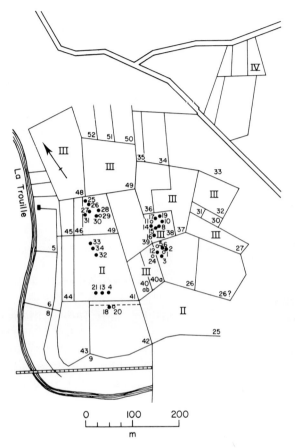

Fig. 47. Camp à Cayaux near Spiennes. Mine Shaft (●), uncompleted mine shaft (○);
II, III, IV, phases after Verheyleweghen. Reproduced from Helinium by permission of
Universa sprl.

domesticated animals, bones of which have been found on 35 of the
mining sites. Farming was evidently carried on during mining or were the
miners also farmers or vice versa? An unpleasant side of the picture
appears when consideration is given to the number of human bones on
some of the sites which were often used as tools. Human skulls found often
showed signs of battering so could the inhabitants of Spiennes 5000–4000
years ago, whether they were farmers predominately or miners, also have
had cannibalistic instincts?

   Grimes Graves and Spiennes are the two chief examples of large scale
mining activities in existence long ago. Many excavations and pit
clearances have been carried out and much interesting evidence on types

of mining and the tools produced has emanated from the work and indeed much more will be done. Despite all this there is still controversy concerning the way of life and the habitation sites of early Neolithic industrialists. Habitation sites and henge monuments, which are said to be contemporary with mining sites have been fully excavated, but there still hangs a cloud over the actual way of life of the miner. It is easy to put the blame on nineteenth century archaeolgists who, keen to explore the shafts and galleries, generally neglected the environmental aspect, but they did not have the assistance of present day specialists and advances in physics, botany and biology. The approach by today's archaeologists is slowly changing the picture, but the work involves time consuming studies and interpretation.

Obourg

Of the Belgian flint mining sites this is probably second in importance to Spiennes. Obourg lies 5 km north-east of Mons and was excavated by de Munck during the period 1880–1886. The flint was of excellent quality and 3–4 m deep, was not extracted by shafts. Instead it was worked by parallel trenches 5 m long, 6 m wide at the top and 4–5 m at the bottom. As soon as the flint was dug out of one trench another was made in close proximity. The chalk was of weak quality and it is surprising that occasional galleries were driven to connect up the trenches probably to obtain maximum flint extraction. These galleries were normally only 60 cm × 70 cm in size although one was reported by de Munck (1886) to be 3 m long and 1 m square. A skeleton was discovered in a 1·55 m high gallery apparently that of a miner killed by a roof fall. An antler pick was still held in his hand. As suggested in Fig. 48 he had probably broken out chalk directly below an unidentified filled in pit and the roof caved in. It is difficult to understand why the body was not recovered from such a shallow depth and given suitable burial or was human life considered

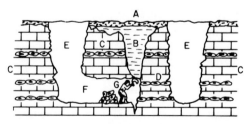

Fig. 48. Method of working at Obourg. A soil, B filled-in trench, C chalk, D seam of nodular silex, E trench, F gallery, G site of skeleton of miner found *in situ*.

very expendable? It could be possible that no check was kept on men working below ground, who might have come from a distant area, had no means of identification, came and went hardly noticed. This will never be verified or ever proved. It is incredible that no apparent attempt was made to support the roof or sides with timber. However, Clarke (1952) states that "their judgement (i.e. the miners'), based as it was on practical experience of the work in hand, was generally sound and can be judged by the skill with which they cut the galleries at such sites as Grimes Graves, Champignolles and Spiennes leaving pillars to support the roof".

After completion of the work of extracting flint from a trench it was filled in with chalk, clay sand and disused mining tools including worn or damaged antler picks. At Obourg, unlike Spiennes, there is no sign of flint picks having been used. Instead single and double handled picks, rakes, combined rake and lever, all made from the horns of deer, were employed exlusively. Numerous flakes, chips and cores remaining from flint tool manufacture were found. Durreaux found a workshop with tools made from the fine quality black Obourg flint.

Rutot (1921) presumed that Obourg was older than Spiennes. He even referred to the site as being Campignian (see p. 106), and of the same date as Grimes Graves! Radiocarbon dates appear to show that Spiennes is older than Grimes Graves and as there is no available date for Obourg it is not possible to relate the three sites. However, there is no doubt that the method of mining used at Obourg is more primitive than either at Spiennes or Grimes Graves which might put the site back to an earlier date, possibly to the Early Neolithic.

Strépy

This site lies roughly 12 km almost due east of Mons, 8 km east-south-east of Obourg and 10 km north-east of Spiennes.

Strépy has much in common with Obourg for trenches were dug and attempts made to drive galleries between them. Two skeletons were found, one of a miner face downwards and the other of a child about four years old. Sanders states that the teeth were worn flat which is characteristic of Neolithic populations in that part of Belgium Sanders (1910). Some of the teeth had been destroyed by a disease which had even extended and affected the bone of the lower jaw.

No flint tools were found, but both single and double handled and many other implements from the horns of deer came to light. The remains of a wild boar were found with the skeletons. In the report on Grimes Graves, (see Clark 1915a) several of the European sites are described briefly. In the section on Strépy it is suggested that as no workshops were found the flint blocks might have been transported to Obourg 8 km away, to be cut. At the time of the excavations there appeared to be some controversy over the date of the skull of the skeleton. Rutot (1921) claimed that it was of the Furfooz race and was Magdalenian, whereas Professor A. Keith, in a letter to the author of the Strépy report, stated that it was of the Bronze Age. Without the assistance of radiocarbon dates it is not possible to estimate the chronological implications.

La Flénu

This lesser known site is located approximately 6 km south-west of Mons and reference to it completes the group around the city. It is mentioned in two publications Clark (1915) and de Loë (1928). On the strength of discoveries at Avennes Rutot places the industries of La Flénu before those of Spiennes.

Avennes, Braives and Meefe

According to de Loë, who carried out some work at Avennes en Hesbaye (Warenne) these three mining sites in the Liege area, although not rivalling Spiennes, do represent a true centre of Neolithic industry.

In 1880 the site of Avennes was exposed, as in the case of Spiennes, by trenches made during the construction of a railway, i.e. between Landen and Ciney. Trenches were also being dug for the erection of new houses and these two undertakings exposed numerous pits some of which were interconnected by underground galleries.

One pit and two galleries were intensively explored in 1885, the pit being sunk through 6 m of marly chalk with flint, a humus bed and about 3 m of sand. The average diameter was about 90 cm. De Loë and fellow workers explored two galleries at the base which had a height of only 80–90 cm and had to be enlarged to 1·65 m. They penetrated 2·75 m to the bottom of another pit. In 1888 foundations, being made for a house exposed underground galleries and in 1891 a new pit was found. A marl pit had also encountered underground galleries.

Six kilometres from Avennes old pits and underground galleries were found in Meefe village.

De Loë also stated that Professor Max Loest had discovered and explored an old pit at Braives adjacent to the commune of Avennes en Hesbaye.

Although all traces of the sites have long disappeared an interesting collection of horn picks, flint tools, axes in used, discarded or badly made condition was obtained including a spherical hammering tool and a large polished axe. There were also fragments of pottery and large blocks of chalk showing marks indicating cuts made to extract the flint.

Rutot also mentions the existence of hut circles at Hesbaye west of Liege.

Grand Pressigny

Fifty kilometres south of Tours in Indre-Loire lies Grand Pressigny on a tributary of the river Creuse. Here was one of the most famous and probably best known prehistoric quarries in France and indeed in Europe. It is well known first and foremost for the excellent quality of the mined flint and also for the wide distribution of the finished products all over western Europe.

Clark and Piggott (1933) mention a fine narrow flake about 15 cm in length in the Blackmore collection at Salisbury, which they say is of the unmistakable honey coloured flint of Grand Pressigny. It is of shallow triangular section with a central ridge of intersection opposite bulbar surface and butt facetted.

The material extracted was used from the late Palaeolithic to the Bronze Age, but mainly from the third to the second millennium BC. The type of flint worked has been described as reddish brown (Cole 1970), honey coloured (Sieveking et al. 1973) and caramel coloured (Bray and Trump 1973), and was exported as far away as Spain to Holland, north to the Channel coast and to Switzerland in the form of blocks or unfinished blanks. Knives, sickles, polished axes, daggers, heads of lances etc. found all over Europe have been traced to Grand Pressigny.

Patricia Phillips (1975) states that the period of the slow introduction of copper in some areas is also that of the most intensive flint mining and this is true also of the Grand Pressigny industries. In fact the quarry is said to have started on a large scale in the Chalcolithic or Copper age which follows the Neolithic and precedes the Bronze Age and was characterized by Corded Ware and Beaker Cultures and also probably the introduction of the Indo-European languages, but of this there is unlikely to be any evidence. However, it has been stated that the exceptionally high standard of the flat polished axeheads of Grand Pressigny display a unique high standard of execution and are often found associated with early Neolithic burials in Scandinavia. Childe (1957) also states that the flint implements found in Switzerland are Middle Neolithic.

De Saint-Venant (1900) describes an investigation he made concerning the distribution and utilization of Grand Pressigny flints. Although his work is probably now outdated his account is interesting mainly because his description is so concise and his enquiries so thorough. He estimates that the material was extracted in Palaeolithic times and during his investigations he sent questionnaires to most of the relevant large museums in western Europe. His conclusions were that the flint from Grand Pressigny was not found in Britain, Italy or Spain, but very large quantities in Brittany, northern France and northern Switzerland. In a discussion on de Saint-Venant's paper, Rutot mentioned that very great quantities had been found in Belgium. De Saint-Venant describes the flint as having a large grain and possessing a little of the texture of sandstone with disseminated mica. It is nearly opaque and the reddish yellow colour of pure wax. On the site there are sometimes veins of jasper generally blood coloured and often spotted with small specks of chalcedony. Based on this one should properly refer to the material as "silex", but most writers prefer the term "flint". Unlike the chalk flints patination is only occasionally found. The best qualities are usually found farthest from the site in the form of polished axes, barbed arrowheads, scrapers and beautiful blades.

Jahn (1956) in an article concerned with the trade in flint, shows a map of western Europe which suggests an even wider range of exportation of the product from Grand Pressigny. It is highly probable that the flint was bartered for goods and in fact even served as a form of currency so highly was it prized. It has been found in gallery graves built by the warlike populations of the SOM cultures and Jersey shows important links between the Beaker cultures and Grand Pressigny flint, but surprisingly no such flint has been found in any of the other islands of the Channel Island Group. On the Breton peninsula Grand Pressigny flint has been found at Morbihan.

Clark and Piggott mention other flint mines in France such as Champignolles, Mur de Barrez, Bas Meudon, Nointel, Petite Garenne and Valennes. France is a large country and has vast deposits of chalk and limestone. Consequently it is surprising that so far not very many prehistoric flint and chert mines have been discovered and this probably indicates a need for closer examination of the terrain and more intensive investigation.

Champignolles

Champignolles is situated near Sérifontaine in the Département de l'Oise. It is probably one of the better known French sites and has been

Fig. 49. Cross section through an openpit working at Champignolles (x 1/35). A infilling with chalk debris and block, B soil, C chalk with flints, D charcoal debris, E unfinished flint tools, F deer horn pick.

extensively investigated. It was discovered in 1890 in a chalk pit, 11 shafts being identified of which nine were cleared including two openpit workings. Bessin and Fouja found the shafts and established that they were bottle shaped, 4 m deep, 52 cm in diameter at the top, 1 m at the centre and 1·5 m at the bottom from which 61 cm square galleries radiated outwards. The openpit workings had an average depth of 5·65 m. Figure 49 shows a cross section through an openpit working. As with many other European flint mines the miner had the advantage of being able to observe outcrops of seams before deciding to sink shafts. These were on the slopes of a ravine the third in depth being worked. Sanders (1910) says that shafted flint picks were used although Bessin and Fouju, according to Clark (1915), found marks on the gallery walls said to have been made by deer horn picks which may have been used as levers. The shafts had been filled in with the natural layers of strata in reverse order. On the surface about 250 000 m² were covered with debris from flint workshops. Several flint axes were found in the galleries and at the bases of shafts. Some charcoal was also present.

Mur de Barrez

These mines in the Département de l'Aveyron were discovered, as in the case of many others, purely by accident. However, the flint or chert, referred to as silex, lay horizontal in a calcareous marl bed. A quarry 25 m long exposed the mines and Boule and Cartailhac excavated the area. There had been no indication of the presence of old mines on the surface.

The site is located in an area with hills at heights of 700–850 m surrounding the valley of the River Goul which flows into the Trwyehe and later joins the River Lot. The area was once subjected to volcanic activity in pliocene times and the hills are capped with volcanic tuffs, andesites and a stepped plateau of basalt caps the ridge of mountains at a height of 826 m. The town of Mur de Barrez lies across a valley from the mines on a hill at a height of 812 m. Below in the valley as on the hillsides are many erratic boulders of basalt.

Geological formations on the hill, 788 m high, where the quarry was worked, were volcanic tuffs and andesites, alluvial, calcareous marl and clay. The numerous mines found were 4 m deep and sunk into the calcareous marl, according to Boule (1884). Five pits were located first with many more later. The chert is about 60 cm thick and lenticular. Galleries were found to have been driven radially to follow the chert which, being thick, could be left in as pillars to give effective roof support.

Tools used were deer horn wedges, picks and hammer heads. Being extremely hard chert it is difficult to understand or visualize the method of extraction used. No flint tools have been found nor any refuse, so the blocks excavated must have been exported elsewhere for finishing. The

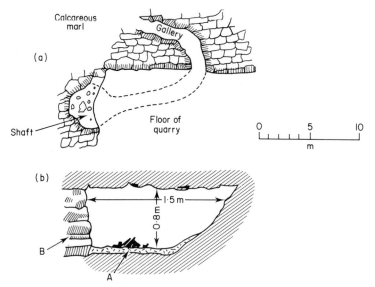

Fig. 50. Shaft and gallery at Mur de Barrez exposed by stone quarry. (a) plan; (b) enlarged section across gallery in (a) not to scale, A-debris and charcoal, B wear on gallery sides from haulage rope.

colour of the chert is grey, described as *café au lait*, the composition as homogeneous and claimed to be easily worked despite its hardness. Boule (1887) says that a polished andesite axe was found having a length of 196 mm.

One interesting feature of the Mur de Barrez mines was the presence of grooves on the gallery sides, evidently, according to Boule and one of his co-workers Griffoul, made by the rubbing of ropes (see Fig. 50). These were probably used for hauling out of large blocks of chert. Griffoul suggested that the ropes could have been run round blocks of chert to facilitate pulling around corners. Charcoal dust was found on the floors and probably indicated the use of fires.

Other French Silex Mining Sites

Baron Joseph de Baye (1885) in 1865 visited a cave at Corzard in the Department of Marne south of Paris, and after investigating the presence of bones there, was able to establish that the Petit Morin district contained extensive old flint mines. He concluded that not only long term habitation had existed in the region, but that the industry and living sites were Neolithic. A field, known as Haie Jeanneton, contained an entire prehistoric mining area. The initial evidence was the presence of rejects of flint having distinct bulbs of percussion. Excavations at depressions revealed pits connected by galleries and the flint had obviously been exploited over a long period. De Baye suggests that the flint of Le Champagne had been transported to the valley of the Lesse in Belgium. The pits at Le Petit Morin were 2 m in diameter and 3 m in depth.

Other mines were 5 km away near to Vert la Gravelle. The flint outcropped on the mountain side and owing to denudation the exposures were clear and not too deep to extract safely without shafts. Amongst the debris found on the surface was Neolithic pottery. De Baye thought that the more sophisticated approach in the workshop phase here of flint finishing, represented the end of the polished flint epoch. Without the assistance of radiocarbon dates it is not possible to be certain about the approximate age of the site, but maybe the working could have extended into the Chalcolithic or even the Bronze Age.

De Baye also reports the existence at Courgeonnet, near Menhir, of defences in the form of ditches 2 m deep and he commented that there were indications of long term habitation. It is difficult to understand whom the Neolithic settlers were defending themselves against.

The underground caves in the centre of the Petit Morin group were apparently used for the storage of provisions. Reference has been made earlier to the paucity of evidence concerning the living sites of Neolithic mining communities and if the material is reliable there is some recognition at least in France that non-itinerant miners were common. No such evidence is forthcoming from other countries and it must be concluded in the absence of such living sites near the mines that permanent habitation was some distance away.

Circular pits were found from 2–3 m in depth at Villevenard and here there was evidence of fire action on the chalk.

A large excavation over 8 m in diameter, explored at Courgeonnet, was thought to have been a depository for flint tools, pottery and deer horns. At St Gourd 75 flint arrowheads were found.

Clark and Piggott (1933) also mention mines at Petite Garenne and Les Martins in east central France, Clermont and Nointel in Oise, Fricourt in the Somme valley, Valennes near Champignolles and Bas Meudon near Paris.

At Petite Garenne, galleries were 3–5 m in length, 2–3·5 m wide and were worked only 1·5 m deep. Andrée (1922) says that Petite Garenne and Les Martins are the only sites in Central France, other than Mur de Barrez, where the silex occurs in rocks other than chalk, in other words the material was chert. At Petite Garenne and Les Martins the ground was too hard for the prehistoric miner to sink shafts so the openpit method was used. In fact at Petite Garenne the miners were probably deterred from making shafts since in more recent times, i.e. 1895, workmen tried to extract flint for road metal and two were killed by a roof fall.

In a short contribution to the French Prehistoric Society, Peyrolles and Peyrolles (1959) described an interesting mining site at la Vigne du Cade, Salinelles, Gard. A possible site in this area was mentioned in 1908 by Dr Marignian to the Society, when he reported finding numerous silex tools, pottery fragments and a grooved mallet on the surface. In 1954 a tractor working to the west of the site accidentally dislodged a horizontal stone slab. Local residents remembered a similar occurrence in 1920 when a hole was disclosed and the slab put back into position for safety. A 2 m circular deep pit in dry stone and 0·75 m diameter was examined and found to communicate by means of a gallery at the base to a second pit which was in a poor state. Other galleries radiated from the base of the second pit. The interesting feature was that the galleries had been used as an ossary or depository for bodies, the skeletons of which were found in various positions. The authors state that the numerous stone tools found had a Campignian style with bifacial retouch and bronze vases were decorated with fluting. Other items were a ring of copper and a metal leaf both of which were found by visitors and so the evidence cannot be corroborated. Little else was found apart from a tooth from a wild boar. The only certain aspect of the mine, according to the authors, was that it was abandoned in the Chalcolithic period.

It is somewhat surprising that there is little evidence of flint mining in the chalk of the Pas de Calais as this is really a continuation of the chalk of the English South Downs. The author has only been able to find one reference to a possible mining site and this was mentioned by Prévost (1959) as Lumbres. A habitation site was buried by piles of chalk. There are several beds of flint on the site, but the miners only worked the top bed as the intervening chalk was very hard. Workings were at the summit of a small hill, 110 m high since the black flint here was easier to extract although it was less favourable for the agricultural community in the locality. The mine, according to Prévost, probably supplied the blocks of stone to build the barrow of Lumbres at the foot of the hill. This represents the first mine to be found in the Pas de Calais and is situated near the limit of the Cretaceous chalk deposits. Both, according to Prévost, the Campignian and Michelsberg cultures are represented, but the domination of the former appears to be the more likely.

Patricia Phillips (1975) gives a useful resumé of the principal features of mining sites in southern France and Elisabeth Schmid (1960) has done extensive work at Malaucène. All the mines were much later in operation than many of the French mines already mentioned, being of the Late Neolithic period or, according to Phillips, belong to the Chasséen especially those in the Rhone valley. At Chateuneuf du Pape waisted quartzite hammers have been found and here the nodules occur over a low hill now under vine cultivation. Such hammers are said to weigh over 10 kg and have been found also by Courtin (1957) by Courtin, at Malaucène and Murs on the southern slopes of Mont Ventoux on which there are several openpit sites.

Other sites lie at Esperelles near the Berne Lagoon and near Eygalieres. Phillips states that with reference to Bordreuil, the most extensive flint mines of southern France are located in the Gard Department at Salinelles where there were many galleries into a seam constituting a flat plaque flint.

Whereas, with a few exceptions, most Neolithic flint or silex mining in Central France was in the customary chalk formations, all the mines in southern France were in limestone, the mined product being therefore chert. Schmid points out that mining in chalk was easy when compared to working in the hard limestone of southern France. She describes the excavation of two trenches at Veaux, near Malaucène (Vaucluse), Schmid (1960), about 50 km north-east of Avignon. Prehistoric quarrying sites on the hills west of Veaux had been discovered over 50 years ago. The object of the work was to compare the site with that of Kleinkems which had already been investigated, and which will be referred to later (see p. 92).

Despite the presence of fragments of chert on the hills west of Veaux and the numerous depressions, no actual excavations had previously been attempted, although Catelan had found on the east flank of the Combe de Leaunier a cave which had been Neolithic living quarters, the evidence being the presence of hearths, pottery and silex tools, dated to the end of the period. The first trench was made down a hillside the second one up the hill into a vertical rock face. In the course of the work numerous mallets, tools and fragments of pottery were found. The chief conclusions drawn from the investigations were that the workings had taken place at different times an early Neolithic mine following an older one. A flint processing factory had been established in late Neolithic times. Not being satisfied with the weathered material, later miners went underground and deeper, but it is not certain whether the chert was worked by shafts or openpits, that is whether or not the depressions are merely large holes. Thus the actual method of working has still to be determined. The depressions were 8–15 m in diameter and 0·5–1·2 m deep. If the limestone was really hard it is difficult to visualize miners digging numerous crude basins to get chert when shafts sunk less frequently and having radiating galleries, as at Grimes Graves, Spiennes and Cissbury would economize in excavation and provide more product per unit volume of containing rock removed. This hypothesis surely would not be beyond the imagination of the Neolithic miners. Furthermore the extreme hardness of the limestone would render unsupported galleries far safer than similarly treated ones in the weaker chalk.

Excavations were resumed by Schmid (1963) at Veaux in 1962. These later investigations had the primary objective of studying the tools used and those produced from the chert extracted from the 30 cm thick layer of nodular bands in the hard limestone. A trench was dug in four steps through a heap of debris appearing as a projection on a hillside. Apparently under the debris was a shaft or old pit. Quartzite hammers were found, the raw materials for which had been transported at least 20 km. The hammers had a ridge or rill cut round the circumference which could have indicated an attachment for a handle.

Willert (1951) conceives that as Palaeolithic man made pits to catch animals he must have noticed the flint beds in the soft chalk below the surface. This might have possibly led him to dig shallow pits especially to reach and to extract such flint which would have been of better quality

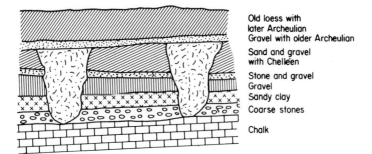

Old loess with
later Archeulian
Gravel with older Archeulian
Sand and gravel
with Chelléen
Stone and gravel
Gravel
Sandy clay
Coarse stones

Chalk

Fig. 51. Funnel shaped pits in the middle terrace of the Somme.

than the exposed beds in chalk cliffs or the weathered flint pebbles in gravel which were already available to him. Figure 51 shows a section of the strata of the Somme terraces in northern France. The pits have been explained by some writers as being the result of eddying of water flows. As Willert points out it is strange that they only go down into the chalk. They are of the Pleistocene since after being filled in they were covered by ice carried gravel and wind blown loess. Probably Palaeolithic man dug Pit A and after being used either for trapping animals or the working of flint it was filled in and later Pit B dug and used for the same purpose.

Rijckholt Saint Gertrude

The only important prehistoric flint mining site in the Netherlands was discovered in 1910 and lies in Limburg, east of Maastricht, about 10 km east of Liege. The mine is Rijckholt St Gertrude which is situated on a chalk plateau forming part of the terrace of the River Meuse. The chalk has been cut through by the river and is covered with loess. Like most other Neolithic sites the area was overgrown at one time with trees and the miners must have had to clear great patches of woodland before shaft sinking could be carried out. The plateau is bounded on the west by the Meuse and by the Eysden woods on the south.

The district around Rijckholt near St Gertrude has been famed for mining, if not for flint, for nearly 1000 years. Engelen (1969) suggests that the oldest coal mine in Europe was in existence near Kerkrade in Wurmtal, near Aachen in AD 1113. In fact modern Dutch coal mining was centred at Heerlen until the 1960s when practically all production ceased from the state mines as a result of increasing costs, competition from Holland's newly found natural gas and their oil reserves and the availability of the cheaper Ruhr coal. The coalfield continuously exploited in Limburg forms an offshoot of the Belgian field around Liege and the German one in the district of Aachen.

Although the presence of old flint mines was not recognized until 1910, the actual associated flint processing workshops were accidentally found as long ago as 1881. Hamal-Nandrin and Servais in 1923 wrote that Marcel de Puydt, when travelling by train between Maastricht and Liege, noticed workshops, but he did not characterize them as constituting a major industry of flint extraction and processing and in fact he delayed investigations until much later.

Clason (1971) discusses the sites of Spiennes and St Gertrude in a single article and states that the geographical setting of both, as were the mining conditions, are approximately the same.

Engelen traces briefly the history of the excavations at St Gertrude and some of the more relevant facts are worth noting from his article. Figure 52 shows a plan of part of the mining area.

There were approximately three phases of working the flint the first representing no more than crude extraction from exposed beds of flint. In 1887 de Puydt discovered an area 54 m by 34 m covered by worked flint and the residue was scattered over 250 m³. Tools which were found were

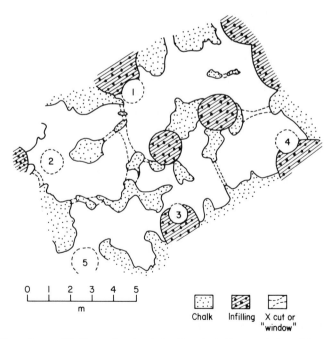

Fig. 52. Plan of part of St Gertrude mine (after Engelen). By permission of Der Anschnitt.

made from flint bone and chert. The chert must have been extracted from some limestone in the vicinity. It was about this time that Spiennes in Belgium was discovered north of the so-called Grand Atelier, by de Puydt. Horizontal galleries constituted the next phase and finally in 1910, after work started by Hamal-Nandrin in 1903, shafts and galleries were discovered. In 1923 Hamal-Nandrin found at a depth of 2 m a skull of a 20–25 year old woman, part of a lower jaw and a portion of a human thigh and in another place a piece of red pottery. Altogether there were nearly 50 years of continuous investigation from 1903. Between 1923 and 1925 the Dutch scientists van Giffen and van der Sleen commenced underground investigations resulting in the finding of charcoal, clay fragments and numerous flint tools. Unfortunately these early investigations attracted little interest in Holland. The early finds of Hamal-Nandrin were thought to be Mousterian and later even merely extended Bronze Age mines. Some work was done by Dominican monks from 1929 to 1932 and they found more than 100 deer horn axes and various deer horn tools. From 1953 to 1964 no work was carried out on the site, but from late 1964 until 1970 probably the most extensive and elaborate investigation of a flint mining site was undertaken. Van Giffen had postulated that settlements had been at the Grand Atelier and it was from here that a tunnel described by Engelen was driven. The availability of local technical mining know-how appears to have been of considerable help. The first phase of the investigations consisted of the driving of a pilot tunnel with wheel barrow transport, then steel props and bars were used for support with tub transport later followed by mechanization including the use of a conveyor. The tunnel was 1·6 m high and 1·6 m wide and was supported by wood props and bars (see Fig. 53). Professor Waterbolk had earlier exposed 10 shafts with a trial trench 97 m long. Professional archaeologists might be doubtful about the wisdom of using mechanized tunnelling on the grounds of possibility of failure to recognize vital small items of evidence. However, if the necessary funds are available to finance such work, positive results can be obtained very quickly. Furthermore, if properly executed and supervized, information can be gathered in a fraction of the time taken up by patient hand and shovel work. The actual drivage machine used in the later excavations was an old converted tractor. In 1964 only 10 m had been driven, but the first stone axe was found and prehistoric workings extended on both sides of the tunnel. By the end of 1965, 18 m of drivage had been achieved. These exceptionally low rates of drivage do not indicate reckless excavation, but it must be stated that as the area was scheduled as a nature reserve no refuse dumps were permitted and so

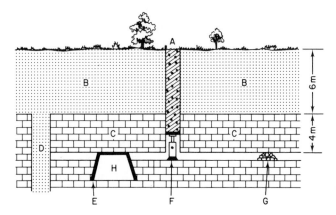

Fig. 53. Cross section showing process of excavation at St Gertrude mine (after Engelen). A filled-in shaft, B gravel, C chalk with flints, D shaft filled in with gravel, E trapezoidal supports installed by excavators, F hydraulic prop installed by excavators, G chalk debris, H exploratory tunnel.

lorries had to be used. This was probably an advantage as slower drivage and transference of debris assisted sorting and insurance against any important extracted material remaining unrecognized. Engelen furthermore states that the very difficult strata control problems encountered resulted in concrete being used to supplement the wood props and bars to prevent falls of the chalk roof. In 1966 there was a further drivage of some 20 m and early in 1967 the thirty-eighth support frame was erected. Up to that time numerous prehistoric working places had been excavated and surveyed. During the same year a conveyor was installed which simplified the removal of the excavated material and at this point 76 m had been driven. At the end of 1968 the length of the tunnel was 106 m, but Engelen states that funds ran out in 1968 and the work was tapered down to 1970, when investigations, the taking of photographs, mapping and cataloguing commenced.

The author has taken the liberty of abstracting much of the article by Engelen, because it represents a unique method of investigating old mining sites and furthermore it is extremely relevant to the present work. Unfortunately funds are becoming less readily available for this type of investigation. However, from an archaeological point of view as opposed to that of mining engineering, the finds are no less impressive. Up to the end of 1968, 35 shafts had been discovered and 20 m on either side of the tunnel a prehistoric working had been investigated. The shafts were circular and 1·2 m in diameter. Shaft 32 had to be supported by sheet metal. Grooves in the shaft side had probably been made by ropes. In the same shaft were found the lower jaw bone and a few vertebrae of a roe deer. Seven thousand tools or fragments of tools were found, and generally these were mostly made from flint. In 1965 the skull of a young woman was found and she had evidently been buried in the mine.

The work showed that the shafts were supported by shaft pillars of chalk, this being unique in prehistoric flint mining. The total extraction of chalk containing flint was approximately 75% so mining must have been very difficult.

It has been postulated that flint mining in the Linearbandkeramic cultural phase had been learned from Mesolithic predecessors, or the residual remnants of these people, but evidence of mining before that of the Michelsberg cultures is lacking. Engelen concludes that flint mining in Holland is older than 5000 years and contemporary with Spiennes, Grimes Graves, Cissbury, Sumeg in Hungary and Kielcein in Poland. This opinion does not strictly conform with the latest radiocarbon dates for many of these sites, both the English sites being somewhat younger. However, a date given by Engelen of 3150 ± 60 BC, one quoted by Clason (1971) of 3120 ± 60 BC and a more recent set of dates from Vögel and Waterbolk in 1971, i.e. 3050 ± 40 BC and 3140 ± 40 BC, coincide to a remarkable degree. The absence of pottery fragments was an obstacle to dating before the radiocarbon method became available.

Layard (1925) has worked on many of the tools found at St Gertrude. She refers to the absence of deer horn picks and had been told by Hamal-Nandrin that horn was not suitable for removing hard stone above the

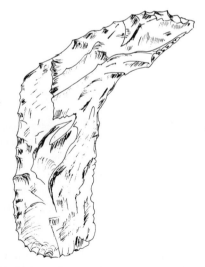

Fig. 54. Pick axe from St Gertrude mine (after Layard).

chalk so stone picks were used. Layard states that implements found at Grimes Graves were of similar form to those found at St Gertrude. A most interesting find mentioned is the sickle shaped implement whose manufacture must have involved the use of much expertise, and was probably used chiefly as a pick axe, although Layard suggests that it could have had multi functions such as for example, axe pick and sickle. The tool exhibits a high degree of perfection in execution such as the minute removal of flakes to produce the cutting edge, the tool being shown in Fig. 54.

It is clear from the work carried out at St Gertrude that there was a large flint mining complex here in Neolithic times, a huge industry involved and possibly a wide trading area.

Kleinkems

In Germany, between the plain of the Rhine and the Black Forest, is a chain of Jurassic limestone hills, the Isteiner Klotz near Kleinkems, from which Neolithic miners extracted jasper. Elisabeth Schmid (1952) describes the first principal investigations at this location and reference has already made to her observations at Veaux in southern France, a site which has been said to have similar characteristics. The rock is a very hard limestone and the nodules of jasper consist of an opaque red coloured variety of quartz containing iron oxide.

Like many other prehistoric mines Kleinkems was discovered partly by chance, due to the building of a railroad 125 years ago at a height of 20 m above the old river bed. About 200 m above the track there is a vertical face of limestone 12–15 m in height. Fifty years ago the vertical face was blasted to form a site for a cement works and during the course of this operation the entrance to a small cave was exposed. The terrace below the face is littered with debris which probably came from similar excavations made 4000 years ago according to earlier investigators such as Professor Robert Lais (see Fig. 55).

The interesting features of the site are the methods of working and the tools used. There are four horizons of jasper lying in nodular seams. Whereas in chalk tools fashioned from antler and sometimes flint were used, it is worth noting that the modern excavations for the cement factory were made with diamond drills and high explosives. Accordingly, the prehistoric miners, not having the availability of such aids, and iron and steel were not yet known, had to improvise. Charcoal debris was found and the presence of baked powdered or sintered limestone and pulped charcoal led to the conclusion that firesetting was used to break

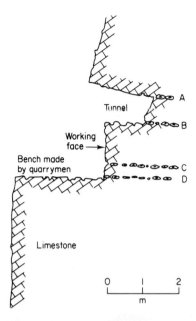

Fig. 55. Cross section through rock face at Kleinkems showing tunnel exposed by quarrying. Reproduced by permission of Professor Elisabeth Schmid.

down the intervening limestone between the jasper horizons. Once tunnels were made the problem of extracting the jasper from the parent rock had to be solved. A unique type of pick, possibly used as a lever, was found and consisted of a stone which had been shaped like a pick head and which was probably attached to a rod or handle by leather thongs or cords. The nodules had to broken up and apparently boulders or stone hammers were used. A sharpened stone was hit by a mallet either held in the hand or complete with handle, to make a hole. The handle end was then pushed into the hole and hafted with leather cords. Schmid points out that such boulders as used are not found *in situ* at Kleinkems or in the vicinity, but only in the bed of the Rhine. These had probably been brought down by the river as it flowed from the Swiss Juras. As indicated earlier any stone foreign to the neighbourhood is described as a "sarsen".

No radiocarbon dates are yet available for the Kleinkems site although Schmid estimates that silex mining took place around 2000 BC. No pottery or bones were found nor any signs of human habitation. What excites curiosity about the site and indeed many others is again the ingenuity of Neolithic man to recognize suitable raw materials for his tools and in fact to labour slowly and arduously in hard rock mines to

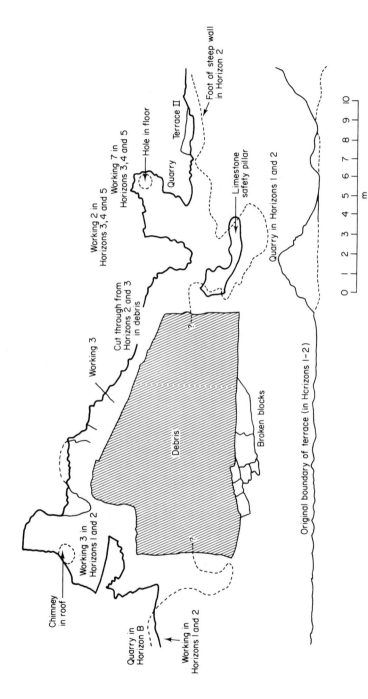

Fig. 56. Plan of Kleinkems. Acknowledgements to the Bergbau-Museum, Bochum.

JASPISBERGWERK DER JUNGEREN STEINZEIT UM 2000 v CHR.
KACHELFLUH BEI KLEINKEMS (SÜDLICHES BADEN)

Fig. 57. Model of Kleinkems mine. Acknowledgements to the Bergbau-Museum, Bochum.

satisfy his requirements for a product which today has no commercial value except in bulk for roadstone, etc. Figure 56 shows a plan of the site and Fig. 57 a model in the Mining Museum at Bochum.

Regensburg

A rich prehistory extending over Neolithic, the Metal Ages and the Early Iron Age, according to Reisch (1974), has been located on the Danube slopes around Regensburg and Kelheim in Bavaria. Gumpert found artefacts here in 1930 after which he drew profiles of the terrain, made trenches and located living quarters, fire places and storage holes. By 1932 he had named the new culture Jurakultur or Jurassic culture after the Jurassic limestone from which at Neumarkt, Amberg, Eichstadt, Hersbruch, Kelheim, Lichtenfels and Regensburg he had collected at least 20 000 artefacts made from quartzite and bluey grey jasper. There was little retouch and hardly any symmetry of form or beauty. At the time the finds attracted much interest from contemporary archaeologists and inevitably there was some controversy over dating. Zotz called the finds Mousterian and included Kachelfluh near Kleinkems, although Birkner supported Gumpert. Patersen and Matthes were convinced that the finds were Mesolithic. Reisch makes no mention of the actual mining or quarrying site for the raw material. It must be assumed that shafts, adits or just quarry faces did exist, but are now no longer exposed.

Scandinavia

The Swedish flint mines near Malmo in the extreme south of the country, Scania are Kvarnby, Gallerup and Tullstorp. The good quality flint was quarried from the chalk which was in the form of glacial rafts. The quarries provided an excellent product which was traded in exchange for other materials from the non-flint areas of Sweden, Norway and Denmark. Working extended through the late Neolithic and even into the Iron Age.

Althin (1951) discussed the age of the flint workings in Scania and actually suggested that they were not really flint mines. They were discovered by Halst in 1904. In 1951 flint was still being mined at Kvarnby, S. Gallerup and Tullstorp. In the same year an ancient pit 3·5 m deep and over 4 m wide was found in a chalk quarry near to the office block at Kvarnby. Iron Age sherds reported to be Roman were found. Although the pit was partly destroyed workmen said the depth was 15–20 m and that it passed through morainic gravel and chalk. Althin based his theories and argument against the pits being flint mines on four factors: (a) the pits went beyond the flint seams, (b) plenty of flint was left unworked and (c) the antler picks were of poor quality compared to those for example found at Grimes Graves. Holst was firm concerning the last factor and said that the pits were flint mines on the basis of the numerous antler picks found there. Althin (1951) said that they were merely chalk pits. Later investigations at Kvarnby at a greater depth showed excellent flint which had been worked.

Only Kvarnby amongst the Scandinavian flint mines has been definitely assigned to a culture, i.e. in this case to the Trichterbeckerkultur (TRB) of the C phase in the Early Neolithic c. 2900 ± 115 BC.

Celts and daggers made from Scania flint have been found in Norway and Finland. In the Arctic north of Norway hoards of such tools have been found along with slate artifacts and associated with megalithic tombs and stone cists according to Becker (1959). There is no doubt that the much sought after flint was a valuable export medium. In exchange Scania could have received furs as a major commodity or even ships' ropes. Seals, whales, otters, bears etc. would have been prolific. Clark (1948) mentions the possible use of skin boats for trade.

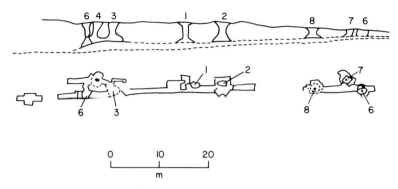

Fig. 58. Sketch and plan of flint mine workings from Aalborg to Hasseris (N. Jutland).

Becker (1959) gives a full account of flint mining in Denmark in Neolithic times. It was not until 1950 that shafts and shallow adits were discovered in chalk near Aalborg in North Jutland off the east coast (see Fig. 58). Here chalk and limestone extend across the peninsula as it does down most of the coast of East Zealand, where to date no prehistoric mining has been reported. It had been known that in Neolithic times the need for flint implements for tree felling was so great that the usual mere collection of raw material from the immense supplies on sea shores would not have been sufficient for this purpose, according to Clark (1948), nor for the large export trade to other parts of Scandinavia. Therefore the existence of underground flint mines was never ruled out. Most of the chalk and limestone is overlain by glacial sand and clay so identification always presents a problem.

An early shaft discovered at Aalborg was 1·85 m in diameter and over 2 m deep. At the belled-out bottom the diameter was increased to about 3 m. The Aalborg Historical Museum later found larger and deeper shafts, i.e. down to a maximum depth of 4·7 m. The system seems to have been to sink the shafts very close together so avoiding excessive tunnelling. Fifteen shafts were cleared away during 1950–1953. Becker suggests a date for daggers of 1800 BC and also for sickles found and the occasional axe. Therefore if the date is valid, mining was probably operating in the Late Neolithic period.

In a modern chalk pit three earlier and more extensive workings than those at Aalborg were discovered at Hov in North West Jutland during 1957 and 1958. The miners here had evidently sunk shafts down to 7 or 8 m and to 4·5 m in diameter, but had found the flint to be inferior and decided to work a seam of small nodules 2–3 m higher up (see Fig. 59). At this level tunnels had been driven 3–5 m in length. There are also filled in shafts

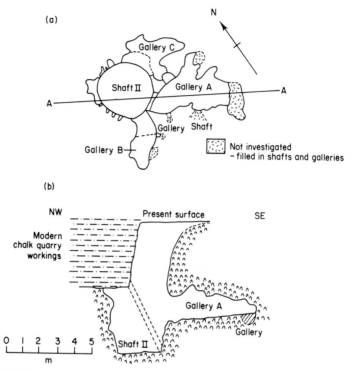

Fig. 59. (a) Plan (after Becker) and (b) section on AB of flint mine (after Becker and Jahn) at Hov. Acknowledgements to Professor J. G. Becker.

where no flint was found by the early miners. According to Becker the Hov workings are dated 2500–2000 BC.

The early shafts had no galleries, but were sunk quite close together there being 36 shafts of this category in an area of only 25 m × 20 m. Where the flint was deeper and of better quality shafts were farther apart and galleries connected them.

In the investigations carried out by Professor Becker, which were extended to 1959, it was found that Shafts 1 and 2 had been partly damaged by modern workings, Shaft 5 was not completed for some unknown reason whereas Shaft 7 was entirely intact. Later, in 1965 Shaft 7 was uncovered and galleries examined. Here very highly developed workings were found as shown in Fig. 60 (Becker 1976, 1977). At the surface the shaft mouth was truly circular and 4·5 metres in diameter and through the soft chalk was funnel shaped, but when the rock became firmer was continued with vertical walls and diameter 3 m. There was some evidence at a depth of 2·3 m of a wooden platform having been used

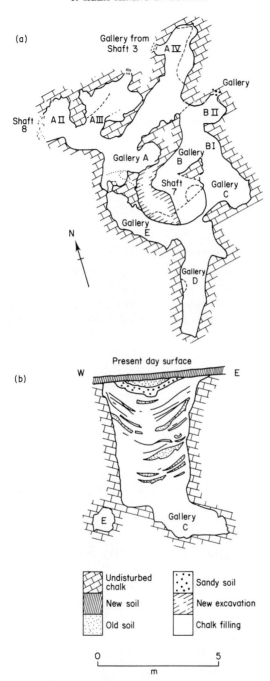

Fig. 60. Shaft No. 7 at Hov, NW. Jutland. Acknowledgements to Professor J. G. Becker.

for there was a horizontal row of small holes which had presumably been made for the insertion of pointed poles for supporting the platform. Across half the shaft 3 m farther down was a bench or platform of solid chalk across half the width of the shaft. Such platforms might have been used for transferring the rough flint nodules possibly for preliminary shaping before they were raised to the surface. The galleries leading from the shaft, e.g. B, were almost the height of a man initially, but farther in, as in the case of BI to BIII and AII to AIII were very uneven. AII is probably a gallery from Shaft 8 and not from Shaft 7. Gallery A was from 0·8 to 1·1 m high over its full length. In the vicinity of Gallery D the chalk was found to be very hard and so the profile is very uneven. In the east and south of Shaft 7 the flint disappeared and so here working came to an abrupt end.

For a long time during the investigations no antler picks had been found and so it was presumed that the chalk was too hard so stone or bone tools which also had not been discovered, must have been used. However, late in the work a large pointed tool, presumably a pick, from a red deer antler and 29·8 cm long was found. The problem is why no more were located. All the larger shafts had been filled in with soil and broken chalk, presumably from gallery excavations and here and there cultural remains such as pot fragments were found in the debris. These were, however, all of Bronze Age date, i.e. much later than that of the TRB culture associated with the mines.

In the summer of 1958 a third flint mining site was found at Bjerre 11 km north-west of Hov. So far in Denmark, as on mining sites in many other countries, there is scant evidence of extensive Neolithic human habitation.

Flint mining in Norway appears to have been non-existent and the raw material which could be picked up in the gravels was not of very good quality, probably it is similar to that weathered variety found amongst Thames gravels today.

Other European Prehistoric Silex Mines

Flint mines have been found in an isolated Cretaceous area at Rocio, Lisbon in Portugal.

Clark and Piggott (1933) refer to Chalcolithic mines at Monte Tabuto in Sicily, near Syracuse. Here the chert was extracted by lateral galleries driven into the hillside in Tertiary limestone for 50 m and excavated with the aid of basalt axes (see Fig. 61).

Sulimirski is quoted by Clark (1952) as saying that flint was actually

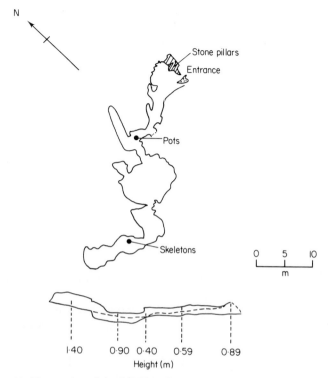

Fig. 61. Plan and section of Gallery System V at Monte Tabuto, Sicily.

mined in Mesolithic times in Poland. A more recent article by Schild (1976) refers to mining even in the Final Palaeolithic era and which also continued into the Mesolithic. The site is in the Holy Cross Mountains which lie in Central Poland in the middle of a line drawn from Warsaw to Cracow. Here a unique type of flint, light brown to dark brown in colour and known as chocolate flint or possibly chert, was worked in the Mesozoic limestones and clays. Several mining sites have been found and at Oronsko shafts were sunk to a depth of 3 m. At habitation sites, dating back to 9000 BC, the same type of material has been found and these are within 100 km of the Holy Cross Mountains. By 8500 BC the same material had been found 200–400 km from the source. Schild gives a useful summary of these finds, and is of the opinion that the Late Dryas* people (c. 8800–8300 BC) were more nomadic than those living during the Allerød Oscillation* (c. 10 000–8000 BC). It is possible that a return to colder climatic conditions induced the Late Palaeolithic peoples to move

* See Ch. 1 for an explanation of these terms.

around in search of more favourable sites for habitation, but this cannot be verified.

Jahn (1956) mentions a massive silex mine of Neolithic times in the Polish Jurassic limestones at the east end of the Lysa-Gora at Krzemionki in the Opatow district in which a strongly banded chert or jasper was won and worked into beautiful polished axes. Much controversy has arisen concerning the validity of the concept of widespread trading of silex in the Neolithic era, but as Jahn postulates, the immense size of the undertakings in all the European countries lends credulity to the theory and it cannot be lightly discounted. Krezemionki has about 1000 shafts of 10 m average depth with galleries and extend over 4 km. This is claimed by Jazdzewski to be the oldest flint mine in Europe (Jazdzewski 1965), which would contradict Sulimirski's theory concerning the Mesolithic age of the Oronsko mine although this did not have shafts and galleries. The mining tools used at Krzemionki included hammers, chisels, antler wedges and wedges made from Silesian basalt and gabbro. Torches of resinous wood were used for lighting purposes similar to those employed as late as 700 BC in the Hallstatt salt mines in Austria.

Jacek Lech (1975) at the Second International Symposium on Flint at Maastricht in 1975, reported on Neolithic flint mines at Saspow 25 km north-west of Cracow in Poland. Ten shafts have been discovered in the Jurassic limestone of the area excavated to a depth of 4–6 m. Flint nodules were said to have been mined in karstic clay pits having been filled in with loess which covered the area in the final glaciation. The pits were oval, 8 m × 5 m, at the surface decreasing in size towards the bottom. According to Lech it had been thought that flint mining in the area was linked with the Funnel Beaker Culture, but radiocarbon dates for charcoal in the infilling of Shaft 6 of 3096 ± 102 BC and from Shaft 1 of 3375 ± 90 BC would put flint mining back to the Lengyel-Olgar cultures. Lech quotes the mass production of mined flint at the large Olszanica settlement of the Linear Bandkeramik culture (LBK). To date there is no reference to the actual mining of flint in this area in Neolithic times before the Michelsberg cultures, but the colonial expansionists of the LBK must have extracted flint or chert for their agricultural needs.

Reference has already been made several times to early theories concerning the age of flint mining. After much controversy over many decades the consensus of opinion is that actual underground mining with shafts did not start, at least in Europe before the Neolithic. Schmid (1972) reintroduced the controversy in a paper presented at a Paris Symposium on the theme "The origin of Homo-Sapiens", the report of which was published by Unesco in 1972. In the paper she reports on a possible

Mousterian silex mine and dwelling site between Laufen and Porrentruy in the Swiss Jura Mountains at Löwenburg in the canton of Berne. Here the limestone is reported as Upper Kimmeridgian in which the silex (i.e. chert) outcrops. Now it is covered with loam and soil which in pre-glaciation times would not have been present. The site was discovered as a result of the finds in 1968 of artefacts resembling those of Mousterian age and many fragments left over from tool making. A quarry face was said to have marks made by man during the extraction of chert nodules. If the theories of Schmid, which are based primarily on finds similar to Mousterian, are correct mining activity would be pushed back 35 000 years and according to the author open up the important question of whether the miners were Neanderthals or modern man.

Artefacts resembling those of the Mousterian would not in themselves be sufficient evidence of such early mining. Quarrying, however, was a strong possibility even in the Palaeolithic, and the existence of a Mousterian dwelling site would add weight to the argument. Another factor in favour of the theory is the reported evidence of wind deposited loam said to have been left as sediment during the advance of the last glaciation. A date of 410 000 BP, i.e. the middle of the Würm interstadial is given for the quarry. However, Schmid (1975) later published three radiocarbon dates for Löwenburg from the Berne laboratories. They were 2990 ± 240 BC and 3070 ± 100 BC, both for charcoal in the waste at a depth of 1·75 m and 3260 ± 100 BC for charcoal on the excavation wall. Either the mine and possible quarry had a long history right through the Middle Palaeolithic, glacial epochs and Neolithic or the earlier theory of Mousterian working is unfounded.

Probably the best known silex mine in Austria and also the only one known to the author in that country at the time of writing is located at Antonshöhe, 3 km from Mauer near Vienna, where mining took place in Neolithic times in the Jurassic limestones. Bayers excavated on the site between 1929 and 1930, but he died in 1931 before the results of his work could be fully published. He left no plans only his notebooks. Neumann also dug on the site in 1949, but Kirnbauer (1958) describes the geology and finds in an article and Elisabeth Ruttkay (1970) discusses the associated burials on the site and the finds of pottery.

No radiocarbon dates have so far been reported for the site, but the numerous mining tools painted pottery and skeletons and associated additions give conclusive proof of their Neolithic age especially when they are considered in the context of other sites and habitations declared to be of the same period. Jahn (1960) suggests that Mauer is associated with the Lengyel culture which could make the mine one of the oldest

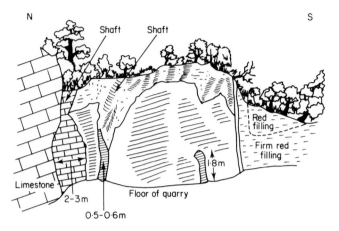

Fig. 62. Sketch of shafts exposed in limestone quarry face at Mauer (after Kirnbauer). By permission of Franz Deuticke, Vienna.

Neolithic workings in Europe. A radiocarbon date for the Lengyel habitation site of Unterpullendorf in Austria is 4180 ± 140 BC.

The prehistoric mining site of Mauer lies in a wood on a 356 m high limestone cliff. The cliff covers an area of 400 m × 120 m and the mines an area of 120 m × 40 m stretching north-east to south-west. Figure 62 shows a sketch of the shafts exposed in the limestone face. There are two beds of red chert and one of white and these were cut by vertical and sloping shafts. The vertical shafts were 4–8 m deep with a surface diameter of 2·6–3 m and a lower one of 1 m. The method appears to have consisted in sinking one shaft and a second 4 m or so away with connections, the debris from the second being disposed of in the first shaft followed by the sinking of a third shaft and so on. Inclined shafts at 60–80° to the horizontal and 10–12 m in diameter were also sunk. Kirnbauer says that in no other place in the Austrian Jurassic limestones have such compact beds of chert been found. The principle of working is shown in Fig. 63.

Deer horn picks have been found and these were used presumably to break out the chert nodules. On this basis the limestone must have been much softer or more jointed and broken than that found on many other European silex mining sites. Pebbles from the Danube were utilized, together with those of quartzite, diabase hammers and greenstone mallets to break up the nodules of chert into pieces 8–10 cm. long for easy transport.

Mauer is also known for the finds of skeletons and for painted pottery. Skeletons were located in a 4·20 m shaft together with animal bones. One was of a man 35–40 years old, of yellow appearance with badly worn

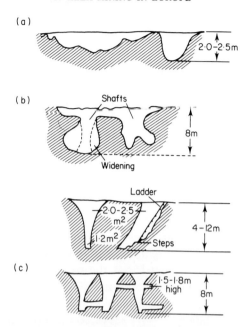

Fig. 63. Profile of working at Mauer (after Kirnbauer). (a) opencut, (b) opencut and shaft mining, (c) shafts with galleries. By permission of Franz Deuticke, Vienna.

teeth, but no dental caries were evident. The skull had been eaten into by snails. Only two graves contained pottery. Pittioni in "Urgeschichte des österreichischen Raumes" said that it was dated from the Moravian-Lower Austrian Mountain Group age of painted pottery. Ruttkay notes that this division of prehistory came after the Bandkeramic and before the Baden culture which has often been encountered in Central European investigations.

The site has prolific refuse dumps, but the problem of the site appears to concern the skeletons. Were they normal burials in shafts as skeletons of women and children or were they bodies left as a result of mining accidents? It is possible that women and children did work in the mines and the conditions of rock excavation without artificial support would lend credence to the theory. Although skeletons and so-called grave goods have been found there is unfortunately no sign of any human settlement.

Fülöp (1973) describes two quarries in the Tata region of Hungary about 65 km north-west of Budapest. Neolithic man here worked a thick bed of chert in a quarry underlying Oxford limestone and resting on an oolitic limestone and in the other under a crinoid limestone, Kimmeridge clay and Oxford limestone. Three distinct holes have been found and these have been made deep into the limestone and infilled over a length of 40–60 m. One excavated quarry site had been backfilled with unsorted chert debris and reddish brown clay material. Amongst the broken debris were four hammer stones and one deer horn tool. The second quarry south of the first was 1 m wide and 6 m long. Burleigh (1975) quotes a radiocarbon date of 1860 ± 65 BC, supplied to him by Miss E. Bácskay of Budapest, for this site.

Further south of Budapest, i.e. about 160 km south west of the city and roughly 30 km north-west of Lake Balaton lies Magyorósdomb, near Sümeg, the site of a prehistoric silex mine which is described by Vertes (1964). This mine was discovered accidentally during the excavation of a trench 50 m long and 0·5 m deep down to a calcareous marl bed rock. The observer noted that part of the floor gave way at one place and in another part of the trench the filling contained deer horn fragments and charcoal. Vertes was convinced that the trench had uncovered an old silex mine and that the deer horns represented old mining tools. During a rescue dig in 1960 three old mines were uncovered constituting a method of working intermediate between Clark and Piggott's Group I mines, i.e. "old bell shaped pits" and their Group II galleried pits (Clark and Piggott 1933). An interesting feature was that the seam of silex was nearly vertical and the process of undercutting into it had created a room 1·2–1·4 m high. The calcareous marl had probably been broken out by firesetting as charcoal was found, but strangely no trace of fire. Samples of charcoal yielded radiocarbon dates of 2560 ± 160 BC with a halflife of 5568 years and 2729 ± 160 BC with a half life of 5760 years. This date would set the working in Neolithic times. No pottery or traces of domestic refuse were found. The silex was broken out of blocks with the aid of hammers made from quartz pebbles or by discoids of quartzite. Without radiocarbon dating Magyorósdomb could easily have been considered to be of Palaeolithic age, Mesolithic or at least pre-Neolithic. As it is the mine was probably worked through the Late Neolithic into the Eneolithic or even into the Bronze Age.

The Campignian Tradition

In the 1950s and 1960s some controversy prevailed over the age and culture associated with the group of mines and sites in Belgium, north of Liege. Some of these have already been mentioned.

Campigny is a site in northern France where, in 1872, crude pottery and pits containing worked flint was discovered. The tools consisted mainly of large picks and tranchet axes. These were crude and unpolished and were assigned by different investigators to the Mesolithic or Neolithic. They were likened to those found in the Danish Mesolithic kitchen middens. In due course the mines of Grimes Graves and Spiennes were assigned to the Neolithic of Campignian tradition. In fact the Campignian tradition of unpolished axes was deemed to persist right through into the Bronze Age. The tradition seems to be stronger in the Neolithic cultures with a Mesolithic heritage, particularly those having flint mining.

The Campignian tradition is not confined to flint, but has its counterpart in the stone axe industry such as at Graig Llwyd, according to Gabel (1957). Schwantes (1932) appears not to attach much importance to the concept and regards it as simply chance that has given axes produced from Neolithic mines their resemblance to Palaeolithic and Mesolithic versions. Abundance of flint rendered finishing superfluous and tools were intended for use in an unfinished state.

In referring to the sites north of Liège near the Dutch frontier de Laet (1958) notes that these have been called Campignian, but he says these are much more archaic than those of the French Campignian and renames the tradition pre-Campignian. If as de Laet concludes the pre-Campignian is Mesolithic for reason of non-farming activity and lack of finish on the flints then flint mining by underground methods, even if primitive, would have started much earlier. He implies that Obourg could have been pre-Campignian or Mesolithic, whereas Spiennes is much later than the Bandkeramic and definitely Michelsberg.

Moreover it is known that Mesolithic peoples occupied the areas adjacent to those of the farming or Linear Bandkeramic cultures, so would probably pre-Campignians, with no interacting influences.

Piggott (1954) points out that the use of the expression "Campignian" has unfortunately serious drawbacks. In French archaeological circles *le Campignian* is culturally between the Mesolithic and the true Neolithic. He goes on to suggest that instead of Campignian the phrase "secondary Neolithic" should be used for cultures containing some element of Mesolithic heritage.

Even with the valuable development in radiocarbon dating the true derivation of age can never be absolute. In other words the actual dates of starting and termination of a flint mine can never be determined accurately, therefore some controversy must always prevail.

5
Sources and Trading of Obsidian and Other Hard Stones

Although silex mining was a very advanced and important activity in Neolithic times, flint, chert and jasper were not the only important materials used in the manufacture of tools and other equipment. There was possibly a wide and extensive trade in flint especially, but even so some regions were beyond the reach of possible trade routes and many producing areas could not satisfy all the requirements of the Neolithic and other communities. The two chief alternatives used were obsidian and special varieties of hard igneous and other rocks.

Obsidian

This variety of volcanic glass, although not in very wide use on account of its comparative scarcity, has all the useful properties of many of the better grades of flint, i.e. conchoidal fracture and ease of chipping to a required finish. In fact it is superior to flint and other sedimentary based materials especially for the making of axes and arrowheads. Furthermore it has an additional property in being suitable for the production of vases and jewellery, often being inlaced in metals to enhance their appearance.

   Obsidian was known as far back as Upper Palaeolithic times, being found in Level C of Shanidar Cave in Iraq and dated $28\,700 \pm 700$ $-33\,000 \pm 1000$ BP. These are reputed, by Renfrew *et al.* (1966), to be the very earliest stratified finds in the Near East. Both in the Near East and the Mediterranean area and in later Neolithic times in South and Central Europe obsidian was an important item of trading. It formed a basis for exchange and was transported over great distances to the non-productive area of Mesopotamia by caravans, being traded for woven goods, shells and pottery. A beautiful example of an obsidian jar was found at Byblos and was said to be a gift to the princes of Byblos from the Egyptian pharoahs. This together with a gold embellished obsidian box was found

108

in the Royal tombs at the excavations there, according to Cullican (1966) dating between 1840 and 1700 BC.

Obsidian is found in dykes and the best variety occurs near later volcanoes. It is formed by the rapid cooling of high silica (i.e. greater than 65%) volcanic lavas. Extraction is relatively easy as it occurs mostly near the surface and it had been quarried over many millennia BC. It absorbs water readily so can be dated by the degree of hydration (see Appendix Two for a brief explanation of the method).

Over the last 15–20 years much has been learned about the sources of the obsidian found on habitation sites, and the possible extent of trading, by the use of trace element analyses. Basically this method consists of measuring the wavelength of light emitted from elements when heated to incandescence. The trace elements, barium and zirconium have been used by Renfrew *et al.* (1966) as a means of identifying sources of obsidian found on Central Mediterranean and Aegean sites. Obsidian has been found on almost every Early Neolithic site in the Mediterranean area and was imported from at least one of the following extraction districts:

Acigöl	Central/East Turkey
Bingol	East Turkey
Ciftlik	Central/East Turkey
Giali	Island off South West Turkey
Lipari	Island off Sicily
Melos	Island off southern Greece
Nemrut Dag	Near Lake Van in eastern Turkey
Pantellaria	Island between North African coast and Sicily
Sardinia	

In Armenia obsidian was obtained from Erevan and Kars. Obsidian artefacts found in Europe came chiefly from Hegyalya near Tokaj in Hungary and the Carpathians.

The association of obsidian made implements and crop cultivation is often difficult to establish without additional evidence. This derives from the property of silica gloss retention which, although existent with silex, is not possessed by obsidian.

The source at Nemrut Dag has been known for some considerable time and the obsidian found at Shanidar, previously mentioned, is reputed to have originated at this Lake Van site, which continued to supply the material until late Bronze Age times. According to Renfrew *et al.* (1966) the obsidian occurs in a bed 1·2–2·5 m thick and varies in colour from clear black to opaque olive green.

The Aegean islands, known as the Cyclades, had a vast export trade in quarried obsidian, the chief and probably the only major supplier being Melos. In fact 60% of the obsidian on Greek Neolithic sites originated there, a notable example being at Nea Nikomedeia where obsidian from Melos was found in the late Neolithic phase c. 3600 BC. Rodden (1962) states that none was found in the early Neolithic on this site. Similarly an obsidian blade from Melos was found by J. D. Evans (1971) at Knossos on the island of Crete. This was dated c. 6000 BC and in this case was 80 miles from Melos. During the megalithic civilization of Malta obsidian was imported from Lipari which also supplied Italy in both Neolithic and Bronze Age times. Sardinia provided natural sources of obsidian for the farming communities there during the Neolithic period.

During the sixth-seventh millennia BC the proportion of obsidian to flint used for the manufacture of tools at Çatal Hüyük in Anatolia reached 80% compared to 40% at Jarmo in Mesopotamia and less than 1% at Byblos and Jericho in the Levant. According to Renfrew et al. (1966) the Levant finds are chiefly from Cappodocia and the others from Armenia.

North of the Balkans during the Temperate Neolithic period the colonists moving north had to obtain their obsidian from sources other than the Mediterranean area. Much obsidian has been found on excavated sites and between 5140 ± 150 and 4500 ± 100 BC at Gyralaret in Hungary during Köros times much was obtained from new sources in the Carpathians. Childe (1957) writes that during the period of the Starcevo culture trade brought obsidian to the encampments on the Pruth and along the Tisza and Köros. In the Milojoić phase B supplies came from North East Hungary down the Tisza. The Bukkians controlled obsidian deposits of the Hegyala near Tokaj and from the volcanic glass made knives and scrapers, but no bifacial arrowheads. The mountains of South East Slovakia and North Hungary were the main sources of obsidian which occurs as intrusive dykes in the limestone. It had a wide usage in the Bandkeramic cultural phase of North East Hungary. Ruth Tringham (1971) suggests that fine hard pottery with red burnished slip and also coarser wares were traded for obsidian and that painted wares occur particularly on those sites where a large number of artefacts of obsidian have been found in excavations. In the Second Middle Neolithic in South East Europe, from 4500 to 4000 BC, there was an even greater use of obsidian. Axes were made from the material and the Carpathian sources were exploited on a much greater scale.

In the north and particularly on later sites in the Lengyel culture, around 4000 BC, obsidian is less frequent and there is none in the Tisza culture. Despite the introduction of native copper after the end of the Neolithic period, the use of obsidian and silex continued through the Chalcolithic or Eneolithic period into the Bronze Age. With the discovery of metals the uses of obsidian declined at least for toolmaking. Early man found that copper tools could be melted down when blunted and then remoulded and native copper could be rebeaten. Whereas the use of flint tended to decline at the start of the Early Bronze Age, being suitable only for tool manufacture, that of obsidian continued right through the era, not for tools, but for luxury items, including vases. Beautiful examples are contained in the treasures from the tombs at Dorak in Anatolia, discovered (Lloyd 1967) reportedly by Mellaart, but unfortunately these have presumably vanished completely without trace.

Many sources of obsidian have been mentioned in books and papers concerning the Neolithic and Bronze Age settlements in Central Europe. Nandris (1975) examined many of these reported sources in Hungary and Rumania and concluded that the majority in Southeast Europe are literary rather than geological. Of the regions examined by Nandris only Tokaj-Hegyalja in Hungary could be regarded as an authentic source.

Since most of the obsidian used in prehistoric times in Europe and the Near East apparently originated from quarries or was merely picked out at visible locations on the surface, it is not possible to find evidence of workings as they will have been obliterated with the passage of time. Consequently there is no record in scientific journals, at least in Europe, of actual obsidian quarries or mines. However, Coe and Flannery (1964) describe extensive obsidian workshop sites and evidence of underground obsidian mining activity at El Chayal in North East Guatemala. The authors say that the sites date from c. 5000 BC to 1500 BC. A highway cutting revealed vast quantities of obsidian nodules and exposed several wide pits which had apparently been used to mine underground deposits of the material. The age of the sites was assessed on the grounds of the site having no pottery, i.e. they were aceramic; 31 cores were collected and flakes consisting of shouldered knives; large discoidal scrapers, heavy choppers and bifacial utility instruments unearthed. The cores were triangular 6–11·5 cm in diameter with a striking platform 4–11 cm in diameter.

A later article by Sheets (1975) refutes the claims of Coe and his co-author and gives a revised date of 800–1500 AD. Sheets points out that the existence of an aceramic site does not imply a pre-ceramic culture. There was probably no pottery found because the inhabitants would have lived some way from the workshops. So there is some controversy over the dating of this particular site, but there is no doubt concerning the existence of an underground obsidian mine and workshop.

The significant feature concerning obsidian is that although it is a superior product to flint and chert for the manufacture of tools and had a more varied application, it was a valuable commodity for trade. Despite the fact that flint was traded locally in vast quantities from the very numerous flint mines, obsidian sources were comparatively limited. Being in great demand it was traded over great distances and became a symbol of cultural prestige as demonstrated by its appearance in the royal tombs and palaces of Egypt, Mesopotamia and Anatolia.

Hard Rocks

Despite the widespread occurrence of flint in chalk and other derivatives of silica in limestone, communities in prehistoric times made use of rocks mostly of the igneous types. It is understandable that supplies of flint, chert, jasper etc. were limited to tool and weapon manufacture whereas hard rocks could have a variety of additional applications such as for vessels, monuments, burial chambers etc.

Supplies of rocks were obtained by quarrying or they were merely collected from screes such as at the Pike of Stickle, Great Langdale in Westmorland. Although reputed sources can be investigated at site the actual quarries have, if they existed at all, been removed by later workings over the years, except in a very few cases. Why did the inhabitants of the Neolithic and even those of the Bronze Age go to the trouble of obtaining rock and fashioning it when good flint was often readily accessible? The answer must be that the rock was in certain cases easily available in quantity, or transportable, as compared to the deep mining required for high grade flint.

The use of stone for the manufacture of vessels was known over 8000 years ago. For example the pre-pottery Neolithic people at Jarmo in Mesopotamia, in 6500 BC fashioned drinking and storage vessels from stone which was probably obtained from Persia. At Troy in Anatolia stone was used throughout the Early to Late Bronze Ages for the manufacture of vessels and tools. In fact marble was carved into vases and traded as far as Egypt as were stone battle axes copied from metal ones. Marble is plentiful in Anatolia and over 47 varieties have been found to date and as there is a proliferation of igneous rocks it is also understandable that such materials should also have been used. Furthermore flint is scarce in Anatolia and copper and more so tin appears to have been in short supply and so in Early Bronze Age times, even in the Middle and Near East, was used primarily for luxury goods.

During the Early Bronze Age in Europe, axes, adzes, arrowheads and other tools and weapons made of flint and stone were still being used despite the introduction of metals. Copper and tin were even scarcer and more costly than in the Near East. In fact in Britain copper does not appear until as late as 2500 BC. Although stone axes are more brittle than those made from pure copper and cannot be recycled when badly worn, they can be given cutting edges just as good as those of copper tools. Great skill was developed in the polishing of stone axes using sand and water. It is hardly surprising therefore, that prehistoric man made use of easily acquired stone.

Unlike Neolithic flint mining and later copper mining there was no particular technique required to extract rock especially in scree areas. In fact it has been said that great use was made of erratic boulders south of the line of the last glaciation in Britain. These are reported to have originated in the north and west of Britain and Scandinavia. When stones are found in areas foreign to their environment, in a geological context, they, in some cases, could have been transported by human agencies or by glaciers. This has been a source of controversy for many decades. A typical example is the stone from which the prehistoric monument at Stonehenge in Wiltshire was made. This is known as preselite and is a spotted dolerite in which the dominant felspar is albutized. It is reputed to have originated at the Prescelly blue mountains in Pembrokeshire. Eighty two stones were erected in 1620 ± 110 BC, in the form of two concentric rings. The famous ring at Avebury, also in Wiltshire, is another example of the use of such stones.

The interesting feature concerning the finds of stone axes and stone weapons in burial sites and the use of stones in monument and barrow building is not merely that of mining and quarrying the stone, but the distance it was transported, i.e. the trade aspect if any was involved. Much controversy concerning the origin of the stones used to make axes in Britain still prevails and since the axes have been found all over Britain, especially in the south of England in Wiltshire, occasionally in flint mine workings, in barrows, camps, ditches and so on, some effort has been expended in attempting to indicate the possible sources of the stone used. In 1941 the First Report of the Sub-Committee of the South Western Group of Museums and Art Galleries on the Petrological Identification of Stone Axes was published (Keiller *et al.* 1941).

The work done by the investigators consisted basically in making a microscopic examination of thin slices cut from an axe and then pinpointing a rock source or factory workshop where the rock *in situ* has the same petrological composition or properties. Macroscopic examination in isolation does not offer a reliable method of rock identification as every petrologist knows. For example, the implement when completed would have a different appearance produced by polishing etc. and in addition thousands of years of surface weathering. The main difficulty in microscopic examination is the problem of obtaining thin sections from valuable specimens or from museum exhibits. Several subsequent reports have been issued. It was decided to group the rocks initially into nine groups, but now 25 groups have been established.

In the reports the distribution of the sources of the rocks used for axe manufacture is shown on maps. Briefly the characteristics of the rocks in each group are as follows:

Group I. This is a uralitized gabbro, epidorite or greenstone presumably from Mounts Bay area, near Penzance in Cornwall. An axe in Avebury Museum found at Windmill Hill in Wiltshire and also some recognized in Gloucestershire, Dorset and Devon were manufactured from the rock.

Group II. The rock in this group is also reported to be a greenstone of fine texture. An axe found at Otterton in South Devon was matched with a section of the rock taken between Lay Point and St Ives in Cornwall.

Group III. A section of rock at a quarry near Marazion in Cornwall was matched with a stone implement of greenstone found at Beckhampton in Wiltshire. Canon Greenwell found an axe of this group from Cornwall at Grimes Graves in 1868–1870.

Group IV. This rock macroscopically resembles those of Groups I and II. An axe from Grimes Graves found by Peake in 1917 in Pit 15 has been allotted to this group.

Group V. Axes of this greenish grey altered sedimentary rock are similar to pebble from Porthmeor beach, St Ives and a rock sample from Hellesveor Cliff.

Group VI. This group contains volcanic tuffs from the famous Langdale Pikes screes and workshops in the Lake District. There is a very wide distribution of axes made from this rock such as found in Hampshire, Windmill Hill, Dorset, Oxfordshire, Berkshire and Abingdon. Six broken axes at various stages of trimming were found near Langdale according to Clough and Green (1972). These authors quote radiocarbon dates for a chipping site of this group at Thunacar Knott as 2730 ± 135 BC and 2524 ± 52 BC.

Group VII. The igneous rock, known as porphyritic microdiorite, found constituting the crags of Graig Llwd on the northern slopes of Penmaenmawr facing the sea, is the type rock of this group. Axes have been found at Windmill Hill, West Kennet, Stow on the Wold, Cambridgeshire and in Anglesey.

Group VIII. This rock is a silicified rhyolitic glass, a fine tuff or sediment and constituting the material of an axe found at Windmill Hill.

Group IX. Tievebulliagh Hill near Cushendale in County Antrim is formed out of dolerite, but the rock type is porcellanite found in the screes amongst the dolerite. Axes made from such porcellanite have been found at Andoversford in Gloucestershire, Dorset, Kent and at Cushendale itself.

Group X. This is a hard flinty black rock and occurs as baked lias shales at Portrush, County Antrim. Implements have been found at Ham Hill, Somerset, Dorset and Newquay, according to Stone and Wallis (1947).

Group XI. This is a stone occurring as that in Group VIII on Ramsay Island (Grinsell 1958).

Group XII. Two outcrops of rock at Cummawr in Montgomery have similarities to Bronze Age hammers.

Group XIII. A rock attributed to this group occurs near Carn Meine on the Prescelly Hills in Pembrokeshire and is the famous spotted dolerite used for the construction of the bluestone segments of Stonehenge to which reference has previously been made. It was also transported to Wessex in the form of axes found near Stonehenge, Backhampton and Stockton earthworks in Wiltshire, near Bournemouth, in the Neolithic levels at Maiden Castle, Dorset and near Winchester.

Group XIV. An axe hammer of comptonite found in the Cambrian beds at Nuneaton falls in this group.

Group XV. This rock is a grit from Coniston in the Lake District and has a similarity with the material from which an axe found in the North Midlands was made.

Group XVI. This rock is an amphibole from near Camborne in Cornwall and was apparently utilized according to Cummins (1974) in making axes for local use.

Group XVII. A St Austell greenstone falls in this group and is similar to Group VII rocks used in the making of axes found at Hembury and Maiden Castle.

Group XIX. The rock in this group is a coarse sedimentary type with so far no located source.

Group XX. This rock is a coarse sandy tuff probably from Charnwood Forest in Leicestershire. Axes from this rock were abundant mainly in the Peak District of Derbyshire and in Norfolk.

Group XXI. This group contains a rock from a quarry site on Mynydd Rhiw, on the Lleyn peninsula in North Wales, in Ordovician shales.

Houlder (1961). The full geographical distribution of axes from this site is not fully known, although polished varieties arising there have been found in Merioneth, Montgomery, Shropshire and in South and Central Wales.

A brief description of many of the rocks mentioned here is given in Ch. 9.

The most important sites at present known from which rock was obtained are probably Langdale Pikes (Group VI), Graig Llwd (Group VII), Tievebulligh (Group IX) and Prescelly (Group XIII).

Bush and Fell (1949) describe the Pike of Stickle, as it was actually known, near Great Langdale in Westmorland. The Pikes themselves are in the Borrowdale series of volcanic rocks and lie over 2300 ft O.D. The extraction site at South Scree, 700 ft O.D. to 2000 ft O.D., was discovered in 1947. Axe roughouts and worked flakes were discovered over the whole area. A hammer stone of granite was found at the site and the worked material resembled flint, the axe developing a patina when recovered from under peat.

Ritchie (1968) has conducted an investigation into a stone implement trade in the third millennium in Scotland. Vast quantities of Group IX axes were found all over Central, South and North East Scotland with a remarkable concentration of the Irish porcellanite in Aberdeenshire.

Other rocks worked or extracted in Scotland during the third millennium include bloodstone from the Isle of Rhum, pitchstone from Arran, hornfels from Craig na Caillich in Perthshire and a riebeckite felsite from the Shetlands.

If it is correct to assume that there was in the third and later millennia BC a wide trade in rocks and both finished and unfinished implements, the next problem is to determine, or hazard a guess at the precise trade routes and the mode of transport. Unfortunately, unlike the later trade in copper and other metals, there is no evidence of either the route or actual process of barter and especially is there no evidence on the means of carriage of the associated loads, which would have been very heavy. So far as the latter point is concerned it is unlikely that transport could have been other than by foot, or did prehistoric man use sliding vehicles? There is no evidence that the wheel had been invented by this time and in any case the wood of any vehicle would have disappeared without trace.

As Cummins points out (1974), the distances by Neolithic standards were vast. For example Group I axes have been found 350 miles from their point of origin in Cornwall, i.e. in Yorkshire. Clough and Green (1972) suggest trading by sea along the south coast and north to Flamborough Head in Yorkshire.

Group VII axes from Langdale have been found in large concentrations in Lincolnshire and Cummins suggests a trade route by Windermere, Kirkby Lonsdale and Settle, through the Aire Gap, down the River Aire and out into the Humber estuary. Much of this route might have been by water.

Much has been written concerning the location and trade routes of Group VII Graig Llwd axes. Glenn (1935) postulated that unlike Groups I and VI, axes of those and of other groups, they were distributed direct to the user instead of via a "wholesale centre".

No theories for axe distribution from the other groups can be reliably postulated until more petrological work has been done. Indeed without more evidence it is not possible to accept or deny the idea of long distance trade by our Neolithic ancestors. Briggs (1976), however, goes even further and is strongly opposed to the concept of large scale distant trading. He gives cogent reasons for his theories and one question to be asked, for example, is why did early man trade over such long distances if he had suitable supplies of raw materials close at hand? Great Langdale axes (Group VI) are related to known scatters of Lakeland derived erratic boulders. The greenstone of Lincolnshire would have provided a better alternative to Langdale tuff for axe making, so it is difficult to visualize bags of stone being carried, to quote Briggs, over the Pennines and over the Vale of York. On the other hand it is not easy to accept his contention that axe texture and rock texture cannot be related on account of weathering. With thin section examination surely this problem does not arise. Briggs also refutes the idea of long distance pottery trading as a means of barter in exchange for rocks or implements. He is of the opinion that 30 km is the maximum distance pottery can be carried without breakage. One outstanding feature of the origin and trading of Group XX rocks is that apparently they were found in the Peak District of Derbyshire and Norfolk, having originated in Charnwood Forest. Derbyshire has suitable qualities of rock for axe manufacture and Grimes Graves in Norfolk has excellent flint.

On the subject of Stonehenge there are still today two vastly differing opinions regarding the origin of the rocks used in construction. They have been petrologically examined and it is agreed that they are sarsen stones or, in other words, foreign to Wiltshire. What is not agreed is the mode of transport. Kellaway (1971) argues strongly in favour of transport by ice sheets or glaciers during the penultimate ice age. Furthermore he postulates that all the sarsens (Group VIII), stone implements and monumental stones found in Wiltshire, particularly those at Avebury, were so transported. Evans et al. (1972) quote Kellaway's theory and, although admitting some evidence for ice action, say there is also strong

evidence (Evans 1972), for the exploitation of spotted dolerite at Carn
Meine or Cerrig Marcogian by distribution. However, there are no
visible signs of quarries or workings having existed at these two places and
it is extemely doubtful that early man could have broken out the large
blocks of hard rock with the primitive tools, such as antler picks, which
were the only ones to hand at the time. Fire setting does not appear to
have been used at that particular time in Britain, although as has been
shown earlier, it had an application in Neolithic times on the continent of
Europe. Transport is also another problem and numerous attempts have
been made to suggest how this might have been solved. There is not the
slightest doubt that huge blocks of rock could have been carried by
moving ice sheets. Kellaway quotes the transport by glaciers of a huge
block of tabular limestone of area 1858 m² and 1·5 m thick in Warren
County, Ohio. Also the erratic boulders found in Brittany at Carnac, and
used as monumental stones, are said to weigh nearly 325 t each. It does
seem extremely unlikely that prehistoric man even thought of
manhandling huge blocks of stone all the way from Pembroke to
Wiltshire, when he had ample supplies of suitable Jurassic limestone
about 30 miles away from Avebury or Stonehenge.

The whole concept is clouded with doubts and uncertainties and may
never be finally and satisfactorily elucidated. For example why was there
not an alternative and wide flung trade in flint from the many British and
European flint mines and chalk quarries? If stone could have been
transported why not flint? Flint is certainly less difficult to work into
implements than hard igneous or metamorphic rock.

Kopper and Rossello-Bordoy (1974) suggest three methods by which
dimensioned blocks of limestone were quarried for the construction of the
megaliths of eastern Europe and in the Ballearic Islands. Two of these
make use of the natural vertical joints, mechanical cuts being made in the
first example, at right angles to the joints. The second method involved
joint continuation by a mechanical cut until this intersected another cross
joint. In this case some form of cutter or saw would have been necessary,
but in Britain there is no evidence of such a device having been used in
prehistoric times. Soft limestone or chalk could have been cut by some
form of arrangement of flints resembling a saw, but the process would
have been slow which, however, might not have been a such a serious
drawback in those laborious times. Hammering of flint wedges into joints
using increasing sizes of wedge, would have been feasible. Firesetting
could have been a much more satisfactory method, but evidence of its use
would have disappeared when the rock face was worked later with more
modern processes. The third method suggested by Kopper and his co-

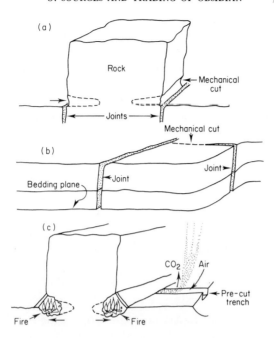

Fig. 64. Suggested methods of extracting dimensioned stone for megalithic construction according to Kopper and Rosello-Bordoy. Acknowledgements to the Journal of Field Archaeology.

author is a form of concentrated fire setting in precuts or joints and is illustrated in the sketch shown in Fig. 64 and reproduced from their paper. Application of 1368 B.Th.u lb $^{-1}$ on calcium carbonate produces quicklime and carbon dioxide. Application of water on the quicklime gives slaked lime and excess heat. The slaked lime is then acted on by the carbon dioxide to give a wet mortar like deposit. It is, according to the authors, necessary to have precut trenches communicating with the precuts which contain the fire, to draw off the surplus carbon dioxide and to provide air entries.

There have been few examples of prehistoric excavations at actual quarry sites, but there are two, according to Houlder (1961), on Mynydd Rhiw in Caernarvonshire and one near Sélédin in Brittany. The rock at the latter site is a fine grained epidioritized dolerite. In the 1950s Cogné and Giot examined many Breton polished stone axes and decided that 40% could be identified as being shaped from this rock, which was formerly allocated to Group IXa in the South Western Committee Classification and later to Group X. Apparently such axes have been found in many megalithic graves in France, but not in the early passage graves. The radiocarbon dates for Sélédin vary from 3800 ± 140 BC to 2050 ± 130 BC so the quarry could have been in use for at least 1000 years. The site is important not only because of its long life, but by the nearness of Neolithic dwelling places and megalithic tombs.

Le Roux (1971, 1973) and co-workers not only carried out extensive prospecting between 1966 and 1970 to define the exact location of axe workshops in the area, but in 1969 and 1970 excavated at the main visible outcrops of the fine grained dolerite and discovered distinct evidence of actual quarrying. The dolerite has been classified as Type A and contains fine black spots of ilmenite which are often recognizable by naked eye. This rock has been the raw material for axes found over the whole of France from Alsace to the Pyrenees and to the valley of the Rhone and even in southern England. Such large production implied extensive quarrying and possible workshops on site. The excavations had to be made through clay to reach the rock which was found to have been worked by benches. (see Fig. 65) Tools were found to have been shaped both on the site and some distance away.

No pottery, flint or bone tools were found and dating was done mainly on charcoal found in large hearths on the site. The dolerite was extracted in blocks often 1 m average width and two to three metres in length, and might have been obtained by the use of fire. Le Roux carried out an experiment on the heat effect on dolerite. He heated the rock for 1·5 h to 400° C for 0·5 h and slow cooling in three hours resulted in no deterioration in the qualities required for tool manufacture, whereas rapid heating to 400° C for 0·5 h or very rapid cooling by water sprinkling caused fractures which rendered flaking useless. Several abandoned blocks probably lend credence to this conclusion.

Delibrias and Le Roux in 1975 had 19 radiocarbon dates for the quarry and workshop at Plussulien, Sélédin, and were able to interpret the phases of working in the quarry as shown in Fig. 65. The working started around 3800 BC and was carried on as shown by Phase I in fracture zones or in solid rock embedded in altered clay. This therefore was as easy to work as flint from weak chalk. The first phase corresponded to the appearance of Type A axes on Neolithic sites although none had been found in earlier passage graves. Later in Phase II above the newer soil level work continued, the blocks there being extracted over the period 3500–3000 BC by percussion methods. After 3000 BC the site was abandoned and vegetation took over. The work was resumed in 2500 BC, but after 2000 BC there was a noticeable reduction in working probably due to the increasing availability of metal tools.

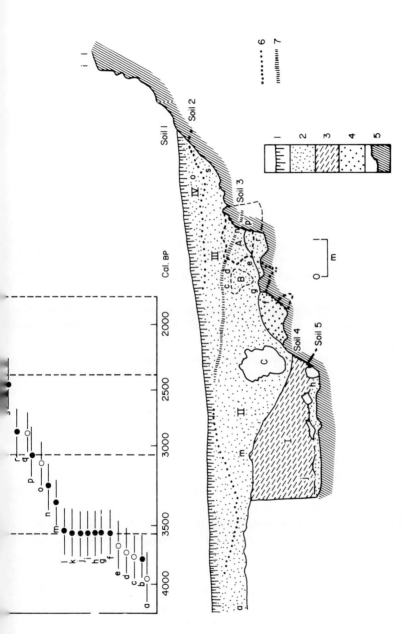

Fig. 65. Quarry works at Plusselien (Sélédin) simplified, 1 soil, 2 waste cuttings, 3 waste clay and cuttings, 4 concretionary altered clays, 5 undisturbed rock, 6 original rock level, 7 soil horizon, A–B–C blocks on benches, (a)–(s) sites of dating samples. Open circles on upper diagram refer to problems discussed by Delibrias and Le Roux (1975). Acknowledgements to C-T. Le Roux.

Delibrias and Le Roux (1975) mention other Breton Neolithic production sites including both quarries and workshops, i.e. Type B epidiorite at Brieverien in the region of Glomel, hornblendite Type C at Kerlevot in Pleuven, south of Quimper and fibrolite (sillimanite) at Plouguin north of Brest.

Further east in the Low Countries there was a wide trade in volcanic rock for the production of implements of various sorts during Danubian or Bandkeramic times around 4000–3600 BC. This certainly took place a few hundred years before the famous flint mines at Spiennes began production. Some authorities, however, place the more primitive mines at Obourg in the pre-Campignian. These facts are not strictly significant when discussing the importation of rocks such as basalt, phtanite and tephrite, etc., but supplies of known flint could have been available, as in the case of Wessex, for the manufacture of suitable polished axes. In exchange for such volcanic rocks, the Rhineland peoples could have imported pottery and such pottery, reputed to have come from Belgian Hesbaye, has been found at the well-known Linearbandkeramic site of Köln Linderthal.

Prehistoric man from the Neolithic era onwards right into the Iron Age, required rock to make querns for the grinding of corn. Indeed querns were used much later through Roman and medieval times. The rock had to be sufficiently soft to enable the varieties of mortars, grain rubbers and saddle and rotary querns to be easily shaped. Sketches of some of these items are shown in Fig. 66. Mortars were used even as far back as Palaeolithic times and as recent as in Roman Britain. Grain rubbers were used by Neolithic man. Saddle querns which enabled two hands to be used, extended into the Early Iron Age in Britain when the rotary type took over.

Soft basalt was ideal for the production of both the saddle and the rotary quern, although late Neolithic sandstone querns were found in the Eifel district of Germany at Kollig. Hörter et al. (1950) describe quern quarries of the Eifel made in the basalt deposits at Mayen. These quarries were discovered when modern machinery was being used to extract basalt. The earliest quarries had been worked in the Middle Hallstatt times (800–600 BC) of the Iron Age, although primitive diggings of Mayen basalt took place. in the Bandkeramic cultures of the Early Neolithic. Querns made of Mayen basalt have been found alongside datable objects in settlements and graves.

The lava field of Mayen is known as Bellerberg and lies within the triangle formed by the three towns of Mayen, Ettringen and Kottenheim. There are two streams of lava from the crater, one flowing

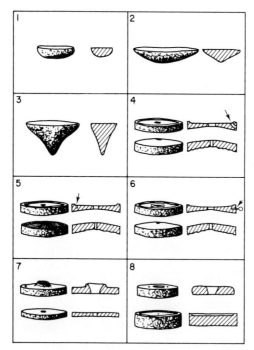

Fig. 66. Types of querns. 1 leaf shaped rubbing stone (Neolithic–Middle Hallstatt), 2 beet shaped rubbing stone (Late Hallstatt), 3 Napoleon Hat (Early and Middle La Tène), 4 oscillating rotary quern (Early–Late La Tène), 5 and 6 fully rotating quern (Roman), 7 Early Middle Age quern, 8 Later Middle Age quern (c. AD 1000).

south to the Mayen quarries and the other north to Kottenheim (see Fig. 67).

The Middle Hallstatt quarries were identified by the debris left behind on a platform on basalt indicating that only the softer upper section had been worked. Parts of querns, which had evidently been made on site were found in the debris.

Hard basalt hammers were used and these weighed up to 17 kg, to break out the rock and lever out the columns of basalt. Röder (1955) states that the hard basalt used for the hammers had been petrologically examined and found to come from the Hochsimmer lava flows. It is suggested that the charcoal found indicated the use of fire setting to break out the hard basalt. If this is correct it is difficult to understand why such a method was not used at Mayen. The Mayen basalt has a compressive strength of 900–1500 kg cm^{-2} compared to that used in tools of 3500 kg cm^{-2}. In the La Tène period iron tools were introduced.

It is significant that the Mayen basalt must have been in great demand

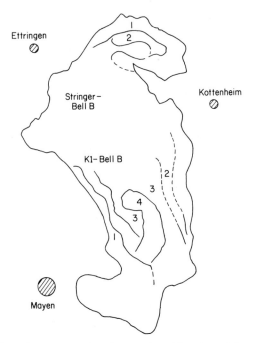

Fig. 67. Bellerberg lava stream locations and prehistoric and later working zones of Mayen quarries. 1 prehistoric, 2 Roman, 3 Early middle Ages, 4 Middle Ages and recent.

for a face of nearly 5000 m, 1·5 m high, had been worked for a distance of 46 m, up to the onset of the Roman period, with primitive tools. The basalt was traded over North West Europe, southern England, where a Mayen quern was found on Overton Hill circle, in the Shetlands and over Belgium and North West Germany.

Shale was also used for the manufacture of beads and was presumably worked at Kimmeridge Bay at Purbeck, although Henrietta Davies (1937) postulates two distinct shale industries here, i.e. that starting in the Early Iron Age and one during the initial period of the Roman occupation of Britain. She says that early Iron Age man found no evidence of earlier occupation, i.e. by Bronze Age cultures. However, shale beads of oval shape have been found at the Hembury, Maiden Castle and Windmill causewayed enclosures.

Apart from silex, obsidian and hard igneous rocks one development was the use of jadeite for the manufacture of implements. Such products were chiefly reserved for ceremonial or exhibition purposes, the raw material being in relative short supply. In Britain jadeite artefacts have been found near Stonehenge and in other parts of Wiltshire as well as in

Hampshire. Finds of jadeite implements are in fact, in Britain, mostly confined to chalk areas of East Anglia and the Southampton area.

The major source of supply were Brittany and probably Switzerland. One hundred celts of jadeite have been found at Morbihan and several hoards in Thuringia and near Mainz in Germany. In 1930 a polished jadeite instrument was found 1 m below the surface in undisturbed clay at Lyme Park in North East Cheshire according to Fox (1932). It was actually 27 cm in length.

6
Chronology and Customs Associated with Silex and Stone Mining

In Chs 3 and 4 occasional passing reference has been made to mode of habitation of flint and silex miners and to the actual finds of associated pottery. At this stage it might be relevant to attempt to bring the available material into general perspective, even at the risk of some repetition of certain aspects of flint mining, in order to consider the cultures and social background to prehistoric mining.

Anyone visiting the site of an ancient flint mine for the very first time, and having no knowledge whatever of prehistory, may be tempted to ask one or more of the following questions:

(1) Where did the miners live?
(2) What did they wear?
(3) What did they eat?
(4) How did they speak?
(5) How long were the mines in use?
(6) What is the age of the mine in calendar years?
(7) What happened to the products of the mine?
(8) Did the miners have currency or did they barter their products?
(9) Was there a high risk factor and a high mortality rate amongst the miners?
(10) Was the miner a skilled craftsmen or just a labourer and were there class divisions?

At one time the reply to any of these questions would be simply "we do not know". This may still be the answer to many of the queries and the same difficulties still exist. For example the period of major silex mining, at least in Europe and Britain, is one of continued pre-literacy, no written records have been left and so none are available, and not surprisingly, as even with history knowledge of the actual sound or nature of prehistoric speech will always be a mystery.

Another major drawback to interpretation is the absence of perishable items such as clothing, timber etc. although signs of postholes on habitation sites, recesses on shaft and gallery walls and imprints on pottery often provide useful clues.

On the other hand the method of disposal of the dead give indications of religious beliefs and the presence of grave goods yield valuable evidence of social customs and lifestyles. Barrows, megalithic tombs, passage graves etc. are most easily recognizable, but gaps in knowledge arise if flat graves are not found. The normal process of sinking of the surface and natural infilling with humus, soil, peat etc. obliterate any obvious signs and often flat graves are only observed when they accompany habitation sites which are in the process of being excavated.

When searching for evidence of flint mining there are definite guidelines to be followed. Any area of Mesolithic settlement, such as for example in Sussex, Belgium and western France, and within easy reach of chalk exposures, was a possible habitation site, probably for the succeeding Neolithic farmers. The Mesolithic and earlier Palaeolithic folk generally dug their flint from exposed outcrops in the chalk and may have dug very shallow holes. The succeeding Neolithic peoples continued this practice, but later tended to work the deeper deposits in the chalk either with bell pits, adits or deep shafts, with or without galleries. Neolithic habitation sites were later constructed on the chalk uplands and remains of these are occasionally found in a flint mining area. Widespread heaps of debris containing flint may indicate a workshop floor near a possible old shaft or at least a shallow hole in the ground. Depressions in the ground, often overgrown and of no interest to later farmers may represent filled in shafts. Mounds of chalk debris near such depressions could well be chalk dumps superfluous to the infilling of such shafts. These dumps might contain pottery, discarded or broken antler picks, scapula shovels or even chalk lamps. Charcoal and antler picks provide scope for possible radiocarbon dating.

An outcrop of good quality flint might have been worked and if depressions occur in line with the dip of the seam, they can be a good indicator of abandoned mine shafts.

Chronology of Silex and Stone Mining

In Chs 3 and 4, covering British and European silex mines, and in Ch. 5 on extraction of minerals other than silex, no attempt has been made to give exhaustive descriptions of all known mines and quarries. Instead a selective appraisal covered the best known sites. For a complete list the reader is referred to Appendix One.

The advent of radiocarbon dating, despite its imperfections, and these are mentioned in Appendix Two, has assisted in confirming the general age of mining sites, i.e. in respect of most of them having been assigned specifically to the Neolithic culture, although some are known to have been of an earlier origin. At first glance it might be tempting to use the dates in a relative sense, but this is fraught with difficulties. For example upwards of 11 laboratories have dated sites and different methods of counting, including acetylene, carbon dioxide, methane and liquid scintillation have been used. This is only one drawback and another is the method of selection of material to be dated. The dating of shaft filling, for example, might have been several hundreds of years later than the actual process of mining. Charcoal is one of the best materials for dating purposes, but wood age may bear little relationship to mining dates. With antler tools dating can be much nearer the true date provided they have not been discarded and deposited in pits or dumps a considerable time after mining took place.

Despite these obvious drawbacks, until some more efficient and reliable method is proved, radiocarbon dating will continue to be used. In fact it is the best method currently available in spite of it not fulfilling all the expectations at its inception.

When all the deficiencies have been considered a prudent question might be "what can be the value of the method?". Another temptation is to average the dates for a particular site or culture and to compare the result with averages from other sites or cultures. The problem in this case is to know exactly what is being averaged and how to deal with the recognized scatter around each date.

Age of Silex Mining and Associated Cultures

Despite the similarity of Mousterian, Aurignacian, Campignian etc. artifacts, to those produced from mined silex, there can be no doubt today that the majority of underground silex mines and many quarries were worked specifically during Neolithic times and that many extended their period of active operation into the later Chalcolithic and Bronze Ages. This fact has been accepted for many decades and radiocarbon dating not only confirmed the general calendar dating for many post Palaeolithic sites, but established once and for all the general Neolithic dating for the majority of known flint mines.

Students and research workers are continually being warned not to read too much into actual radiocarbon dates and this is advisable for the reasons already suggested, but also on the grounds of deficiency of basic knowledge related to the actual determinations which will be discussed later in this book.

Unfortunately there is still a paucity of radiocarbon dates for silex mines. This is understandable since many mines were excavated and backfilled long before this method of dating became available, and furthermore charcoal and other datable material was mostly not retained. Appendix One lists the majority of available dates and the relevant sites represent a very small proportion of the total silex and hard stone mines known. The dates given place the mines mostly in the Neolithic period and what is more significant, within a narrow time range, the general dates covering a period of roughly 3500–1340 BC, representing a slight incursion into the Bronze Age. Generally most underground silex mining commenced with the appearance of Post Lindbandkeramic cultures signified by the widening and regionalization of the LBK corridor and extending into the so called western Neolithic cultures such as the Michelsberg, Windmill Hill, Trichterbecher, Chassey etc. in the fourth millennium BC.

Despite the analytical limitations of radiocarbon dating it is interesting to examine certain aspects in a little detail.

At the time of writing seventeen dates are so far available for Grimes Graves, six for the Sussex mines, one for Easton Down and seven for the Netherlands and Belgium.

The relevant ranges and average dates are as follows:

	Range	Average dates
Netherlands and Belgium	3470–2280 BC	3109 BC
Sussex	3390–2700 BC	2940 BC
Easton Down	2530 BC	2530 BC
Grimes Graves	2340–1340 BC	1978 BC

Despite the caution which must be observed when trying to explain the implications of certain radiocarbon dates, the ones quoted can indicate some agreement with the climate of archaeological opinion. Therefore the acceptance of the dates at face value result in the following general conclusions:

(1) Flint mining started with the Michelsberg cultures in northern Europe around 3500 BC.

(2) Approximately 200 years later flint mining had started in Britain at the time of the Windmill Hill culture.

(3) Flint mining in Sussex continued for at least 700 years and after a

period of probably 800 years after its introduction spread north into Hampshire and Wiltshire.

(4) Flint mining did not start in Norfolk on any large scale until 1000 years after its appearance in Britain. Grimes Graves was worked for at least 1000 years, maybe intermittently, and continued into the Bronze Age.

(5) So for northern Europe and Britain flint mining can be said to have been operative from *c*. 3500 BC until *c*. 1300 BC, a period of over 1000 years.

Similarly mining of silex was in operation in Poland around 3100 BC during the time of the Lengyel-Polgar cultural phase, in the same period up to *c*. 2000 BC by the Chassey cultures of France, in *c*. 3000 BC in Sweden in the Trichterbecher phase, in Switzerland by the Cortaillord cultures in *c*. 3000 BC and as late as *c*. 2000 BC in Hungary at Tata.

Cultures

It is probably relevant at this stage to consider the term "culture". This has already been used in several contexts and it will be necessary to adopt it in this and subsequent chapters. Culture really implies, a general sense, a form or degree of intellectual development. More broadly it includes customs, material development and way of life, but not a period in time, although it is somewhat easy to use it to denote a time scale without specific reference to the culture involved. Industry and culture are two separate identities and are often subject to a certain degree of confusion. Two or more cultures may have similar industries, but practice different life styles. Childe (1948) said that "archaeology is liable to become a study of cultures rather than that of culture". Lüning (1972) considers what comprises a culture and is of the opinion that some culture groups, in spite of all contacts and exchange influences, basically develop clearly independently, i.e. they go their own ways. Some cultural groups appear identical mainly because they have identical pottery and often this is the only evidence which has survived.

In 1819 the Danish Museum of Antiquities set up the Three Age System, i.e. (1) Stone, (2) Bronze and (3) Iron. For many years this sufficed, but today the complexity of evidence requires the splitting up of these into different phases and then into cultures. It is inevitable that such groups are often referred to as peoples and folk and often this cannot be avoided in discussions. However, as Lüning points out, culture is a

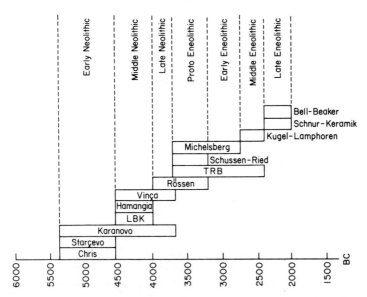

Fig. 68. Culture development in western Europe based on radiocarbon dates (after Galley). By permission of Romisch Germarisches Kommission, Frankfurt.

totality which cannot be split up and to attempt to adopt sub-cultures would add another complication to the problem. When more knowledge becomes available or is nearer completion it might be necessary to subdivide, but for the present would serve no useful purpose.

Galley (1971) summarizes the chronology of the more important cultures on the European continent and these are incorporated in Fig. 68.

The possibility of silex mining and quarrying in pre-Neolithic times has been mentioned several times in this and earlier chapters. Amongst the sites considered, examples of such mines are few in number. Obviously work was carried out in Palaeolithic and Mesolithic times, but known cases are rare owing to destruction, weathering and resultant obliteration. Mention has, however, been made of Findesbury in Kent and the mining site in the Holy Cross Mountains in Poland. The latter extended its operation into the Mesolithic period, starting work on a semi-intensive basis in the Final Palaeolithic, i.e. in the Allerød climatic phase, c. 9800 BC. Then the vegetation was mainly pine forest and the people, mainly hunters and gatherers, collected sufficient flint for their needs and distributed it on a small scale. It is conceivable, therefore, that the mines were only worked on an intermittent basis. Schild (1976) is of the opinion that the forest people rarely travelled more than 100 km to visit the mines or engage in flint trafficking. However, the position appears to have changed for 90% of the flint was found on Late Dryas sites* within 200 km of the mines and a small amount 400 km away. Schild suggests that obsidian from the Tokay area of Hungary and jasper from Czechoslovakia, may have been used as barter for the chocolate flint of the Holy Cross Mountains. In Late Dryas times from *c.* 8800 BC to *c.* 8300 BC, there was a return to cooler conditions and birch pine forests in Northern Europe and the people hunted reindeer and adopted a more nomadic form of life.

Little is known of any mining during the time of the Linear Bandkeramic cultures in the Neolithic and this is rather surprising. However, the site of Olszanica in Poland, is thought to have been an LBK flint mine. Many archaeologists consider that the Linearband-keramikultur, so named after its distinctive pottery style, formed the primary basis for civilization in Central and northern Europe. Referred to as the Danubian I phase by Childe (1957) it lasted only 400 years, i.e. from *c.* 4400 BC to *c.* 4000 BC and spread northwards from the Danube valley in the south, into Poland, the Rhine valley, the Low Countries and northern France. At approximately the same time the Impressed Ware cultures spread eastwards through north and south Italy, the Mediterranean islands, southern France and into Iberia. The two chief points of interest concerning the LBK group is its development and northern expansion, i.e. along a narrow corridor roughly 20 miles wide, and the regionalization at the end of the cultural period with the incoming of definite silex mining groups. The LBK peoples were predominantly agriculturalists working chiefly loess soils. The neighbouring chalklands and limestone areas, where they existed, were mostly avoided. They lived in long houses with central posts and hearths and having wattle and daub finish, this mode of building probably proved to provide a basis for succeeding cultural groups. There is no evidence for LBK silex mining, but it is quite possible that these people did crude extraction by openpits or quarrying along the margins of their corridors. Mention has been made of the Kleinkems silex mines (see pp. 92–95), in the Isteiner Jurassic limestone range, which worked jasper. Although no radiocarbon dates are available it is known that there were workings here in late Neolithic times and possible galleries and crude holes have been found in the limestone. Large quantities of flint

* See Ch. 1.

implements have been found on the Dutch and Belgian LBK (Omalian) sites which are in marked contrast to sites in the Rhineland. Obsidian, probably from the Carpathian Slovako-Hungary field, has been found in the east, but none in the west.

The Mayen basalt quarries in the Eifel district of West Germany are thought to be of the LBK cultural period, but are known to have been worked right through, probably with intermissions, into Hallstatt times.

Regionalization and extension of the corridor followed the LBK cultures and the Stichbandkeramic appeared at the end of the fourth millennium and running almost contemporary with this culture from Austria westwards is the Lengyel phase. On the Hungarian plains this culture overlaps with the Tisza and farther north is the Vinça culture, whereas in the west there is overlap with the Rössen. At Köln Linderthal in the Rhineland is a well known LBK site where there is stratigraphy showing also Rössen and Stichband according to Meier-Arendt (1975). At the same time in Holland is the Swifterband site of around 3500 BC. Some overlap and diffusion with the Mesolithic Ertobølle cultures occurred about this time. By 3000 BC all the LBK, Impressed Ware and associated cultures had gone and were replaced by the Chassey cultures. In fact Almerian (Spain), Chassey (France), Cortaillod (Switzerland), Michelsberg (Germany and the Low Countries) and the British Neolithic all evolved at approximately the same time. Once these were all included in the embracing term "Western Neolithic". This is now a redundant concept since there are other Neolithic cultures in western Europe.

The foregoing is only intended to give mere background and to pursue all the many theories and concepts concerning all these cultures would be to go far beyond the purposes of the present book. Instead it is considered to be more relevant to mention certain aspects of the various cultures as they pertain to mining of silex and hard stone in order to try and assess the type of existence led by the miners and their families and to attempt to give answers to the questions posted at the beginning of this chapter. To cover all the relevant cultures in the various countries of Europe would be a daunting task and one to be undertaken more appropriately by an archaeologist, in any case proving tedious to the reader so a selective assessment has been made.

Climate

So far as the relevant cultures are concerned the climatic pollen phases are the Atlantic and the sub-boreal, i.e. phases VII and VIII extending from c. 5800 BC. Oak, elm, lime and alder forests prevailed in the Atlantic phase i.e. from *c.* 5800 BC to *c.* 3000 BC. There was some recession of forest during this time, wetness increased, but the weather was warm. There was also a rise in the level of the lakes. There was little grassland. After 3000 BC agriculture came on the scene with the incoming of the Neolithic peoples, and at this time there was an elm decline which so far has been inexplicable. Beech did not become extensive until the Iron Age. Stone (1934, 1937) says damp conditions prevailed at Easton Down around 2500 BC as evidenced by the prevailing molluscs and points to the fact that the rainfall was much heavier than today, but the climate was warm with the winters as today. Consequently he is of the opinion that the water table in the chalk was higher than today. Evans (1969), however, says that there is no clear evidence that during the sub-boreal period the water table was higher. The average temperature around 4000 BC was higher than it is today.

Vertes (1964) refers to the Sümeg silex mining site in Hungary where he says the climate in the year 2570 BC was much milder than at the present time.

The effect of a high water table in chalk, together with very heavy rainfall, would have made flint mining very difficult especially as the flint seams were mostly worked in the floor.

Habitation Sites

Linearbandkeramic Culture c. 4400–3900 BC

There are no definitely proved flint mining sites associated with this culture, but the Mayan basalt quarries in the Eifel district of Germany were worked by the LBK cultural groups and as indicated they continued to be worked right into Hallstatt times. Many habitation sites have been found on loess soils in the Low Countries, Germany and also in Czechoslovakia. Typical sites inhabited at the same time as the Mayen quarries were worked are Sittard, Elso, Geleen, Stein, Beek and Köln Linderthal. In fact much basalt from the quarries has been found on these sites. Köln Linderthal had seven settlements over a period of 430 years and here querns made from Mayen basalt were found. It has moreover been estimated that 85% of the polished rocks found on Belgian sites alone are from outside the country.

The principal type of house was 5–7 m in width, this dimension varying very little, and from 8 to as much as 45 m in length the average being 20 m, hence the term long house. The structure was basically of massive timbers with five rows of posts and three internal ones for the ridge as in

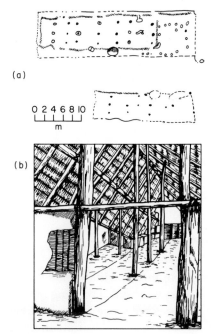

(a)

0 2 4 6 8 10
m

(b)

Fig. 69. A Linearbanderkeramik house. (a) Ground plan, (b) sketch. Acknowledgements to Museum der Stadt, Koen.

Fig. 69. Occasionally there were subsidiary structures, 8 m long with raised floors. The site at Sittard in Holland had a pallisade fortification and a radiocarbon date for this site is 4450 ± 150 BC. Shallow pits were often dug alongside the site for clay for plastering the walls (wattle and daub), and these were once classed by Van den Breek (1956–1959) as rubbish pits. As at Bylany, in Czechoslovakia, where 21 habitation layers were found, storage pits for grain were used.

Houses were generally oriented NW–SE for protection against the prevailing winds. Köln Linderthal site was enclosed by a bank and ditch.

All the LBK settlements are away from the edges of rivers and lakes so there was no fishing, and although hunting is said not to have been prevalent, there was widespread use of antler hoes. Domesticated cattle were kept and oats, wheat and rye cultivated.

The pottery produced had wavy or angular lines with a filling of colouring matter while at Köln Linderthal there was spiral or meander design.

Van den Breek (1956) in discussing the settlements on loesss states that since the loess has good water holding properties the crops do not fail if the water table is low.

Use of Mayen basalt, as already mentioned, was widespread in LBK times and may have been traded for spondylus shells, from which for example bracelets were made, from the Aegean.

Stichbankeramic Culture c. 4000 BC

In Central Germany, Hungary, Austria and Czechoslovakia, although sites were still on loess soils, this culture replaced the LBK. Two sites which typify this innovation are Bylany (3860 ± 165 BC) and Zalany (3931 ± 100 BC) in Czechoslovakia. There was an adaptation of the musical note decoration on Stichbandkeramic pottery. Long houses were still in use and hunting increased, although only to the extent of about 10%. There is no record of mining sites associated with this culture.

Lengyel c. 4000 BC

This culture is contemporaneous with Stichbandkeramik and both had common ancestry. Houses were still of the long type with an adaptation to a trapezoidal plan with storage space at the wide end. At Bylany wattle fences surrounded the houses. The Austrian chert mining site of Mauer was worked by the peoples of the Lengyel culture and a habitation site in Austria, Unterpullendorf has been given a radiocarbon date of 4180 ± 140 BC, and typifies this culture. Another Lengyel mining site Saspow in Poland, has radiocarbon dates of 3096 ± 90 BC and 3375 ± 90 BC. At Bresc-Kujavsky, in Poland, there are 400 houses 15–40 m in length and 10 m wide, and at Strelice there is a fine gabled house with a head at one end. At Hluboke, in Silesia, there is a 60 acre settlement with a causeway 1·5 m wide and 1 m deep together with a stockade and gates. Contemporaneous with the Lengyel culture in Austria and Poland were Swifterband, Rössen and Tichterbecher (TRB) in the Low Countries with some overlap with remnant Mesolithic cultures of Ertobølle-Ellerbeck in Scandinavia and North Germany (c. 3600–3400 BC).

Trichterbecher c. 3000 BC

The Swedish flint quarries of Kvarnby, Gallerup and Tullstrop (2900 ± 115 BC) were exploited by the TRB peoples although they continued to be worked into the Iron Age.

Known also as the Funnel Beaker Cultures, TRB is also associated with the introduction of new religious functions from western Europe such as the construction of dolmens, graves for the dead with the use of large

Fig. 70. A Swedish butted flint axe.

stones, i.e. megaliths. These are principally found in Scania, at Halland and Bohnslan. Flint was exported widely, especially into Norway and Sweden, where in the north of that country there was a lack of flint resources. Scania became the centre for the production of the butted flint axe which, according to Stenberger (1962), became a magnificent tool for forest clearance, Fig. 70. The later Pitted Ware and Boat Axe cultures represented peoples who settled around the coasts of East Sweden and practised seal hunting and fishing, and controlled the flint extraction and flint trade. The dwelling sites of the Pitted Ware peoples are said to be like a necklace around the Swedish coasts. Since flint was lacking in the north the peoples there used bones and slate for tools and weaponry apart from imported flints from the south. The typical pottery consisted of bowls in the case of the Pitted Ware culture with a pointed base and row of depressions below the rim. The Boat Axe cultures, c. 2000 BC, although primarily renowned for the stone axe shaped like a boat, produced hemispherical bowls with handsome band ornaments beneath the rim and angle patterns on the body executed by string and comb stamps.

Around 2950 BC the flint mines of Krzemioniki in Poland were worked by the TRB cultures. Here 1000 shafts about 10 m deep with galleries have been identified.

Principally the TRB peoples were farmers having 60% cattle and the wild animals hunted constituted not more than 5%. There was evidence of oxen being yoked together at Kreznica for ploughing.

Houses were still rectangular as found at Dummerlshausen in West Germany to the extent of 40 6 m × 4 m to 7 m × 5 m in dimension on a lake shore surrounded by a palisade. Wattle and daub were also used. In

Denmark at Barkauer long houses were each 80 m long and divided into spacious structures.

Western Neolithic Cultures c. 3500 BC

Although the term "Western Neolithic" is today regarded as a redundant concept, as already stated, it is used here since it embraces all the more important cultures which were contemporary and which actually were responsible for the greatest number of silex and stone mining sites so far identified.

The cultures in this context are:

Chassey	France
Cortaillod	Switzerland
Michelsberg	Low Countries and Germany
British Neolithic (Windmill Hill)	Britain

These all evolved in the fourth millennium BC when a population explosion took place, the LBK and developed cultures gave way to the Chassey and the rest. Although the above list is approximately correct, there is an appreciable geographical overlap. One characteristic is that all these cultures are associated with similar basic features in respect to their pottery. In this book roughly 68 silex and stone mining sites have been mentioned or discussed and of these 62 were worked by peoples of one of the Western Neolithic cultures.

Chassey

The famous dolerite quarries of Sélédin in Brittany were worked by the Chassey or Chasseen cultures of northern France, between 3200 and 2000 BC. The dolerite was used chiefly to make Grade X axes which were widely traded. Habitation sites of this culture were Le Curnic (3560 ± 250–2650 ± 200 BC) and Vailly sur Aisne (3520 ± 300 BC). A habitation site at Valiciennes had small rectangular houses of timber and causeway enclosures as found in Neolithic Britain. Other significant features of the Chassey culture was the breeding of horned cattle, pigs, goats and sheep. There was no hunting or fishing. Many megalithic tombs and long barrows were constructed and some clay female figurines have been found in addition to flints reputed to have originated at Grand Pressigny. The famous passage graves and megaliths at Carnac in Brittany have been dated 3850 ± 300 BC.

Cortaillod

This culture is much better documented than the North Chassey of France and is principally confined to Switzerland being known chiefly for its lake side dwellings. The chert mining site of Löwenborg was worked by the people of this culture around 3000 BC and two relevant radiocarbon dates from Schmid (1972, 1975) are 2990 ± 240 BC and 3070 ± 100 BC. One feature of the Cortaillod habitation sites is that they are well preserved, being below the water level and there is a wealth of undecayed cereals, leather and wood. Two sites which have been excavated are at Egelzwil which was first occupied about 3630 ± 130 BC although there are radiocarbon dates ranging from 3420 ± 160 BC to 3090 ± 100 BC. There is some relation to the Rössen culture and Childe (1957) quotes a radiocarbon date of as late as 2740 ± 90 BC. Another habitation site is Burgaschise with a radiocarbon date of 3035 ± 110 BC to 2764 ± 90 BC.

Most of the houses were set on piles which were erected to stabilize the platforms as the lake levels rose. There are, however, some habitation sites in the higher meadow lands. There was rearing of cattle, pigs and sheep and hunting, i.e. of red deer, wild cattle and wild pig. Wheat, barley, peas, beans and lentils were cultivated and wild hazel nuts, berries and wild apples gathered.

Childe (1957) states that on all Cortaillod sites flint implements were made of a translucent yellow flint exclusively which was strange to the Neuchâtel basin, but of unknown provenance. Some cherts are translucent and yellow in colour and Löwenburg might have been the source of this material since it was found on most Swiss Cortaillod sites.

Michelsberg c. 3500 BC

Regional developments in western Europe took place after the demise of the cultures already outlined. The original concept or derivation of the Michelsberg from Chassey or Bandkeramic cultures is not now accepted. The development of silex mining including the sinking of deeper pits and shafts with interconnecting galleries characterises the Michelsberg phase and it would not be too dogmatic to infer that this culture actually founded the concept of mining from shafts which provided expertise for the later mining of metallic ores, coal and non-metals by shafts and adits on an ever increasing sophisticated scale through a continuous period of over 5000 years.

The area occupied by the Michelsberg peoples includes the central part of Germany, the Rhineland, Belgium, Bohemia and East Switzerland. One or two authors have referred to an absence of Michelsberg cultural evidence in the Netherlands, but the well known flint mines of Rijckholt St Gertrude in South Limburg and the lesser well known ones of Savelsbos and Valkenburg Cadier en Keer are within the present day boundaries of Holland.

Nine radiocarbon dates have been extracted from various publications for Michelsberg silex mines ranging from 3390 ± 150 to 2240 ± 45 BC with an average of 2980 ± 105 BC. De Laet (1958) comments that Michelsberg cultures originated in western Europe as late as c. 2750 BC, but this hardly conforms with the radiocarbon dates which are now available.

Scollar (1959) in a lengthy article covers a wide area of Michelsberg settlements and discusses regional variations in Belgium, the Rhineland, North Hesse, South Hesse, North Baden, West Wurtenberg, Alsace and South Baden.

A significant feature is the rural economy which is the same as for the Cortaillod culture. Barley and wheat were grown and strawberries, apples and other wild fruits gathered. Apparently there was more hunting and the bones of wild animals including those of horses have been found with high proportions of food refuse.

Most of the Belgian flint mining sites were worked by the Michelsberg cultures, but some workers mention SOM cultures in this context especially with reference to the mines north of Liege. What is certain, however, is that Spiennes was worked around c. 3000 BC and can be assigned to the Michelsberg cultural phase.

Childe (1957) characterizes Spiennes and its environs as a specialized industrial community. Axes made from excellent Spiennes flint have been found as far south as Coblenz and they measure 23 cm in length with an 8 cm wide blade. In the north they were probably hafted on to wooden handles, but in the south according to Scollar (1959), probably had antler sleeves.

Coleman (1957) remarks that several authors refer to poverty of habitations near Spiennes, Verheyleweghen (1962) mentions evidence for wind break shelters which the miners used for a day on the plateau, meals being eaten around the camp fire and the camps quickly abandoned. The same author states that the miners' houses were some distance away near Marais de la Trouille. It is surprising, if Verheyleweghen's hypothesis is correct, that the miners in those times did not live nearer their work or was such work of a seasonal nature and performed by farmers in their non-productive interludes? The density of population is remarkably high and Verheyleweghen comments on the number and characteristics of skulls he found in the shallow Spiennes pits. The number of skeletons found were far less than would be expected. Scollar (1955) reported on an enclosure or a causeway camp 200 m long, at Spiennes and he says this is reminiscent of the Windmill Hill causeway camps and flint mines at Grimes Graves. He took aerial photographs and noted that the white streaks on the photographs inside the enclosure were found to be due to large quantities of flint debris of half finished implements turned up by the plough.

Habitation sites of the Palaeolithic era, such as caves, were often used by the Michelsberg peoples as tombs for their collective burials.

There are several Michelsberg habitation sites in Belgium which, unlike their counterparts in southern England, could have had association with flint mining. At Boitsfort which compared to English sites was not a fortified town, there were cremations under long mounds. Other sites are Saint Servais, near Namur, Til Chateau at Hotton, Insemont near Hastiere and Furfooz. Scollar (1957) describes some undulations at Boitsfort, in the Forest de Soignes near Brussels, in sandy loess and comments on the similarity of these with the banks and ditches of a hill fort. In Belgium there is a strong western influence and the most common pottery shape is the bowl. Many variants of these are found in southern England and northern France (Early Chassey). Hemispherical bowls are uncommon, but are found at Spiennes with unusual flat bottoms. Coleman (1957) says these are attributable to the SOM culture and not to Michelsberg! Grain imprints on pottery are very common. Tulip beakers are frequently found in Belgium and so called flat "baking

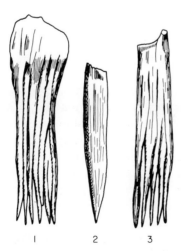

Fig. 71. Implements found at Spiennes. 1 and 3 antler combs, 2 bone tool from rib bone.

plates" are also prolific, but have been proved to be merely lids for jars. Antler combs were used for leather dressing (Fig. 71). Villages were occupied over long periods and correspondingly deserted over similarly long periods which may indicate intermittent mining activity. At Ehrenstein near Ulm in western Germany (3447 ± 100 BC to 3190 ± 80 BC) the floors in the houses were renewed as many as 13 times.

Scollar comments on the lack of silex in the Rhineland–North Hesse Group and says that flint had to be imported. However, jasper was available from Kleinkems in large quantities and it is surprising that this has not been found. Settlements had stout palisades and ditches with big stock compounds. Houses were 11 m × 6 m and rectangular with substantial log floors. Urmitz had double bank and ditches. Mayen continued the same features as for the LBK culture overlying the same enclosure site.

Much flint was imported to factories at Aachen and Luxembourg. There are no bone tools as these are said to survive only rarely in the acid Rhineland soils. In the Rhineland the villages were fortified with banks and ditches and of dimension 3 m × 5 m often with only four corner posts for simple roof support. Burials are unknown and Scollar attributes this also to the poor preserving properties of the soils of the Rhineland.

Scollar also mentions the classical group of South Hesse, North Baden and West Wurttenberg so called as here is the classical hill top camp of Michelsberg in Baden the type site for the culture. It is surprising that here also is there a lack of good silex considering the nearness of the Kleinkems jasper mines. In fact in a comprehensive list of sites of the Michelsberg culture Scollar places Kleinkems in the Alsace–South Baden Group.

The Windmill Hill Culture

Flint mining in Britain in Neolithic times appears to have had much in common with European practices and is said to be attributable to the Windmill Hill culture so named after the type site in Wiltshire. This is probably the salient feature to be considered when discussing the habitat of British flint miners, but in the context of uniform cohesion and to avoid isolation in tight compartments in a discussional sense, it is probably pertinent to attempt to consider, however, briefly, the relationship between European and British derivation of flint producing communities.

Piggott (1955) referred to the Neolithic cult of the British Isles and said ". . . it is now abundantly clear that the Windmill Hill culture is a member of the great Western family". The controversy concerning the origin of the Windmill Hill culture raged for some time from the 1930s onwards. Some workers postulated a derivation via the Chassey cultures in Brittany and Northern France and others via the Rhineland. In fact Hawkes (1934a) suggested a route from southern France up the Rhone valley to Switzerland and thence to Britain by a route which did not touch Brittany, this early culture being established on the western Swiss lakes during Bandkeramic times. The same author Hawkes (1934b) had denied a Michelsberg ancestry on the grounds of chronology, Michelsberg being too late to be ancestral to the Windmill Hill culture. Two factors strongly mitigate against this theory, i.e. the presence of similar pottery on Windmill Hill sites and Spiennes and the advent of radiocarbon dating, as discussed earlier in this chapter. Piggott (1955) however, postulates a concurrent development. The similarity of causewayed camps of Urmitz and Mayen in Germany with those in Britain and the flint mining similarity of Britain and Belgium, while they do not prove ancestry, do indicate an affinity.

It is extremely likely that peoples of the Michelsberg cultures did cross the sea and colonize parts of Sussex and Wessex and might have initiated deeper flint mining. The subject of the origin of the Windmill Hill culture can safely be left at this stage as it does not strictly affect the characteristics of the habitation of flint miners in Britain.

There is inevitably some problem in considering the mode of settlement associated with the activity of the Neolithic flint miner in Britain. The chief difficulty is the dearth of occupational sites of the type found in Europe. Post hole evidence is rare as are the traces of houses or turf. Conversely causewayed camps with bank and ditch enclosures and strangely sacred sites such as Woodhenge were contemporaneous with the flint mines. Another problem is the absence of occupational evidence near the actual flint mines, with a few exceptions, although this is true also of many of the European flint mines.

Stone (1934, 1937), when describing excavations at Easton Down, said that there was proof beyond doubt that the site was inhabited and used by the peoples of the Windmill Hill and Peterborough cultures and reached its zenith in the hands of the Beaker folk. There were 10 dwellings only 200 m from Pit No. 82 and these were sometimes circular and occasionally elongated. If circular they were 1·5 m in diameter and if elongated 3 m × 1·5 m, and dug about 0·5 m into the chalk. They actually resembled temporary shelters which would have been necessary if the miners had remained on the site at night. Mostly the settlement pits had been filled with rubbish and Stone remarks that the men must have had

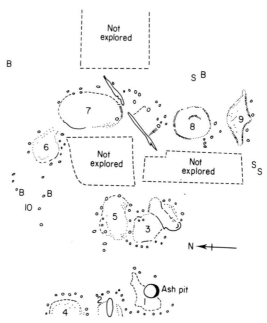

Fig. 72. Pit dwellings at Easton Down. S Pottery, B Beaker pottery. Acknowledgements to Wiltshire Archaeological and Natural History Society.

unclean habits. Some evidence of stake holes for perpendicular support suggests the provision of flat roofs. The circular pits could have been cooking pits or they could have been used for storage. The pottery found was of the Windmill Hill, Peterborough and Beaker types. Fig. 72 shows a habitation site at Easton Down.

At Blackpatch, north-east of the mining area, shallow depressions mark the existence of supposed dwelling sites. These were found to contain bones of animals and flint scrapers, but no pottery. The disused shafts had been used for the disposal of the dead, both inhumations and cremations had been carried out. However, as cremation was not practised until the Bronze Age, as already indicated, mining probably continued until this era at Blackpatch.

In order to study the possible mode of life of the peoples of the Windmill Hill culture it is necessary to look beyond the actual mining sites. Piggott (1954) cites the existence of three types of evidence; (a) flint mines, (b) causewayed camps and (c) long barrows. Flint mines have been discussed in adequate detail and it is interesting to look briefly at the two other sources of evidence. To detail all the characteristics would be to go far beyond the intended purpose of this book.

Causewayed camps are similar to their counterparts of the Michels-berg culture of Europe. They consist of up to four circular or oval ditches with breakages for causeways usually at irregular intervals with banks. It has been claimed that the habitation sites were the actual ditches for here have been found arrowheads, pottery and antler combs. On the other hand within the enclosure have often been found evidence of buildings, i.e. postholes for wooden supports. One theory is that the enclosures were used for penning cattle during seasonal occupation. If occupation indeed had been seasonal one question to be posed concerns where the people actually lived when the causewayed camps were not in use. At the time of writing a major Neolithic camp is being excavated near Northampton, and reported by Hammond (1978), where pottery evidence suggests a long period of use of over one or two millennia. The site is at Briar Hill and two acres have been stripped. Graig Llwd axes as well as evidence of post holes have been found.

Curwen (1934) describes a Neolithic dwelling site on the south-east spur of Barrow Hill with an area of 40 m² enclosed by a large bank or ditch with five shallow pits. There were no post holes, but ashes from a hearth were found and soot and charcoal remains. Sherds of Neolithic Windmill Hill type pottery without lugs or carination were recovered. The dwelling could have been that of a miner (see Fig. 73).

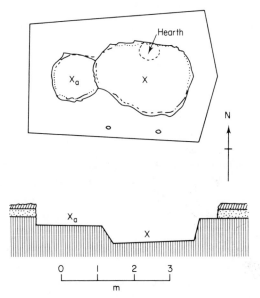

Fig. 73. Two pits at New Barn Down, Harrow Hill. Acknowledgements to Sussex Archaeological Society.

The long barrows are mounds of an elongated nature up to 100 m in length oriented east–west with collective burials. They were lined with wood and turf.

Evans (1969) gives a useful list of Neolithic habitats, etc. and some of the more important are given here:

Ascott under Wychwood	pit	2810 ± 130 BC
Beckhampton Road	long barrow	3250 ± 160 BC
		2517 ± 90 BC
Brook	partial forest clearance	2590 ± 100 BC
Durrington Walls	henge monument	2450 ± 150 BC
Hambledon Hill	causewayed camp and long barrows	2880 – 2700 BC
High Peak, Devon	settlement	3010–2710 BC
Kilham	long barrow	c. 3000 BC
Horslip	long barrow	3240 ± 150 BC
Knap Hill	causewayed enclosure	2760 ± 115 BC
Marden	henge monument	1989 ± 50 BC
Silbury Hill	mound	2145 ± 95 BC
South Street	long barrow	2810 ± 130 BC
Waylands Smithy	chambered tomb	c.3500–2500 BC
West Kennet	long barrow	2820 ± 130 BC
Willerby Wood	long barrow	c. 3000 BC
Windmill Hill	causewayed enclosure	2570 ± 150 BC
		2950 ± 150 BC

Curwen (1929) gives a comprehensive account of excavations carried out at the Trundle near Goodwood racecourse, 4 miles north of Chichester in 1928. This is a Neolithic camp shaped in the form of a nine sided polygon occupying 12·5 acres as seen in Fig. 74. There is a large inner and small outer bank separated by a ditch 5 m below the crest which is 27 m high. Amongst the finds was a Neolithic burial of a woman whose body was laid upon its back with knees drawn up to the right and the head turned slightly to the west. The pottery found was of the round bottomed bowl type with small ledges for handles. An interesting feature of Curwen's report was that he was of the opinion that the people of the Trundle were the same as those who worked the flint mines. He cites Lavant Caves which are only 1 mile south-west of the site. Other reasons given are that the chalk cups are similar to those found at Cissbury and Grimes Graves, the pottery similar to that of Grimes Graves as also were the bone points and flint types. Thomas (1976) gives a date of c. 3500 BC for this camp which is earlier than any of the radiocarbon dates quoted for

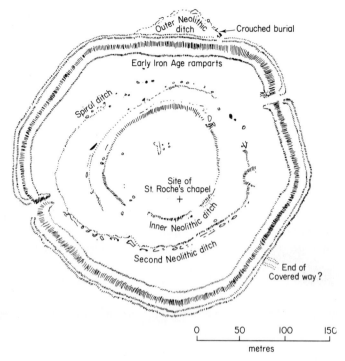

Fig. 74. The Trundle, Sussex.

the British flint mines although Church Hill, London, has a radiocarbon
date of 3390 ± 150 BC.

Succeeding Cultures

Around 1800 BC a new race of peoples colonized parts of Britain, at first
chiefly Wessex and the South from the Continent of Europe. Known as
the Bell Beaker people, after their characteristic shape of pottery and
drinking vessels, they came from Portugal and moved rapidly northwards
probably up the North Atlantic coast to Britain and through Central
Europe also. They were round headed peoples, strongly built and
essentially agriculturists, although their beakers have been found at
Easton Down flint mining site. By 2000 BC they had reached Holland and
Germany. Beaker folk brought with them a knowledge of metalwork
although flint mining still continued. In Scotland and Ireland they
exploited local copper and gold. The culture can be assigned to the
Eneolithic which is sometimes referred to as the Copper or Chalcolithic

Age. Colonization appears to have been peaceful and the Beaker folk settled alongside the peoples responsible for the Peterborough ware in Britain and they exercised a degree of influence. Grimes Graves flint mines continued to be worked through the Beaker phase and into the Bronze Age. Further consideration of the Eneolithic and Bronze Age cultures with reference to mining, especially as these cultures heralded true metallurgy, is more appropriately covered in the later chapters on prehistoric mining and metal working.

Food and Health

Arable farming, as compared to hunting and fishing, introduced more stability into the diet of prehistoric man. Although Palaeolithic man derived adequate protein from hunted animals and his successor, Mesolithic man, had added fishing and the gathering of wild fruits and cereals, diet was intermittent according to man's ability to find and catch. Conversely Neolithic man was more static and made the earth work to suit his needs and accordingly he could plan to the limit of the produce available. In addition he could supplement his diet by hunting and gathering.

Whether the conditions of nutrition for the farming communities were the same as for the mining groups or whether the farmers were miners or vice versa, is still an open question. It could well have been a matriarchal society with the men folk mining and hunting or conversely whole families could have been employed seasonally in all the tasks of farming and mining.

Brothwell (1969) makes the point that the early agriculturists had an opportunity to overfeed on carbohydrates. It is estimated that an average adult had a mean daily intake of 2000–3000 kcal (dietary calories) which is approximately the same as today, but the ratio of protein, fat and carbohydrate to total food intake must have been very variable in prehistoric times.

There is strong evidence for arable farming near the flint mines in Neolithic times. Michelsberg pottery is often found with grain imprints. Bread, according to Childe's (1957) quotation of Güyan was not made, the flour produced was not converted into bread, but eaten as a sort of gruel. Childe, however, refers to the ovens found in many Neolithic villages which surely must have been used for baking. The principal crop in Wurttenberg was barley, but wheat was also grown. Querns have been found at Windmill Hill, Whitehawk, The Trundle, Hambledon Hill, Hembury and at Stoke Down flint mines. Fine grained sandstone rubbers were also recovered at New Barn Down. Grain storage pits on British sites are evidence of arable farming. Hazel nut shells and apple pips have been found at Windmill Hill and crab apple remains at Hembury and Hazard Hill settlements in Devon. The use of sickle flints appears to have been a rarity, only one being found, i.e. at Windmill Hill. Marine shells were unearthed at Maiden Castle and mussels at Whitehawk Camp.

Meat was an important part of the diet of the prehistoric flint miner as evidenced by finds of bone of cattle, pig, sheep etc. It is also considered that cannibalism was common amongst Neolithic communities. Before burying at Spiennes and at Furfooz, near Namur in Belgium, the flesh had been removed from human bones. Brothwell (1969) also remarks that from the glowing recommendations of recent cannibals, human flesh is known to be tasty to eat and no less nutritious than that of other mammals. As Brothwell also states, the fight for survival in difficult times might have led prehistoric man not to waste a deceased's flesh, be it friend or enemy. At Maiden Castle (Clark *et al.* 1937) in Dorset, a dismembered skeleton of a young man was found to have axe marks on the bone. evidence of having been cut up as by a butcher for the stewpot. The skull was hacked to pieces, a suggestion that the body was cut up and eaten, There was very little respect for the dead and bodies were thrown into flint mine shafts at Cissbury and Grimes Graves. In fact Pull (1932b) describes the miners as slaves although there can be little definite evidence for this assertion. The skeleton of a miner in a working position, with antler pick in hand and already referred to, however, adds some credibility to this conjecture.

It is highly possible that disease was quite prevalent and Brothwell and Brothwell (1969) deals with the health hazards of prehistoric man in some detail. He comments that prehistoric hair when found is generally auburn and that this colour is often produced by protein deficiency. Neolithic man, as compared to his predecessors, tended to settle more in small groups in villages so that the tendency to spread infection was more pronounced than amongst nomadic groups. Two common diseases were club foot and gastroenteritis, the latter being caused probably by the use of unclean cooking pots and utensils. When the mode of life is considered it is not surprising that dental and bodily diseases were rampant. Mining itself must have been a very hazardous occupation compared with the standards of the present day. Stagnant ventilation, damp conditions, poor illumination, cramped working, falls of roof and side and the use of inefficient and primitive tools must have played their part in contributing to physical disabilities and probably premature death according to standards of today.

Most of the evidence available has been obtained from an examination of skeletal remains, but despite this little is known concerning the actual health of Neolithic miners. However, Lottin in "Le Materiaux pour L'Histoire Primitive et Naturelle de l'Homme" gives information concerning the health of flint miners in the Meuane commune of Loire et Cher at a mine working around AD 1740. Apparently entire families, up to 150, worked in the mine, made shafts and worked the flint in horizontal galleries. The fathers extracted the chalk blocks and the mothers and children removed the flints and finished the tools at home. Before flint mining started, i.e. between 1680 and 1709 the average life expectancy was 24 years 3 months and 13 days, between 1761 and 1790 it was only 19 years 2 months and 2 days, but as the mines flagged and finally closed in the 1880s, the figure had risen to 36 years 2 months between 1853 and 1882. For the same three periods the infant mortality rates (up to 5 years of age) were 13, 24 and 5·66 per thousand population. If such high mortality rates existed in the seventeenth and eighteenth centuries AD, how high would they have been in Neolithic times, i.e. say 4000–5000 years earlier? Living conditions outside mining would not have been conducive to the maintenance of good health nor would the conditions cited for the actual mines have helped.

Mode of Dress and Customs

There has been no evidence of weaving or spinning found on British Neolithic sites, such as loom weights or spindle whorls although at Spiennes in Belgium, bone awls were recovered and weaving combs for wool were found on several Michelsberg sites.

Many sketches showing imaginary operations at prehistoric silex mines portray miners working nearly naked except for loin coverings possibly of leather. It is quite likely that all miners worked unclothed. If weaving was not carried out the only possible dress would have been skins of hide. Pittioni (1950) uses his imagination and shows a sketch of a miner wearing a fur cap, leather jacket and sandals (see Fig. 87). This he says would have been typical garb for the copper and salt miners in Bronze Age Austria. Andrée (1922) produced a sketch of relics of miners' leather clothes found at Dürenberg.

Despite the lack of evidence for weaving on British sites, there is ample indication that skins were dressed for use as dress attire, similar to the practice of the Mesolithic peoples, and for the covering of huts and dwelling places. Bone objects were found at The Trundle, at Grimes Graves and at many sites flint scrapers have been recovered. Ox bones for piercers, awls and needles are common finds on British Neolithic sites. Some of the bone objects were probably used for dress fasteners as well as for the preparation of skins.

Antler combs for preparing skins are common at Windmill Hill, Easton Down and Harrow Hill as well as in Belgian flint mining dwellings. Sheep provides poor leather compared with that from pig and ox.

Steatite beads have been recovered at Hembury similar to those found in the Cortaillod sites in Switzerland.

There is some controversy concerning the implication of the Neolithic chamber tomb as these have often been ripped open by vandals and the contents removed. They therefore give little indication of the style of life. It is outside the scope of this book to consider burial customs. There is little or no indication of religious practices and as has been indicated there was little if any respect for the dead. Durrington Walls is a sacred site dating from c. 1700 BC, but its significance is still uncertain. Absence of goods found on religious sites is a problem.

It is claimed that miners built an altar of flints in one shaft at Grimes Graves and placed a carving of a pregnant woman before it with a phallus and chalk balls, possibly to provide an omen for the finding of good flint in future shafts. This probably is mere supposition and it is extremely unlikely.

Conclusions Concerning Flint Mining Communities

The bulk of flint mining was carried out in Neolithic times chiefly by the Windmill Hill and Michelsberg culture groups and these were essentially farming people, not necessarily of settled stock and who did the actual mining must remain a strongly debatable question.

The prevalence of trade must be regarded as hypothetical partly for reasons given by Briggs and discussed in Ch. 5, and also from a consideration of locality. As with many other archaeological concepts, the worker enthusiastically devoted to his subject and his need to assign a reason or meaning to any piece of evidence, tends to interpret what he finds on the basis of present day standards. For example it is commonly thought that there was a large body of specialist full time miners producing vast quantities of silex, most of which was traded far and wide or bartered. The miners on this basis would have been sustained by the farming communities. A far more feasible explanation, in the author's opinion, is the existence of tribes who visited the mines from time to time, extracted enough silex for their needs and then moved back to their bases or farmlands. Lack of systematic working, neglect of human life, the taking of major risks and the scarcity of dwelling sites near the actual mines adds logic to the argument. It was probably a hurried operation with little or no attention to ground support and the mines would be left unattended until the next individuals or tribes came, probably on a seasonal basis. The miners would camp with their herds near the mines and go away loaded with flint or chert either in a rough state or in a semi-finished condition. There is now strong evidence for this arising from recent finds at Grimes Graves (see Ch. 3). The only treatment given to the raw material would be making rough outs of tools to get rid of the surplus material in the interests of weight reduction. Probably many miners with their families would be working at the mines at one and the same time and any signs of habitation such as at Spiennes, Blackpatch and Easton Down would represent mere camping sites. The filled in shafts in many cases became mere rubbish pits.

7
Copper and Bronze Age Mining

Although mining of silex commenced principally in the Neolithic era, it continued in many countries through the Eneolithic into the Bronze Age and in some cases into the Iron Age. In fact some flint mines were worked in historical times and as late as the present century. Customs and practices, especially in technological terms, change gradually. It is therefore unjustifiable to assume that at the end of the Neolithic era, there was an abrupt changeover to the working, for example, of native copper and similarly at the commencement of the Bronze Age a sudden transition to bronze technology. Likewise the Iron Age was far from a 100% age of iron production and usage. Nor is it valid to regard the boundaries of the four ages as fixed and rigid any more than to assume that in Britain Victorian age customs ended abruptly with the accession of Edward VII. In fact progress with the discovery of settlement sites, radiocarbon dating developments, etc. is tending to establish a possible lengthening of the Neolithic and an earlier and notable transition to Iron Age customs.

Unfortunately evidence for the prehistoric mining of copper and tin is scarce. There are exceptions, e.g. in Ireland, Austria, Yugoslavia, Bulgaria, Sinai etc. but compared with silex mining, examples of remains of extensive underground metal mines are lacking at the present time. The first worked copper was the native variety and was dug out at the surface so providing vast supplies for the first metallic articles. On the other hand an appreciable amount of work has been done on, for example, prehistoric metallurgy, the identification of smelting sites, ovens, slag heaps and the study of constituents of copper and bronzes from which early metal implements were made. In some cases it has been possible to identify the sources of the metals, but only rarely have the actual mining sites been found. Two outstanding exceptions are discoveries of Eneolithic copper mines at Rudna Glava in Yugoslavia and

Aibunar in Bulgaria about which more will be said later. The significance of these finds was establishment of definite evidence of underground copper mining in the fourth millennium BC, at a date possibly before underground flint mining started in Britain. It had been thought, prior to these discoveries, that the first underground mining of copper commenced in Anatolia in c. 2000 BC, and provided origins of copper metallurgy in the Balkans. It is now believed possible that copper artefacts found at Troy in western Turkey were made from Balkan copper.

Much has been written concerning finds of copper and bronze items, including tools and weaponry, and the underlying metallurgical considerations. Accordingly it might be useful to deal first with the ages and cultures associated with these developments and then the actual metallurgical aspects before considering some known prehistoric copper mines.

Ages and Cultures

In the early stages copper usage and availability were somewhat dependent on flint technology. Away from the sources of copper available flint continued to be used for all tools and implements. Copper, being scarce was reserved for production of prestige items. Some areas never received copper since there was no available barter exchange material. Conversely Sweden had little flint and no copper resources so copper items were received in exchange for furs, timber etc. Britain did not receive any copper goods until well after 1800 BC, the date of the arrival of Beaker pioneering settlers.

The Near East

The technique of metalworking seems to have been discovered in the Near East at a relatively early date. For example, at Cayönu, which is only 20 km from Ergani Maden, a well known source of native copper and malachite ores, drilled beads, straight pins and a square sectioned reamer were found neatly hammered from native copper and the pins ground. Mellaart (1975) says this is the first attested use of native copper in the Near East and precedes the use of hammered and later smelted copper at Catal Hüyük by a thousand years, i.e. Cayönu dates from c. 7000 BC whereas Catal Hüyük is dated c. 6000 BC. So the remarkable fact is that copper items were being fashioned at a time when northern Europe was still inhabited by Mesolithic hunter, gatherer and fisher folk. Native copper was still being hammered for trinkets and beads at Catal Hüyük around 6000 BC. At Mersin XVI the first heavy copper tools and axes were found. Cast copper objects were found in Mesopotamia dating from c. 4200 BC. The earliest crucibles for copper smelting were found at Iblis in Iran and possibly date before 4000 BC. From Siyalk, c. 5500 BC, were the first copper artefacts found in Iran, a hammered awl with a round section and another with a flat bulbous top. Pins and needles with biconical heads were also found. According to Mellaart the copper is thought to have come from the Talmessi mine, 225 km south-east of Kashan in the central desert where native copper occurs in abundance.

Anatolia had, and still has, ample supplies of copper both of the native and ore varieties hence the term "cradle of mining" being given to this major part of Turkey. Iran also has copper and, unlike Anatolia, has tin so the bronze artefacts discovered in abundance in Anatolia and Mesopotamia during the Bronze Age could have been manufactured from Anatolian or Iranian copper and tin from Iran. This implies a network of trade routes across Mesopotamia and Anatolia. In addition Cyprus had immense copper resources and ancient copper mines have been discovered there although to date there is no evidence of prehistoric workings. Crude ingots were probably exported to the mainland during early Bronze Age times. During the Neolithic and Chalcolithic periods there appeared to be no recognition of copper deposits on the island. Bronze in Anatolia appears to have been rare before the third millennium BC.

Dayton (1971) maintains that Turkey is not so rich in minerals by ancient standards especially in copper ores and that Mesopotamia probably looked beyond Anatolia to Bohemia and the Danube for supplies. Against this Muhly and Wertime (1973) point out that Ergani alone today produces 17 000 t of copper per year and so reserves were vast in both the Copper and Bronze Ages.

Although relating more to historical times and therefore outside the scope of this book, it is interesting to note that the copper used to make the Sumer articles in Mesopotamia, was probably obtained from mines which have been discovered at Oman on the Persian Gulf. Likewise the Egyptian Pharoahs sent expeditions to Sinai to prospect for and mine copper from deposits at Timna (Wilson 1977).

The approximate dates for the Bronze Age in Anatolia are:

Early Bronze Age   3000–1950 BC Troy I–V
Middle Bronze Age 1950–1700 BC Troy VI Assyrians
Late Bronze Age   1700–1200 BC Troy VIIa and the Hittites

Europe

Recent work in the Balkan field has now proved beyond any shadow of doubt that copper metallurgy here preceded that of bronze in Anatolia. There is no evidence of contact with Anatolia and it is possible that prosperous peoples started metallurgy independently. It is hardly surprising that, after long experience with flint mining, progress should have been directed towards the extraction of other useful materials. Neolithic cultures were self sufficient, but discovery of uses for native copper, for copper ores and adaptation to copper mining led to the need for craftsmen and traders and the introduction of a more settled pattern of life. This was the dawn of the Eneolithic or Copper Age or, as some prefer to call it, the Chalcolithic. Copper resources are spaced all over Transylvania, Matra Mountains, the Ore Mountains, Yugoslavia, the North Austrian Alps and the Harz Mountains.

The cultures concerned from about 4000 BC onwards are the Karanovo of the East Balkans, the Maritsa of South Bulgaria and Yugoslavia, the Boian of South East Rumania and the Vadestra of North West Bulgaria and South West Rumania. The succeeding phase is that of the Gumelnitza. Houses of post and frame walls with log floors and coated with clay were the customary habitation. There were domed clay ovens outside the houses. The economy was based essentially on cattle, cereals and legumes. Radiocarbon dates vary from 4290 ± 100 BC for Macedonia, 3890 ± 250 BC for Karanovo to 3485 ± 100 BC for Sitagroi and 3350 ± 60 BC for Yulkaneshty.

Over in the West Balkans there was the Vinça Plocnik culture with similar settlements and radiocarbon dates of 3895 ± 160 BC for Vinça itself, 3760 ± 90 BC for Baneija and 3797 ± 60 BC for Gorna Toszla.

Actual ore extraction and smelting had begun by the end of the Vinça period, a typical example being the mine at Rudna Glava.

Mellaart (1960) compares the chronology of the Balkans, especially the Vinça phases, with the Anatolian and Cretan dates. Late Vinça is much earlier than Troy I and contemporary with Early Minoan II of Crete. Karanovo V is not later than Troy II. This is in line with the theory of Dayton (1971) which has been strongly refuted by Muhly and Wertime (1973). The last two authors state that bronze developed late in the Near East partly due to lack of tin. Dayton suggests that the Ur tin–bronze came from Spain. Renfrew (1969) expands the argument in support of Mellaart and suggests the autonomy of the south-eastern Europe Copper Age. The full implication of the latest theory is that the Eneolithic or Copper Age started in south-eastern Europe with copper being mined and prepared in the countries mentioned, plus Transcaucasia, sometime before bronze was discovered in the Near East and possibly even before copper was mined there. M⸱ llaart even suggests trade routes for copper southwards and immigrationᵢ possibly across the Bosphorus into Anatolia. Thus many of the copper goods found on Anatolian sites, such as Troy, were exported from the Balkans. This does not rule out, of course, the possible journeys northwards by prospectors from Anatolia, but it does on the other hand make mass immigration northwards by colonists, as suggested by Childe (1957) less likely.

Another controversy concerned the development of metallurgy in Spain. Blance (1961) suggested that it was introduced by colonists travelling by sea from Italy and the East Mediterranean bringing with them copper and bronze goods some of which were based on the two piece mould used in the Aegean area. Also she suggested that these migrations included prospectors. Renfrew (1967) refutes this and cites the abundance of copper and tin in Iberia and suggests that the metallurgy there could have been well developed by, say, 2600 BC, well before its inception in the Aegean. There was independent and early use of copper in the Vinça culture, so why not in Iberia?

In Scandinavia the end of the Neolithic period was not marked by changes in technology. Absence of native copper or of copper ores resulted in the import of finished products of copper and tin and later of bronze, some from Britain, and flint technology continued with these developments. When supplies dwindled craftsmen made daggers and tools of silex and stone to the design of the actual metal versions.

In Rumania copper was used to make fishhooks, awls, pins, rods, wire, flat axes, chisels, axes, hammers, adzes, strips, beads, bracelets, pendants, amulets and discs as early as 4000 ± 500 BC–3000 ± 500 BC. The sites where 750 objects have been found lie on a band running SW to NE from the River Dnieper and the River Bug to the Carpathians, an area today partly in the USSR. The culture responsible was the Cucuteni-Tripolye according to Grieves (1975).

The Bronze Age in Europe was marked by the appearance of the Bell Beaker cultures. These were represented by round headed peoples who introduced a characteristic bell shaped beaker, presumably intended for the drinking of wine, milk or mead. As mentioned by Harrison (1974), there appears to be no agreed theory concerning their origin. What is known, however, is that they appeared on the European scene about 2000 BC and went northwards leaving behind some settlements and beaker remains, tanged knives, sheet gold ornaments, awls and spiral bracelets. The three main possible origins are: (1) they were of Indo-

German origin and spread rapidly through Germany and then by
maritime routes along the northern coasts and then to the British Isles, (2)
that they were of oriental descent and moved by some unknown route to
Brittany and (3) that they went by Spain, Brittany, Holland, Bohemia
to the British Isles. There is some complexity about the origin of the
culture and various theories are prevalent. For instance Sangmeister
(1966) suggested a "Rückstrom" or "reflux" theory involving the
combination and mixing of two waves of movement, i.e. an origin of the
culture in the south west which spread and radiated north, north-east and
east and one from Bohemia radiating west, south-west and south. The
blending of these two involved a reflux or movement back to the Iberian
peninsula. The origin of the Bohemian Bell Beaker culture is not at all
clear and according to Sangmeister may have involved a source external
to Europe. Lanting *et al.* (1973) produced radiocarbon dates which
appear to refute part of Sangmeister's reflux theory. One salient feature,
however, is that Spain, Central Germany and Brittany had copper and
tin resources and Britain also had both metals. The culture has
radiocarbon dates for Germany of 2200–2100 BC to 1800–1700 BC. At
Heidmoor the dates range over 2020 ± 170 BC. Corded Beaker preceded
the Bell Beaker ware and for Holland the date is 2240 ± 120 BC. Butler
and Van der Waals (1966) suggest that the Bell Beaker smiths introduced
metal working into the Netherlands and quote evidence such as highly
skilled casting, stone anvils, hammers and burnishers. The copper used
probably came from Brittany, but a Central European source is doubtful.
These authors say that there were few points of contact with the Early
Bronze Age peoples which would imply a measure of independence of the
Bell Beaker culture.

The chronology of the European Bronze Age is:

Early Bronze Age	1800–1450 BC
Middle Bronze Age	1450–1250 BC
Late Bronze Age	1250–750 BC

The Bronze Age is especially well documented for Europe although
settlements are very scarce as they are in Britain. Metallurgy became very
well developed in the Early Bronze Age especially during the Unetice
cultural phase such as at Prasklice in Czechoslovakia 1895 ± 80 BC,
Helmsdorf in northern Germany 1775 ± 80 BC and Leki Mali in Poland
1655 ± 40 BC. Vast hoards of tools and weapons have been found and
sociological analyses have been made of the different types of graves,
varying from those of chieftains to mass graves. Cremation appeared in
the Middle Bronze Age and by 1200 BC was almost universal hence the

adoption of the term Urnfield culture. The various periods of the Late Bronze Age are:

1250–1200 BC	Reinecke D
1200–1100 BC	Hallstatt A1
1100–1000 BC	Hallstatt A2
1000–900 BC	Hallstatt B1
900–750 BC	Hallstatt B2

The Late Bronze Age is noted for the excellent documentation of copper and salt mining in the Austrian Alps about which more will be· said in this chapter and in Ch. 8.

The British Isles

About 1800 BC the Bell Beaker peoples arrived in the British Isles. As already indicated various theories have been put forward concerning their possible origin and their routes to and within Britain. Stone (1958) has suggested three possible routes, i.e. from the shores of the Wash to Wessex, from the south and south-east coasts along the Thames and Hampshire Avon valleys to Wessex and from the Netherlands to North East England and South Scotland. Piggott (1973) says that colonization seems to have been concerned primarily with the exploitation of local copper and gold, but settlement of Wessex, where they formed the origin of the Wessex culture, could not have involved the working of such deposits since in that locality they are non-existent. Gold and copper were, however, worked in Scotland and Ireland and metallurgy was more advanced than in England.

In Britain the way of life of Beaker folk was accepted by the inhabitants, i.e. those of the Peterborough culture. This involved different burial customs under round barrows and often with beakers. They introduced stone battle axes, tanged and barbed flint arrowheads, flint daggers and also rivetted knives and daggers. They were definitely agriculturists and grew barley rather than wheat, and kept pigs and sheep.

Bronze, which appears to have been discovered in Iraq in the fourth millennium BC, did not reach Britain before 1750 BC, according to Coghlan (1942).

There is a scarcity of sites which can be assigned to the Beaker period in Britain. According to Simpson (1971), there are two explanations: (1) they were nomadic peoples content to live in light tents or (2) all the post hole evidence has disappeared in Wessex and this can be due to erosion of the chalk and limestone. At Easton Down, in the flint mining area, a settlement is marked by oval pits 3 m long, 2 m wide and 50 cm deep in chalk. Stake holes can be seen, but not in the depressions, see Fig. 72. Belle Trout, also in the flint mining area, had two rectangular enclosures which have been destroyed by coastal erosion. The surviving enclosure is defined by a bank and ditch. Individual post holes within the enclosure marked five further structures.

Prehistoric Metal Working

The archaeology of the Bronze Age, and this is partly true of the preceding Eneolithic or Copper Age, is nearly entirely concerned at present with metallurgy. Unfortunately, therefore more attention is being paid at present to the study of prehistoric metallurgy and the relevant sites of such operations, trade patterns and the related cultures, than to actual sources of metal and the relevant mining sites. However, mining and metallurgy have a very close affinity and in fact prehistoric miners must have had a working knowledge of metallurgy even though this may have been crude. The mining engineer today must also be conversant with the general principles of metallurgy. It is not proposed here to give a comprehensive coverage to prehistoric metal working, but to highlight the salient principles in relation to prehistory before turning to actual known mining sites.

It would seem that there were several distinct phases of development of copper metallurgy:

(1) the first copper to be extracted was the native variety. As this was soft it was easily shaped by cold hammering to give crude ornaments.

(2) It was found that complicated shapes could be more satisfactorily obtained by hammering the native copper. However, this method was unsuitable for tools and weapons as the copper became brittle and tended to crack. Before the advent of heat treatment stone and silex tools were found to me more efficient despite the fact that when copper became blunt a new edge could be produced by hammering. However, during this phase and indeed later phases copper was in short supply as trade routes did not run through areas where copper was available. Consequently copper tended to be reserved solely for the production of prestige goods.

(3) Heating was introduced which gave a hardening of the copper and so increased the range of goods which could be produced.

(4) Smelting was discovered and casting was carried out in stone moulds.

(5) Closed moulds were introduced.

(6) Copper was alloyed with tin to produce bronze.

(7) The *cire perdue* or "lost wax" process was developed.

Native Copper

The first copper to be used by prehistoric man was the native variety and is said to have formed the link between stone or silex and metal for the making of simple objects. Copper still exists today in Cornwall, France, Germany, Hungary, Iran, Ireland and Spain. It is free from impurities and requires no smelting. Hammered native copper was found at the Neolithic habitation site of Catal Hüyük in Anatolia and dates from 6000 to 5000 BC, the copper being 99·83% pure. It exists as primary copper in the oxidation zone and is fairly easy to identify *in situ* being purplish brown or green. Prehistoric man would have had little difficulty in recognizing it and, being free from impurities, he found it exceedingly easy to mould it by hand into crude basic shapes. Coghlan (1951) secured varieties of native copper from many sources and divided them into three groups:

(1)   small grains or pellets and spongy growths

(2)   laminated or arborescent growths and

(3)   massive solid copper from one pound in weight up to large blocks

The largest block of native copper was found in Minnesota in 1857 and according to Alexander and Street (1946) weighed 420 tons. Coghlan (1951) found that a large block, which probably contained impurities, would have been difficult for primitive man to work. In fact Coghlan could not cut it with a steel hacksaw blade or even hammer it.

Reid (1918) comments that narrow veins of native copper can be seen, without the presence of tin, in the cliffs of the Mullion in the Lizard of Cornwall between the tide marks. It can also be found in the St Just district and near Camborne. It is purported to have been worked by Neolithic man as copper implements have been found in Cornwall belonging to that period. Tylecote (1962) says there is little native copper today in Europe as it was probably all used up by early man.

Heat Treatment of Copper

It is highly unlikely that Neolithic or Copper Age man continued for long to manage with cold shaped or hammered copper for his manufacturing requirements. Although hammering enabled him to shape copper implements, and to harden them, they would have remained very brittle. In fact it is quite possible that he soon realized that heat treatment, i.e.

annealing gave him a harder, less brittle and thus a more durable cutting edge. He had experience with pottery firing and so heat treatment might have appeared on the scene very early. Reid suggests that the discovery might have been made as a result of hardening wooden spears with fire. The acquisition of heat treated copper certainly extended the range of goods possible to prehistoric man.

The next stage, i.e. the melting of copper was not reached for some time. A temperature of 1083 °C is needed to melt copper fully and this cannot be obtained in an ordinary fire without some form of forced draught. In fact Coghlan (1942) suggests that smelting of the ore to produce the metal actually preceded melting. To reduce a carbonate of copper ore to the metal requires a temperature of only 500–600 °C as compared to 1083 °C for complete melting of pure copper whereas for tin the relative values are approximately reversed, i.e. 1000–1100 °C and 232 °C respectively (Thompson 1958). Reed (1934) postulates that primitive man did not stumble on to the achievement of a sufficiently high temperature to melt copper, but reached this stage only after trials with various types of furnaces. The pottery kiln, for example, when developed could generate 1200 °C, so why not a furnace for melting copper? Coghlan is of the opinion that at Tepe Sialk melting of copper actually preceded the operation of smelting. This was possible as a result of the early development (c. 3000 BC) of an efficient pottery furnace with controlled draught. Apart from the factual temperatures mentioned it is virtually impossible, as Childe (1951) states to distinguish native copper from smelted copper in artefacts.

Long before primitive man discovered how to melt copper, it was inevitable that he would look for methods of joining together pieces of such metal. According to Grieves (1975) definite evidence of welding was found on 396 out of 464 Tripolye A objects of the Cucuteni-Tripolye culture of south-east Europe in an area today partly in Rumania and partly in the USSR. This culture has a date of c. 4000–3000 ± 500 BC. Grieves suggests a maximum temperature range of c. 300 °C. This for a high lead copper is very near the critical temperature of c. 327 °C when such a copper becomes brittle and fractures during hot forging. For welding, according to Grieves, the flux could have been salt or animal fat or even urine.

The first ores to be smelted were the oxide and carbonate ores such as cuprite and malachite. The sulphide ores, examples of which are copper pyrites and chalcocite, require more advanced metallurgy and it was probably some time before prehistoric man discovered the necessary techniques. Coghlan (1951a) states that the sulphide ores always occur deeper than the oxides and carbonates. This, however, is not always true as there are mines in Turkey working shallow sulphide ores which have not been oxidized. Prehistoric mining of sulphide ores just below the surface also took place in the Austrian Alps.

Coghlan (1951b) carried out an interesting experiment on the smelting of malachite. He made a small hole in the ground which was dried out first with a wood fire before he started a charcoal fire. To do this he made a ring of stones round the hole and about 1 m in diameter and built up a cone of charcoal which contained layers of charcoal and malachite. A strong wind blew on the day chosen for the experiment and after one hour the fire reached bright red heat. The fire was supplied with fresh fuel and kept at full heat for several hours. When the fire was cleared out the malachite had only been reduced to black copper oxide. A temperature of 700–800 °C would have been needed, according to Coghlan, although the failure was not due to low temperature, but to the access of too much air. He then repeated the experiment with a pottery furnace. An ordinary pot of red ware was inverted over a flat pottery dish on which small lumps of malachite were placed. He placed this miniature kiln on a bed of red hot charcoal and ashes and then a cone of burning charcoal was built up all around it until completely covered the kiln. The fire was kept at a good red heat for several hours using no artificial draught. Metallic copper was produced, but not a compact mass. Coghlan produced a compact mass by grinding malachite to a small size. He suggests therefore that copper could have been accidently reduced in a pottery kiln especially as it was used for pottery decoration. The same author elsewhere suggests that the dropping of ore into a camp fire is highly unlikely as a pointer to the discovery of smelting. Two conditions would be required: (1) the temperature would have to be sufficiently high and (2) the fire large enough to exclude air. Thompson (1958), however, refutes much of this reasoning and comments that a temperature of 600 °C is so low that the fire would hardly be visible in strong sunlight whilst as the free energy diagram shows, the temperature at which copper oxide can be reduced is well below 600 °C. According to Thompson there is no reason why the first reduction of copper carbonate could not have occurred in a domestic fire drawn up by a hot dry wind.

Many people have in the past attributed the discovery of smelting to accident. For example, Spielmann (1926) raises an interesting point concerning the ignition of petroleum and the consequent reduction of copper when both occur together, e.g. in Caucasia. Arsenic and arsenical oxides would be liberated, but ancient man had no knowledge of toxicity. In the "Ancient Egyptians" it is stated that an Egyptian lady, according to E. Smith (1911), had inadvertently dropped a piece of malachite paste, a cosmetic, into a charcoal brazier. Ault (1920) maintains that a prehistoric man could have accidently dropped his knife into a camp fire and in trying to recover it detected something gleaming and ruddy yellow among the scattered ashes. It is, however, more likely that prehistoric man dropped a piece of carbonate ore into a camp fire out of curiosity to see what happened.

The smelting of sulphide ores presents additional problems as compared to the treatment of oxides and carbonates. The principal one is that heating a sulphide ore with carbon in the form of charcoal will not lead to the reduction of the ore. In order to carry out the smelting process the ore must be cleaned to get rid of the waste rock and then graded into the correct size. Then the ore is pre-roasted which involves heating at a low temperature with adequate access of air probably for days until volatiles, such as antimony, arsenic and sulphur, have been expelled. Even then some impurities often remain and contaminate the final product of smelting. Once the ore has been converted from the sulphide to the oxide it can be reduced as for a natural oxide or carbonate with charcoal. However, with pyritic ores, after roasting there remains a mixture of copper sulphide and iron oxide and the latter must be removed. This can be done by adding sand to the liquid mass and iron silicate is formed which can be skimmed off the surface leaving the sulphide free to be reduced with charcoal.

After the technique of acquiring the correct minimum temperature to melt copper, either from the native or smelted state, had been found the way was open for casting in moulds. This was actually the greatest breakthrough as the number of objects made possible was unlimited. At first, as would seem logical, open moulds were used, but in order to restrict air admittance to the molten copper and so prevent the formation of bubbles, closed moulds were introduced. In both cases the moulds were of stone. Another advantage of closed moulds was the increase in the range of products in terms of shapes especially when the moulds were produced from clay, A more sophisticated process was the pouring of molten copper round a charcoal mould.

Bronze

The presence of impurities in copper, intentional or otherwise, has a hardening effect and an increasing casting ability. Thompson (1958) accordingly says that bronzes are impure coppers and nothing more.

Tin often occurs naturally with copper in lodes, especially in Cornwall, so that extraction and subsequent reduction would give a tin–copper bronze, which had a high value in exchange like a good chalk flint. Primitive man probably discovered that impurities associated with "natural" copper ores such as arsenic, antimony, tin etc. tended to harden the copper. Later he·probably experimented to find out what proportions of pure metals were necessary to give a hard alloy with good casting properties. Coghlan and Case (1957) quote a hardness number of Br 79 for the high arsenical copper constituting a halberd which when fully worked gave Br 132. For a modern pure copper the figure for a casting was Br 50 and Br 110 when cold worked. A 10% tin bronze casting gave Br 70–100 and Br 230 when fully cold worked. Arsenic tends to lessen the porosity in castings and to give a higher hardness value. The addition of tin gives even better results than that of arsenic. Some Central European workers, when discussing copper–arsenic bronzes, argue in support of an extra age, even before the Eneolithic, i.e. a Kupfer-Arsen Zeit. Particular reference is to Transcaucasia around 4000 BC where arsenic in copper objects has been discovered.

Reid (1918) states that "copper" from Cornwall, though extremely variable, is often much tougher and harder than foreign copper. A possible reason is that except in the Lizard area, all Cornish copper contains tin. Brown and Blin-Stoyle (1959) carried out 438 analyses of British Middle and Late Bronze Age material containing copper, tin, lead, arsenic, antimony, nickel, bismuth, iron, zinc, silver, gold and magnesium. They found that whereas in the Middle Bronze Age lead was only a trace element in the bronze, in the Late Bronze Age it was present in substantial quantities. Metallurgically up to 2% lead facilitates the working of bronze, but over 2% lead tends to reduce the mechanical properties such as lowering the strength and ductility and the resistance to corrosion. So the result of adding lead would be to facilitate working and to save copper and tin. The authors also state mostly Middle and Late Bronze Age bronzes have 15% tin whereas Desch in the discussion of the article by Piesse (1927) says many ancient bronzes have the usual 90% copper and 10% tin. The same author shows how a small increase in the amount of tin adds to the Vickers hardness values:

	Before hammering	After hammering
Copper	87	135
9·31% tin–bronze	136	257
10·34% tin–bronze	171	275

It is certainly untrue to suggest, as Ramin does (1977), that bronze appeared fairly late on the scene owing to the relative scarcity of tin. As mentioned earlier, bronze could have been discovered accidentally when a copper–tin ore was worked. There is hardly any tin in the Middle East yet true bronze appeared on sites in Anatolia well before 3000 BC.

The addition of tin to copper lowers the melting point, i.e. according to Coghlan 100% copper melts at 1085 °C (1083) whereas a 10% tin-copper bronze melts at 1000 °C. Likewise according to Coghlan (1939), the tenacity increases from 10 tons/sq. in to 15 tons/sq. in.

Rickard (1932) says that alloying probably occurred by accident for example copper in Egypt was modified by arsenic, in Germany by nickel, in Hungary by antimony, in India by zinc and in Saxony by tin. Saxo-Thuringian ores contained sufficient tin to make a natural tin bronze, but far too low for the alloying to be fully effective. According to Clark (1952) this represents the first region to develop tin–bronze.

Cire Perdue

This was one of the final processes to be developed by prehistoric man and was used for the casting of objects in metal. It is also known as the "lost wax" process. The main advantage of its use is that it is especially suitable for the casting of complicated objects such as statuettes and figurines, complex jewellery etc. The object to be cast is first modelled in wax around a small clay core. It is then totally enclosed in clay and baked, the molten wax escaping through orifices, which are left in the clay. By this means a cavity between the original clay core and enclosing baked clay is left into which the molten copper or other metal is poured through the existing orifices which are then plugged. The baked clay after the metal is set is then broken and the cast object removed. There is evidence of the method having been used at Ur in Mesopotamia around 3000 BC.

Sources of Copper and Tin and Mining Processes

Mining preceded metallurgy since native copper required no underground extraction. As copper and tin lodes usually occur in hard igneous rocks access had to be made below the surface before any metallurgical reduction of the ore could be attempted. The most important copper ores are:

1. Oxidized ores

Azurite (Chessylite), blue copper carbonate $2CuCO_3Cu(OH)_2$
Chrysocolla, hydrated orthosilicate of copper, $SiO_2CuO \cdot 2H_2O$

Cuprite (Ruby copper), monoxide of copper, Cu_2O

Malachite, green copper carbonate, $CuCO_3$ $Cu(OH)_2$

Melaconite (Tenorite), black monoxide of copper, CuO

2. Sulphide ores

Bornite or Peacock ore (Erubescite), sulphoferrite of copper, $3Cu_2SFe_2S_3$

Chalcocite (Copper glance), Cu_2S

Chalcopyrite (Copper pyrites), sulphoferrite of copper, $CuFeS_2$

Fahl (Tetrahedrite) grey copper ore, Cu_2SbS_3

The only commercially important tin ore is the dioxide of tin, cassiterite, also known as tinstone, SnO_2. The sulphide of tin or tin pyrites is virtually useless and is known as stannite Sn S_2 Cu_2 S Fe S.

Of the copper ores malachite is the most important although cuprite and chalcopyrite are very plentiful. Gowland (1902) was of the opinion that the sulphide ores were probably unworked in prehistoric times, but that there is a possibility that the Romans worked them in Cyprus. However, there is now ample evidence that such ores were worked in the Bronze Age in Austria and elsewhere.

The degree of purity of the most common copper ores is as follows:

	Copper
Azurite	55·30%
Chrysocolla	36·00%
Cuprite	88·80%
Malachite	59·30%
Melaconite	79·86%
Bornite	55·57%
Chalcocite	79·83%
Fahl	51·00%
Chalcopyrite	34·56%

Of the tin ores cassiterite contains 78·82% tin and stannite 27·68% tin.

As Childe (1930) has pointed out Neolithic communities were usually self sufficient. Flint, chert and suitable stone for the manufacture of tools and weapons were generally available not too far from the habitation sites. Despite this, however, there are now recognized patterns of trade. Comparatively Bronze Age peoples were not usually self sufficient. The intervening Chalcolithic or Eneolithic merely continued the silex using traditions of the earlier periods with use of copper where available. Bronze Age communities also continued to use silex, but there was greater emphasis on replacement by copper and copper alloys. Unlike flint etc. copper was not widely distributed in workable horizons and shallow copper is scarce today. Political stability was therefore essential for the maintenance of efficient and necessary trade patterns.

Although the quantitative analyses of copper and other elements in artefacts have been carried out spectographically since 1950, there are still problems concerned with the identification of copper sources. Compared with the determination of the sources of hard rocks by petrographic analyses (see Ch. 5), the origin of the copper from which specific axes were made is still more problematical. The same rocks, as in prehistoric times, are still existent *en masse*, but copper deposits, especially those of native copper, are largely worked out or are no longer accessible for comparative analyses.

Trace elements quantified include chiefly tin (Sn), lead (Pb), arsenic (As), silver (Ag), nickel (Ni), bismuth (Bi), and iron (Fe). There are two theories concerning this approach, but these are governed essentially by national requirements. For example the Austrian school insists on the absolute composition so minute trace elements are important. The origin is not so critical as proved prehistoric mines are existent in the Tirol. Pittioni (1957) claims remarkable consistency with his sources of the metal from which picks and adzes were made. He, for example, related a Muhlbach bun ingot to a Mitterberg pick and an axe adze, found in Austria, to a Slovakian copper ore. Tylecote (1970), however, points out that ore composition and hence ore quality varies with depth. Pittioni worked on the basis of average depth which would tend to inhibit accurate correlation. Conversely the Stuttgart school ignores trace elements on the ground that knowledge of sources of ores will always be deficient and so justify a concentration on composition, i.e. % Cu or % Sn (Waterbolk and Butler 1965). These approaches will not be entirely satisfactory until there are more known mines with copper deposits still residual and so available for sample analyses. Such provisions, however, still ignore the complications arising from a situation where a mine has stopped working due to the deterioration of the deposit. Although a knowledge of metallurgy by prehistoric man is not to be presumed, there can be no doubt concerning his ability to make a qualitative assessment.

Brown and Blin-Stoyle (1959) consider the analyses of bronzes of the Late Bronze Age and list a large number of elements which are found in appreciable quantities, e.g. Cu, Sn, Pb, As, Sb, Ni, Bi, Fe, Ag, Au and Mg. They conclude that lead in the Middle Bronze Age artefacts only appears as a trace element, whereas in the Late Bronze Age it was added intentionally in substantial quantities.

Copper is found in veins or lodes in older harder rock and the methods normally employed by flint miners such as the use of antler picks were inadequate. Explosives of course were not available. Consequently the usual method was firesetting which, however, had already been used by

Neolithic miners, as already mentioned, especially for breaking out hard silex from the parent rock. In addition heavy stone hammers had to be used to break up the rock preparatory to its treatment.

Copper ores have been worked in prehistoric times in either the Eneolithic or Bronze Age in Britain, Ireland, the Balkans, Yugoslavia, Bulgaria, Austria, Turkey, Greece, the Aegean, Iran, Oman, Italy and Iberia.

The sources of tin, so necessary for tin–bronze production, has always been a problem and is discussed in detail by Charles (1975). It is known that there is none in the Mediterranean or the Near East but supplies were available in prehistoric times in Italy, Sardinia, Cornwall, Brittany, Central France, Saxony, the Erzgebirge, Iran and Bohemia. Surprisingly Caucasia has no tin, although Childe (1930) wrote that it occurred along with copper here in prehistoric times. There is no evidence that tin was exported to the Near East from Cornwall as early as the third millennium BC, yet tin was used after this date to make bronze. Muhly and Wertime (1973) state that as late as 800 BC tin was listed as a precious material along with gold, silver, iron, elephant hides, ivory, garments, purple dyed

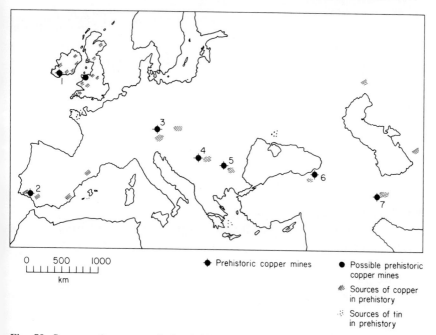

| 0 | 500 | 1000 |

km

◆ Prehistoric copper mines   ● Possible prehistoric copper mines

/// Sources of copper in prehistory

⠃ Sources of tin in prehistory

Fig. 75. Sources of copper and tin. 1 Mount Gabriel, Ireland; 2 Huelva, Spain; 3 Mitterberg, Austria; 4 Rudna Glava, Yugoslavia; 5 Aibunav, Bulgaria; 6 Kozlu, Turkey; 7 Veshnoveh, Iran.

wool and precious woods. Tin right through the Bronze Age was used as currency. Brass, used as an alternative to bronze, does not appear to have existed before the Iron Age. It consists of 40% zinc and 60% copper. Figure 75 shows sources of copper and tin in prehistoric times.

Copper Mines

Compared with silex mining, prehistoric copper mines are rare. Apart from the extensive mines of Austria it was not until Roman times that underground mining of this valuable commodity was carried out on a wide scale. Indeed, if the ancient classical writers are to be believed, the beginning of historical times was marked by massive mineral exploitation. Sagui (1930) discusses this with reference to Spain, Italy and Greece. Pliny, for example, said that Italy was a rich mining field, but, as Sagui points out, Pliny had a greater love for his country than for the truth! Polybius, Strabo, Plutarch, Pausionis and Heredotus all claim that the mining districts in Spain, Italy and Greece were active before the first millennium BC. Sagui says that the Cassandra mines in Greece were worked 2500 years before Alexander the Great which would date them as 2800 BC!

To pursue the subject of ancient mining would be to go outside the scope of this book, which is concerned with earlier times. Whereas there is lack of evidence of wide scale prehistoric mining of copper and tin there is a vast literature on ancient mining much of which is unreliable.

Stayt (1931) describes very old copper workings at the Messina mine in the extreme north of the Transvaal near the Limpopo River and which extend over 25 miles. No dates are given for the working of the mines which had copper sulphide ores, but the methods used resembled those used by prehistoric man. Narrow, shallow, vertical shafts which were circular were sunk and today there are in the same district some nearly 700 m deep. Fire setting was used and round stone hammers, without handles, were employed to break up the ore at the surface to eliminate waste rock. The ore was then sent for roasting and smelting. Broken waste heaps lie alongside the old excavations which were filled in by hand with the debris from the next new shaft as in flint mining.

Since traces of prehistoric copper mine workings have been found to be rare and widely spaced it might be useful to discuss some of these in a geographical context, i.e. according to country or region.

Britain

Many old copper mining sites in Britain, which are still visible, are thought to have been worked in Romano-British times and possibly earlier, but concrete evidence is still lacking. Davies (1935) in his book "Roman Mines in Europe" suggests that the Orme's Head chalcopyrite mines in North Wales were probably opened up before the Roman Conquest and based his opinion on the finding of horn picks, stone mauls and also bronze picks similar to those used in the Late Bronze Age in Austrian Alpine mines. In a later paper Davies (1948) describes some excavations he made on Orme's Head near the Gogarth Hotel and on the basis of finding a Roman coin concluded that copper had been extracted by a deep level adit probably on the line of a modern drainage tunnel. Although evidence was not complete he further suggested that a Romano-British settlement had been in existence. Miners working copper on Orme's Head in the nineteenth century had also found Roman coins and stone mauls. Tyler (1979, pers. comm.) of the Sites and Records Office of the Shropshire County Council has kindly provided the author with unpublished results from some recent work by Duncan James and Keith Griffiths. The work was at Pyllau on Orme's Head on surface tips where Davies had previously found stone mauls, and in a blind heading 1·2 m by 1·2 m. In the heading, along which apparently still circulated air via another unknown shaft or adit, on a ledge 0·3 m above the floor, a stone maul was found and a second in a gallery along with six bone tools. These, however, possibly had been collected together previously by a visitor. In these underground workings there were abundant thin stalactites and thick growths of stalagmites. The latter were underlain by clay containing comminuted charcoal. Although radiocarbon dates are not available it is possible that the mines were at least of Romano-British origin or even earlier. Tyler mentions the lack of shotholes and the general character of the working which is totally different from known nineteenth century mining sites and is of the opinion that they predate them, but by how much is not yet certain.

Davies (1946) describes opencast lead or galena workings at Ystwyth which are said to be Celtic and approximately contemporary with the Roman period. Evidence is based on the hammer and querns found. Such items have been found on Parys Mountain, Anglesey as well as on Orme's Head. At Ystwyth copper pyrites was discovered in the lowest level on Copper Hill although early mining was for galena giving 3·25 oz (101 g) silver per ton of ore and 12% zinc.

In England prehistoric mining certainly took place for copper at Alderley Edge in Cheshire and for tin in Cornwall.

At Alderley Edge on a bold projecting ridge 200 m above sea level, galena and green malachite ores occur in sandstones, marls and conglomerates of the Lower Keuper Series. Old surface workings were discovered here in 1874, during the driving of a new adit, and were said by Professor Dawkins at the time to date from the Bronze Age. The workings were holes in the ground to a depth of 2–3 m, but no galleries had been made. According to Roeder (1901), four sites were found which provided evidence of prehistoric mining, i.e. Brindlow and Windmill Wood to the south of the road running to Macclesfield and Engine Vein and Dicken's Wood to the north. The Neolithic floor was found to be covered with charcoal debris and vitrified copper scoriae. At Brindlow and Windmill Wood stone hammers had been made from brownish green micaceous sandstone and a few were of igneous origin, i.e. greenstone or hornblende. They were grooved and varied in size from 29 cm × 15 cm to 11 cm × 9 cm, their weight being 2–15 lb each. The hammers seemed to have been used for pounding and crushing the fine metalliferous sandstone. Flint knives were found at Engine Vein mine where 2 m diameter earthen circles were seen. Here there were also numerous flint flakes, cores and a scraper together with some implements made from chert. Stone circles were existent at Dicken's Wood, and were located very near to the mines.

The Cornish peninsula is linked with the valuable commodity tin and less so with copper. Although copper and tin occur together in many places it was not until about AD 1740 that actual copper mines with shafts commenced in Cornwall and this continued until about the middle of the last century. Between 1850 and 1860 the copper either diminished to negligible amounts or the copper lodes ran into tin lodes. The copper here occurs adjacent to the familiar Cornish granite and is leached and left as gossan to be worked by miners.

As mentioned earlier native copper is present at Mullion, St Just and near Camborne, but is apparently nearly always mixed with tin ore. In the Lizard native copper occurs free of tin.

The prehistory of the Bronze Age in Europe is linked with Cornish tin and although this ore was no doubt available elsewhere, e.g. in Brittany, Central France, Germany and other countries farther east, there is no doubt that Cornwall was the major source of supplies. There have been many theories regarding trade routes, but what is certain is that tin–bronze in prehistory was used to make tools and implements which are found at great distances from Cornwall. During the Bronze Age there was close affinity between the peoples of Brittany and Cornwall and it is possible that the art of working tin was carried across the English Channel by migrants from Brittany. Irish copper and Cornish tin most probably was used in the manufacture of bronze and Cornwall, being on the trade route from Ireland to Europe, could have constituted not only a supplier of tin, but a trading station for metal tools and implements.

Deep mining of tin with shafts was not known before AD 1400 in Cornwall so the only form of extraction used by prehistoric man was the working of old river gravels or possibly quarrying out cliff faces. A bed of detrital ore, 3 m thick, in the form of heavy black stones and sand from 2 m wide up to the full width of the valley was streamed. These beds occur anywhere from the surface down to a depth of 12 m Hencken (1932). Worth (1874) describes the finds of stone pounders, hewn pieces of wood, a wooden shovel and a deer horn pick in stream works at Carnon. He mentions the finds of R. W. Fox in 1804 12 m below the surface at Carnon on a tin bearing stratum, of human skulls, deer horn picks and a wooden shovel. Around the shovel was a piece of decayed string. A handle had been pierced for the insertion in the tine of a deer horn pick. Worth points out that very few stone hammers have been found. Hencken says the finds at the beginning of the nineteenth century are not necessarily of Stone Age date as the same type of antler pick set in an antler handle was used in Roman times. He suggests a date between 2000 BC and 1800 BC for the start of Cornish tin mining, tin mostly being worked in the densely inhabited west in the Late Bronze Age, the Iron Age and the later part of the Roman period. The first tools were made from horn and wood and in fact stone hammers would not be required for early streaming operations and stones sufficed to pound the ore. The scarcity of stone hammers, grooved for the reception of the handle, as found at Alderley Edge, is explained by the fact that by the time deep mining in hard rock had commenced the pick had been substantially improved.

Ireland

The origin of copper mining and the resultant copper metallurgy in Ireland has been a debatable subject for some time. It has been stated by Herity and Eogen (1977) that pre Beaker people introduced such technology before 2000 BC and traded with the Beaker folk in England, others that these folk travelled north from Europe along the Atlantic seaboard to Ireland landing on the coasts from Kerry to Waterford with another wave travelling across England to Ireland. Coghlan and Case (1957) maintain that there is no evidence of pre Beaker metallurgy in Ireland. Case (1966) points out that there are many primitive objects of smelted copper in Ireland, but few in England and Wales. Although this is not irrefutable evidence it is probable that the Beaker people introduced metallurgy into Ireland and before it spread into England.

Although there are spasmodic occurrences of copper all over Ireland, the main resources are in the south of the country. These occur as Fahl or tetrahedrite, a sulphide ore, and malachite. These two ores impregnate slate and grits overlying the Old Red Sandstone of the Devonian. This irregular concentration of ore stretches west to east across the south of the country from County Kerry to County Waterford. Cole and Hallisey (1924) wrote that many attempts had been made to work the deposits, but without any encouraging results. Post carboniferous copper lodes of chalcopyrite and bornite were mined in the nineteenth century, at Bearhaven, Cappagh, Ballycummisk, Coosbeen and other localities on the coast of County Cork. There are also extensive deposits near the Wicklow Mountains and native copper and copper ores outcrop in the cliffs of Waterford near Bunmabon although Macalister (1949) says there is no native copper in Ireland. Prehistoric copper mines have been proved on Ross Island near Killarney, near Kenmare in County Kerry, at Derrycarhoon in West Cork and in the counties of Tipperary and Waterford. The best known mine is Mount Gabriel in West Cork. Tin is insignificant, a small unimportant mass occurs in County Wicklow, but in general the tin used in bronze metallurgy came from Cornwall. Figure 76 shows the location of the chief copper resources in Ireland.

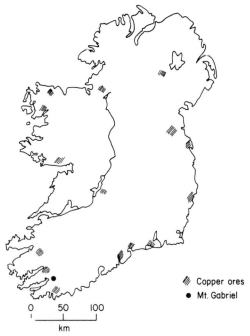

Fig. 76. Locations of Irish copper ores.

John Jackson of the National Museum of Ireland (1968) inspected the Mount Gabriel mines in 1966 and located 25 adits. He reported later that Triphook noticed the mines in 1856 as did Triphook (1856a, b), Kinahan (1861, 1885), Jukes (1861) etc. Kinahan (1885) says the mines were once thought to have been called "Dane's Workings", but not because they were thought to date from the Vikings, but only known according to Mahr (1937) to be old or "Old Men's" workings. Mount Gabriel lies in West County Cork about 2 miles north of Schull, 19 miles west of Skibbereen and 10 miles south-west of Bantry. The hill is approximately 412 m OD and is composed mostly of Old Red Sandstone consisting of purple slates and the upper series of green chlorite grits and is folded anticlinally parallel to the cleavage. The ores are mainly sulphides of copper such as chalcocite, chalcopyrite and tetrahedrite and, according to Jackson (1968) are of low grade. They occur at the junction of the green chlorite grits and the purple slates. At the time of Jackson's first survey in 1966 one adit, No. 1, was easily accessible and was found to be 0·77 m wide and 4·6 m at the stope (Fig. 77) Roof height was little in excess of 1·5 m. Apparently fire setting was used to extract the ore and

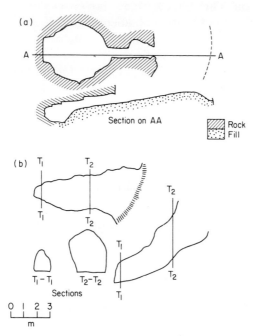

Fig. 77. Mount Gabriel copper mine. (a) Mine No. 1 (after Jackson) (b) Mine No. 4 (after Deady and Doran). Acknowledgements to Cork Historical and Archaeological Society and to Franz Deuticke, Vienna.

although wooden shovels were not found at Mount Gabriel some were recovered from Derrycahoon 8 km to the north-east. Deady and Doran (1972) suggest that fire setting was used possibly only for the making of the entrances owing to lack of oxygen in the deeper adits, and that the stone mauls found could have sufficed for removing projecting pieces of rock from the walls of the adits. The mauls were beach rolled ovoid pebbles 15–20 cm in length and weighing from 5 to 10 lb. The ore from the mine was cobbed on stone paved cobbing floors separated from unwanted gangue which was then discarded probably into the tip heaps.

Deady and Doran (1972) siphoned the water from adit No. 4 in 1970 and proceeded to survey it to its depth of 8 m. These authors obtained a radiocarbon date from a tip heap of adit No. 5 of *c*. 1500 BC which, if correct would date Mount Gabriel as being worked in the Early Bronze Age.

Austria

The best documented copper mines, probably in the world, have been proved in Austria. They have been extensively explored during the past 100 years. The first publication of salient features concerning the mines was written by Much (1879). Since then there have been numerous publications including those of Kyrle (1918), Zschocke and Preuschen (1932) as well as more recent studies by Pittioni (1950, 1954).

The principal centre of prehistoric mining of copper is at Salzburg and in the Tyrol, as shown in Fig. 78. There are three mining areas, i.e. Salzburg and North Tyrol lying just south of Salzburg and east of Innsbruck and East Tyrol and Lower Austria near Eisenstadt. The first is the most famous and includes the mines of Viehofen, Bishopschofen, Mitterberg and Kelchalpe. Viehofen is in the mining district of Sausteigen near Zell am See and was the first prehistoric copper mine to

Fig. 78. Location of Austrian prehistoric copper mining areas. 1 Salzburg and N. Tyrol; 2 E. Tyrol; 3 Lower Austria.

be discovered in the Tyrol. There is claimed to be evidence further west at Brixlegg and Scwaz, but this is not conclusive. East Tyrol has Matreier Becken Virgental, but no exact dating is available. It is claimed that copper mining started during the earlier part of the second millennium BC, about 1700 BC, and early workers claimed that the prospectors came possibly from the Near East, but since this assertion the Eneolithic copper mines of Rudna Glava, dating from the fourth millennium BC, have been found in Yugoslavia. Austrian prehistoric copper mining certainly continued for over 1000 years. East Tyrol mining started somewhat later and continued until the second century AD, according to Pittioni (1954). The region of Schieferalpen (slate mountains) is known as the Grauwacken zone and lies between unstratified rock and the northern limestone alps. This area extends from the Inn Valley to the Alpine eastern margin and contains a copper sulphide ore in the form of pyrites. The best known area is around Bischopshofen, known as the Mitterberg, and the mines were worked here at an altitude of 1800 m. The copper pyrites dips steeply in a north–south direction and strikes west to east. Old workings are marked by, what are called by Pittioni, "pingen", craters being "trichterpinge" and hollow ridge pits "furchtpinge". At Viehofen there are visible signs of the original excavations.

Mining engineers Maczek *et al.* (1952, 1964) in 1930 commenced a systematic and scientific examination of the Mitterberg ridge and as a result there is a vast amount of available information on methods of working and metallurgy which is far in excess of that existent for copper mining in prehistoric times outside Austria. Pittioni (1950) has assembled most of the important information in an English publication.

Estimates of the total production of raw copper vary widely as would be expected. Childe (1948) bases his figures on the ones given by Pittioni, and Zschocke and Preuschen, and quotes 100 tons per year for 1000 years for the whole of the eastern Alps, i.e. from the Bronze Age until the end of the Urnfield phase, the most important period being *c.* 1000 BC. For the whole of the Mitterberg zone of the Salzburg region and the Tyrol 45 000–50 000 tons is estimated.

The salient feature of the underground mining method used is the advanced nature of the operations for such an early period in prehistory. There was no indication of primitive or crude technology and this is probably proof of advantage having been taken of previous experience of silex mining in hard rock. The systematic methods of extraction, drivage, drainage, ventilation and preparation of the product would not be out of place in the nineteenth century, except for developments in illumination and explosives.

Methods of Working

The Austrian copper pyrites ores occur in very hard rock so, as explosives were not available, firesetting, as at the silex mines of Kleinkems and Veaux, was employed. Wherever possible natural mine water was employed for this operation. Heating was only used to break out the rock above the ore as it was more effective, the ore being loosened out once the roof rock had broken.

Andrée (1922) describes briefly the method used at Viehofen. He mentions specifically the use of inclined shafts and says that where vertical shafts were used two or more would be required to regulate the air for ventilation. From this it can be appreciated that prehistoric miners appeared to have some understanding of the basic principles of the flow of warm air. The illustration Fig. 79a shows three shafts with the working place at A. Here a fire would be made to enable the rock to be broken out and the working face advanced to the right or in a southern direction across the lode. The air would be drawn down one or both of two shafts

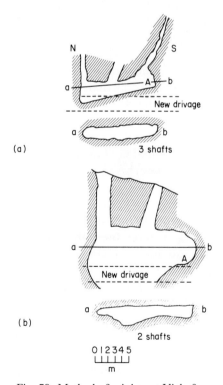

Fig. 79. Method of mining at Viehofen.

Fig. 80. Idealized cross section of prehistoric copper mine.

and the smoke passed up the third shaft which acted as a chimney. All shafts were between 0·8 m and 2 m in diameter. When the working face had been advanced to the limit of the ore body, i.e. up to the country rock, another face would be started lower down and the process repeated. The cooling water gravitated downwards to a sump at E. Figure 79b shows the same system employing only two shafts. Andrée quotes 100 m as being the maximum depth worked. Figure 80 is a sketch made by Kyrle (1918) showing in a comprehensive manner the various operations of firesetting and drivage, and Fig. 81 a model, of a Bronze Age copper mine, at the Bergbau-Museum in Bochum, West Germany.

A method employing adits is described by Pittioni (1950). The author refers to "opencasts", which in mining parlance is incorrect as opencasts are surface excavations in which the whole of the overburden is removed to reach the ore or seam. However, the technique covered by Pittioni, shown in Fig. 82, commenced by making a wide opening in the hillside

Fig. 81. Model of a Bronze Age copper mine (Bergbau-Museum, Bochum).

with firesetting at (a). Drivage commenced when the height of the opening exceeded the man's height and then the opening was timbered over as in (b), the timber being used as a platform for debris. Now the intake air could be drawn in by the fire causing the smoke to rise and pass out

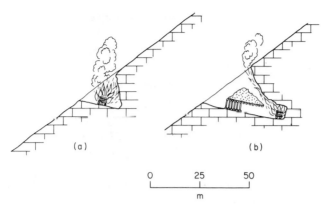

Fig. 82. Early stages of opening up a copper mine in the Austrian Alps.

of the mine along the resulting passageway. Figure 83 (a) and (b) shows how the mine was developed with stowage and ascensional ventilation as the lode was worked deeper into the hillside. The advantages of the method were; (a) the miners were working all the time in fresh air and (b) drainage of the water used in firesetting was

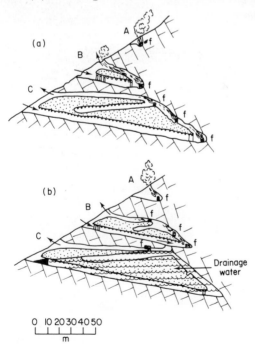

Fig. 83. Later stages of opening up a copper mine in the Austrian Alps. f = fire. Acknowledgements to the Institute of Archaeology, London.

facilitated. The depth of working, measured from the crest of the ridge, was limited to about 100 m. According to Pittioni all the available material was completely extracted so representing a considerable achievement for the Bronze Age miner.

The tools and other equipment used by the miners were the ancestors of tools used in the industry up to a decade ago. Huge pine trunks were cut for ladders as shown in Fig. 80. Various long pointed pick axes with long shafts, made also from scrub, together with heavy bronze hammers to reduce the heavy work, were used. Wooden shovels were probably employed for filling the ore into pine branch barrows and wooden tubs which were also used for carrying water for firesetting and for bailing out the sump when shaft working was adopted as at Viehofen. Splinters, obtained from a hard resined wood, called lighting chips were used for illumination, but gave a very smoky flame. Wooden troughs were used for directing water to the site for the fire and were made from hollowed out round tree trunks. Water was conveyed from the surface of the mine in wooden tubs of 25 cm diameter with a base 2·4 m thick. This base was fixed in a small groove 8–20 mm deep and the side secured with wooden nails. Figure 84 shows examples of equipment found in the copper mines of the Mitterberg.

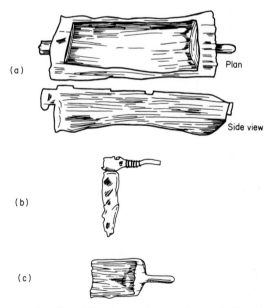

Fig. 84. Equipment found at Mitterburg (a) water barrel hollowed out of tree trunk (1·5 m long, 47 cm wide, 30 cm high) (b) bronze pick with wooden handle (23·8 cm long) (c) wooden shovel (28 cm × 18·7 cm, handle 14 cm long).

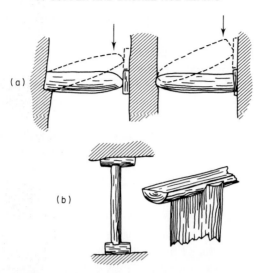

Fig. 85. Method of setting wooden supports in Austrian copper mine. (a) support for vertical shafts, (b) gallery supports.

Timbering was used for supporting the roof and sides of adits and shafts and was very advanced for the time and yet it is surprising that such methods had not been used in the weaker rock worked by the Neolithic flint miners. The copper miner knew how to cut wooden supports to size and how to tighten these between the sides with the aid of "lids" or sole pieces as shown in the sketch at Fig. 85. To erect a water dam he set two props and lids against the roof and floor, built up a wall of planks and then banked up a wall of debris as in Fig. 86. One surprising feature concerning the finds associated with prehistoric mining in the Tyrol is the preservation of timber. As Pittioni (1950) points out, the condition of the

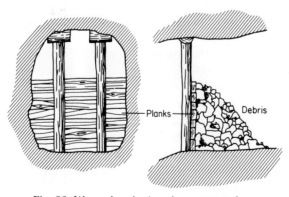

Fig. 86. Water dam in Austrian copper mine.

wood on being laid bare was as fresh as it must have been 3000 or 4000 years earlier.

When the material containing the ore had been broken down separation had to be carried out. First it had to be crushed to separate the ore from the gangue and then the ore ground to a fine size. For both operations hammer stones were used and the ore selected by hand. For grinding, stones were fitted with handles with leather thongs. Separation of the fine material was carried out in submerged sieves in troughs of water. Agitation of the water enabled advantage to be taken of the different specific gravities of the ore and the matrix. This operation marked the forerunner of the modern technique of fine particle separation based on divergent densities.

It is presumed that the material was transported in leather buckets to the surface of the mine, use being made of ladders. Windlasses or hoists were probably introduced much later than prehistorical times.

There is evidence from waste heaps on the surface that the actual smelting was carried out at some distance from the mines, indeed Pittioni mentions that traces of smelting have been found, in the case of the Mitterberg, even away from the actual ore deposits and centralized smelting sites are suggested. Roasting, i.e. heating with charcoal to drive out the sulphur and convert the ore into oxide, preceded the actual smelting.

It is virtually impossible to estimate the actual manpower engaged on mining, transportation and ore preparation with any reliable degree of accuracy although Zschocke *et al.* (1934) attempt an assessment for the Salzburg mining area. For the four stages shown in Figs 82 and 83 these authors suggest 52 men as follows: six men for the preparatory stages (1–2), 14 men for the first production stage and 27 men for the second stage (3) and 5 men for the final stage (4). For a mine having three adits a total manpower of 180 men is suggested comprising:

> 40 miners
> 60 timbermen
> 20 dressing personnel
> 30 ore transporters
> 10 miscellaneous
> 10 cattle men
> 10 foremen
> ——
> 180
> ——

These men are assumed to have moved 4·2 m³ of lode per day giving 12·6 tons of gangue material and 315 kg of raw copper, so that an output per man day would be 1·75 kg. Zschocke and Preuschen estimate that 20 m³ of timber would be required daily. If the estimate of 500–600 workers for the whole of the Salzburg region is reasonable, it is possible to imagine a total daily production of the order of approximately 1 ton of raw copper per day. This represents a remarkable achievement even by later day standards.

The general picture of prehistoric mining in the Austrian Alps which emerges is one of intense production which was well organized from the Bronze Age right into the Iron Age. Based on spectographic examination of hoards of tools and weapons and individual finds in Europe it is evident that the Austrian mines not only supplied the needs of the home country, but exported into Germany and even farther afield. Pittioni postulates a wealthy group of prehistoric mine owners employing free and independent labour. Furthermore as others have often presumed, he suggests little sharp differentiation between rich and poor as is so often significant in later ages when urban civilization began to be based primarily on materialism and monetary possessions. This would imply a measure of socialist society at least below the level of the mine owners. Pittioni (1950) describes the excavation of a large miner's house on the Kelchalpe containing a few old fireplaces. Here presumably near to the

Fig. 87. Dress of Austrian prehistoric copper mine. Acknowledgements to the Institute of Archaeology, London.

mine, the men cooked their meals and there is evidence of bones of cattle, swine, sheep and goats. As mentioned in Ch. 6 Pittioni suggests that the miners wore leather clothing and fur caps as shown in the sketch reproduced from his article (Fig. 87).

The Aegean and the Balkans

There are few remains of prehistoric copper or tin mines in the Aegean region, but many references to classical Greek and Roman mines, have been extensively documented. Sagui (1928) describes the ancient mines of Cassandra in Greece and postulates that they could have been worked 2500 years before Alexander the Great (356–323 BC)! They are mentioned by Herodotus (c. 485–425 BC), but after the conquest by the Roman general Emilius there is no mention of them again until the Middle Ages. Only a little copper was extracted, manganese appearing to have been the chief product.

One interesting feature associated with many of the Greek mines is that apparently under ancient Greek rule the miners actually lived underground, but appeared to come to the surface once a week to breathe fresh air and to see the skies. Abandoned kitchens, traces of fireplaces and holes as cupboards or lamp niches lend some degree of authenticity to this theory, particularly as workings in ancient times often extended appreciable distances underground. Ramin (1977) mentions gallery lengths of from 700 m–2 km and depths of 150 m or more.

Wainwright (1944) mentions a tin bangle found at Lesbos which might have come from the mines worked on the northern shore of the Gulf of Corinth at Crisa and its later representative Cirrha, which in classical times was the port of Delphi. The tin was worked by opencast methods which by c. 2000–1550 BC had become fairly large. Early Helladic III was probably the period according to the Cambridge Ancient History, when the mines were first worked, i.e. 2400 BC.

The foregoing represents references to ancient as opposed to prehistoric mines, although they could have been actual developments of prehistoric mines of which all traces have been obliterated. It is to Yugoslavia that reference must be made for recent evidence of the prehistoric mining of copper. The confirmation of the existence of Eneolithic copper mines at Rudna Glava has contributed much to the theory that copper metallurgy here preceded bronze metallurgy in Anatolia. The diffusionist views of Gordon Childe postulated a migration north from Anatolia and radiocarbon dates for the Vinça culture published in 1960 were rejected by Milojcic as being too early. He said

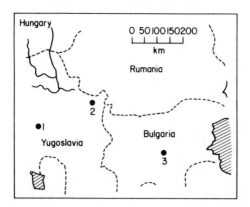

Fig. 88. Location of Rudna Glava. 1 Jarmovoc, 2 Rudna Glava, 3 Aibunor.

that the Vinça culture originated in *c.* 2650 BC and Childe suggested a date of *c.* 2700 BC. Mellaart (1960) gives a date of 4010 ± 85 BC for its commencement so suggests that *c.* 4100 BC could be accepted.

Rudna Glava is located 22 km east of Majdanpek in East Serbia and is reputed to be the oldest prehistoric copper mine in the world, see the map at Fig. 88. There is evidence of several mine shafts which were in operation before 4000 BC. The Eneolithic is associated with the improved dressing of stone tools and the oldest copper and gold metallurgy, and represented either the final stage of the Neolithic or the oldest transitional phase of the Metal Age, lasting from *c.* 4000–*c.* 3500 BC (Jovanovic 1971). The Early Eneolithic was characterized by simple metallurgy of native copper and copper oxides whereas towards the end of the period there was mass processing of sulphide ores. Rudna Glava (ore head or miners' top) lies in a valley known in local tongue as Saska Valley or the valley of the Saxons. It is claimed to be the first copper mine to be based on the experience of the old flint miners according to Jovanovic (1976).

The ores at Rudna Glava are those of magnetite and chalcopyrite impregnations, these being the result of oxidation, and secondary enrichment of copper which meant early exploitation of this metal. Early miners had worked suitable copper veins and there is evidence of this in the terrain. Jovanovic (1976) says that the first minerals to be worked in prehistoric times were magnetite and azurite. Jovanovic and Ottaway (1976) have collected samples of the ore from the mines and classified these into three groups, from the galleries constructed much later by the Romans, from the Early Eneolithic shafts and from an ore vein completely untouched comprising chiefly up to 63% iron ore. They conclude that malachite was worked during the Early Eneolithic and

(a)

(b)

Fig. 89. Shafts at Rudna Glava. Upp: shaft 7d on edge of modern opencast working; lower: working platforms of shafts 6a, 5b and 4d on edge of modern opencast working. Acknowledgements to Professor Jovanovic and Der Anschnitt, Bochum.

magnetite, haematite and pyrite were not sought after and were left behind as gangue.

Excavations by Jovanovic commenced in 1968 and a series of vertical shafts was discovered. The Vinça miners first established themselves on a steep slope as a working platform and dug oval or elliptical shafts. In the south-east there is a zone of Early Eneolithic open pits. The platforms and pit and shaft openings had been made invisible by forest humus. Jovanovic explored mine shafts and found that Shaft 2 was 1·6–1·8 m in diameter and 3·2 m deep. At a certain depth the shaft turned aside following the slope of the limestone layers. Shaft 3 had two sloping galleries 0·50–0·6 m in diameter, which were connected together in the upper part. Pottery found in Shaft 7 shown in Fig. 89a was thought to be that of the end of the older phase of the Vinça group. No traces of ore were found in the shafts which had been filled in with clay earth and small and large size blocks.

The country rock is generally soft and so primitive methods of extraction sufficed, i.e. antler tools and stone hammers as in flint mining. Firesetting in the limestone, even if known, was not necessary. Deer horn picks were mostly used for scraping or raking or to widen breaks in the ore veins. The hammer stones were rounded, right angled or triangular. Shaft 6a, discovered by Jovanovic in 1974–75, proved to be the best example (see Fig. 89b). This was positioned in a horizontal layer between massive limestone blocks and on the walls were side crevices which had been used for storing pottery, large pots, stone and bone tools. Shaft 5b was over 10 m deep.

The present day opencast mines which are worked for magnetite had cut through Eneolithic shafts and adits and also those of late Roman times and partially destroyed them. Many shafts had been found before the opencast face had reached them.

A comparable Late Eneolithic mine is at Aibunar (see Fig. 88) near Stara Zagora in South Bulgaria. This mine was excavated by Cernych with a Bulgarian–Russian team. Renfrew (1978) refers to the mines there as offering an impressive sight having an appearance of narrow fissures in the rock 2 or 3 m deep, and today cleared to a depth of 4–5 m. Two shaft hole tools of copper were found during the excavations. This mine and Rudna Glava are the two oldest known prehistoric copper mines in the world. According to Renfrew the finds at Aibunar and those at Varna, a site on the Bulgarian Black Sea coast, suggest that metal working developed into a considerable industry during the fifth millennium. Cernych (1978) describes the results of excavations carried out there in 1971, when the mines were first discovered, and later in the following year. There are 11 mines along the outcrop of malachite ore although rarely some azurite is present. The workings generally consisted of openpits and shafts. Numerous burials were found and one mine yielded sherds and antler tools. Another had been excavated to 18–20 m and the openpit here was 5·5 m in diameter and 4 m deep. Several interesting facts emerge from Cernych's investigations. The most important is the evidence of an immense working area which was, according to Cernych, exploited by full time or professional miners as evidenced possibly by settlements quite close to the mines. Smelting was carried out at some distance from the mining area as no adjacent furnaces have been found. In settlements some distance away copper ore has been found corresponding to that worked at Aibunar, but numerous copper implements at these sites have chemical compositions not related to the mined ores.

In South East Bulgaria, 7 km south-west of Burgas, is the prehistoric copper mine of Karabajir where there are three veins each about 2 m wide. In prehistoric times the most southerly of these was removed for nearly a kilometre by a series of trenches 50 m long and more than 40 m deep and connected underground by rock arches. Apparently the other two veins were less important and instead of cuts were attacked by rows of shafts 8–15 m apart and probably connected underground. The veins were completely removed in all cases probably by firesetting, Davies (1932). The ore worked was malachite having less than 9% copper, but no arsenic, tin, antimony, silver, bismuth, zinc, cobalt or nickel. The ore was broken up with porphyry hammers. Davies says that the Karabajir mine was of Early Iron Age date. A second mine, Rosenbajir, lies 24 km from Burgas and 4 km south of Cape Atija. This mine was probably worked in prehistoric times, but was certainly exploited by the Romans in a later period of its operation. The technique of working resembled that of Karabajir, i.e. several veins were exploited by trenches and at deeper levels by several shafts sunk from them and there were many underground galleries. The ore consisted of chalcopyrite having 30% copper and 29·8% iron with much sulphur.

Turkey, Iran and Cyprus

Turkey has often been referred to as the "cradle of mining", but essential developments in extraction of minerals are not assumed to have started until the Old Kingdom era in Anatolia, around 1750 BC. Today it is well known that reasonably advanced mining was existent in other countries well before that date. Indeed it is somewhat surprising that copper mining started later in Turkey than in several other countries, especially as today this country has two per cent of the world's copper reserves in addition to important reserves of other essential minerals. In 1973 100 million tons of copper pyrites were discovered at the entrance to the Dardenelles at Canakkale and in the area of Murgul on the North Turkish border, also 50 km from Soviet occupied Batum. The mine production of metallic copper today is approximately 20 000 t per annum, of which about 1000 t is exported. So why was copper not mined much earlier? If it is true that there are no visible workings earlier than those already known, it is possible that extensive native copper deposits of a surfacial nature have long been worked out or are obliterated. On the other hand bronze technology might have developed solely with imported ores. It appears certain that had copper been available in Anatolia, in the time of Troy, it would not have been brought in from the Balkans. Wertime (1964) asserts that native copper lay in a belt stretching east from Ankara, one in the Corum province, one in Tokat and a third in Gümüshäne. Analysis of a deposit from near Ankara gave 99·83% copper. So far tin has not been found in Turkey.

A prehistoric copper mine was discovered at Kozlu in northern Turkey in the 1970s by Giles and Kuijpers (1974) and according to these workers, the Government of Finland gave a radiocarbon date to wood found on the site as 2800 ± 30 BC. This date if correct presents an isolated exception to what has already been said and the site in fact has been described as the oldest radiocarbon dated copper mine. There was evidence of sophisticated sub-surface excavation according to Giles and Kuijpers.

Kozlu lies in the western Pontic mountain range at an elevation of 1300 m, 80 km south of the Black Sea port of Samsun, 30 km north-west of Tokat and 300 km north-east of Ankara. It is interesting that Tokat lies near the Bronze Age sites of Horoztepe and Mahmatlan and 165 km from the ruins of Hattusas (Boghazköy), the ancient Hittite capital.

The deposit is copper sulphide which originally outcropped with a dip of 60°. There is considerable secondary CuO_2 due to percolation of alkaline ground water. The copper sulphide lies in a schist.

Extensive timber was used in the mine and the authors of the article suggest extensive deforestation to supply this requirement. It is not possible to be certain of the actual method of working, but it is suggested that primitive underhand stoping in steps was employed with a stope width of 3–5 m and that with this method the incidence of roof falls was frequent. Probably the vein was exploited for a distance of at least 300 m.

Holzer (1971) describes copper mines in the Veshnoveh area in west central Iran (see Fig. 90). It has always been assumed that Iran was rich in copper and other minerals and supplied Mesopotamia, which had no

Fig. 90. Location of copper mines in Veshnoveh area, W. Central Iran. 1 Mazrayah mine, 2 Laghe Morad mine, 3 Chale Ghar mine. Acknowledgements to Holzer and Franz Deuticke, Vienna.

such raw materials, in exchange for finished goods. Various routes for trade have been suggested, but only vague reference has been made to the actual sources of the minerals. Very old workings were discovered in 1969 in the Veshnoveh area of the highlands of Qom at an altitude of 1120 m. Three deposits were found at Mazrayah 1·5 km south of Veshnoveh, at Chale Ghar 4·5 km south-south-west of that area and at Laghe Morad 4 km to the south-east. The main deposits are of chalcocite and malachite forming thin veins and veinlets along cracks and joints of the host rock which is of igneous origin.

Holzer gives a description of the three mines investigated. At Mazorayeh cave like diggings were exposed and the bottom of the drifts were covered by rock falls in which bones and teeth were found, but no pottery. Chale Ghar had two or three narrow tunnels which after a few metres led to a network of small gophers, narrow stopes and short inclines. A well preserved pot was found. Old drifts at Laghe Morad were investigated in some detail and there were eight or ten such underground

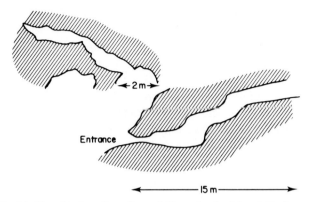

Fig. 91. Sketch of profiles of two drifts at Leghe Morod Veshnoveh.

workings located on the eastern slopes of a ridge, Fig. 91. Some adits had almost been completely filled with rock debris and soil. Entrances were either narrow tunnels or low cave like openings. The walls and roofs were rounded and smooth. Well preserved stone mining mauls were found, but pottery was rare. Holzer (1971) comments on the dearth of signs of mining activity, e.g. no evidence of explosives, metal tool marks from drilling etc. and so he suggests that firesetting was used or hammering with simple stone tools. Usually, however, when firesetting has been used there is some evidence such as soot marks, burnt wood etc. Crude mining tools of dark green magmatic rocks foreign to the area were found. These weighed 1225–1900 g and were well rounded. Holzer makes the astonishing suggestion that as similar stone mauls have been found in China and Russia it might indicate the migration of ancient craftsmen to Europe, Palestine and Central Asia!

An unglazed vessel was found at Chale Ghar which could be correlated with the Djemdat Nasr level of Mesopotamia 3200–3000 BC. If this is correct then Chale Ghar represents an intermediate or transitional phase between the Eneolithic and the Bronze Age as suggested as follows:

Rudna Glava	Yugoslavia	c. 4000 BC Eneolithic
Aibunar	Bulgaria	c. 4000 BC Eneolithic
Chale Ghar	Iran	c. 3200 BC Bronze Age
Mitterberg	Austria	c. 1700 BC Bronze Age
Kozlu	Turkey	c. 2800 BC Bronze Age

Such an assessment is based on very few actual reliable dates, however, and these are moreover spread over a wide geographical area. Holzer goes even further and suggests that the Veshnoveh mines, extending from 3200 BC to AD 1700, represent the oldest metal producers in the world.

Crawford (1939) suggests five possible sources of tin in prehistoric times in the Near East: (1) Turkmenistan, (2) Angert, east of Alikhen Dagt, (3) Tillek, in the vicinity of Surp Carabet, (4) Asterabad and (5) Drangian. These are with the exception of the first, based on visible signs of veined tin.

After c. 2000 BC copper was discovered in Cyprus, but there is no valid evidence of Bronze Age mining on the island. As Davies (1932) points out it must be doubtful if Cyprus supplied copper to the Aegean so early and alternatively Anatolia, Sinai, or Syria might have been involved. Cyprus has always been associated with copper and this is based partly on the name of the island and on the fact that in classical times copper mining flourished. There is no sign of prehistoric mining although the thorough and intensive development of the Roman mines would have destroyed all available evidence. Some stone tools, which could have been dated possibly from the Iron Age were found, but no early type moulds have been discovered. The Bronze Age settlements were located mostly away from the copper deposits on the massif. These facts provide evidence, according to Davies (1928), against prehistoric mining on the island.

Iberia

Some of the most famous ancient copper mines of the world are located near Huelva in South West Spain, but the pyrite deposits here were never worked by prehistoric man. These mines, in the Rio Tinto district, however, are probably the longest worked mines, at least in the western world, being exploited by the Phoenicians and later by the Romans. It is also thought that the Phoenicians mined the gossan for silver and gold. There are Roman shafts and opencuts (43 BC) still visible and the huge Roman slag heaps were once used for the supply of ballast for the local railways according to Bateman (1927).

More recent work has been carried out at the Rio Tinto mines in the Huelva district by the Institute of Archaeo-Metallurgical Studies and described by Wilson (1977). Surprisingly evidence of workings, which were reputed to be much older than even those of the Phoenicians, was found. The investigators had previously worked at Timna in the Sinai Peninsula (see later section in this chapter) and it is noted that there was a similarity both in time and operation to these mines. The deposits stretch from Seville to the Portuguese border and were surveyed somewhat unsystematically many years ago with no discovery of pre-Phoenician workings. There are three types of mineralization, (a) gossan head, i.e. oxidized, (b) overlying strata containing unoxidized copper ore and (c) below sulphide pyritic ore of copper plus silver, iron and gold. A 20 m quartz and calcitic intrusion in the form of a dyke, oxidized on top, was ideal for prehistoric smelting. The dyke can be traced as an outcrop along the surface and is marked by an absence of trees. Apart from smelters' huts and megaliths there is no evidence of habitation of the megalithic period. Early miners of the fourth millennium BC had extracted this malachite vein often only a few centimetres thick from quartz outcrops with primitive rilled stones shaped like axes leaving behind irregular trench like workings several metres deep. There were round hammer marks and the actual tools were discovered on the hill. Only a fragment of a furnace wall was found and the content of the slag was around 2%. There were small pieces of copper and slag. The mine referred to must have had a very low output. In a second mine, which was identical with the first, some Phoenician pottery was found which was of the Early Bronze Age dating possibly from the end of the second millenium BC. The miners of Phoenician times went deeper, but stopped when they reached pyritic ore which according to Professor Rothenberg was not roasted in very early times.

At Cuchellares there are outcrops of rhyolite containing traces of malachite and evidence of many primitive mines including the finds of crude hammers. These represented the very early stages of mining there being no pottery and only a handful of slag. Malachite was sandwiched in red gossan which would have made a good flux giving an excellent copper. Some of the slag heaps in Huelva are 30–40 m high so the undertakings must have been quite large.

The objective behind the work directed by Professor Rothenberg was to map the layout of the industry. It was difficult to convert the quantity of slag to that of copper as too many preparation problems are involved. In the second–third centuries the mining had to be stopped owing to the lack of wood for charcoal all the forests having been cleared.

One of the advantages to the investigator at Huelva is that modern opencast mining is exposing full sections of the slag and so the full history of metal preparation can be deduced. In the Late Bronze Age c. 900 BC, only silver was being worked and chiefly from the galena which was present.

Unfortunately after many years of investigation no complete furnace of prehistoric age has been found at Huelva so the intention is, in order to achieve the proposed objective, to make a mathematical model from the data acquired. The author is grateful to Professor Rothenberg for permitting him to use much of the material concerning both Huelva and Timna (1979, pers. comm.).

Iberia was unique in the development of its mining and metallurgy. Some writers have suggested influence by migrations from the eastern Mediterranean region, but there was no necessity for prospectors to search for Iberian ores as copper deposits are prolific in the Balkans and Near East. Thus Renfrew (1967) strongly suggests an independent development from the Neolithic to the full Chalcolithic or Eneolithic for Iberia with self sufficient identification and the working of extensive mineral ores, especially copper, which is widely scattered and tin of North West Spain. Tin, however, is scarce and was probably imported and Childe (1957) suggests that copper was worked locally on a larger scale in the Bronze Age than in the Eneolithic.

The three areas thought at one time to contain the chief prehistoric copper mines are (1) Asturias in the north, (2) Lerida near the French border in the north-east and (3) Alicante in the south-east. Savory (1968) remarks that up to the present modern work on implement analysis has not been followed up by further work on the numerous ancient copper mines on the peninsula, which have produced waisted mauls like those found at El Argar. Some of these mines appear in fact to have yielded Early Bronze Age implements such as Argaric daggers and flat axes as at the Mina de Milagro (Asturias), a "Palmela" arrowhead and a flat axe at mines in the Alemtejo and flat axe moulds, as shown in Fig. 92, at Riner (Lerida) and the Mola Alta de Serelles (Alicante).

Sanders (1910) describes the experiences in 1888 of Mr Van Straalen who was the manager of copper mines at Mieres de Milagro in the

Fig. 92. Early Bronze Age flat axe moulds from Alicante, Spain. Acknowledgements to Museo Prehistoria de Valencia.

province of Oviedo in North Spain. He noticed the leaves of a tree being agitated violently on a day when there was no wind or even the slightest movement of the atmosphere, and discovered a current of air from an "old man's shaft" which was connected with the old workings of the Aramo copper mine. The shafts were small and vertical and the copper ore was in dolomite. The prehistoric miner was probably attracted by native copper or by the rich nodules of black oxide of copper containing up to 72% of the metal in the outcrop. There had been a fall of ground and a skeleton was found in approximately the same position as the one at Obourg in Belgium. The ore was taken to the surface in wooden hods to which a leather ring or handle was fixed to allow them to be dragged along the ground in very narrow places. Rock was used to make pillars for the support of the roof. For lighting fire sticks of resinous wood were used as at Mitterberg in Austria. These were inserted into lumps of clay and fixed to the gallery sides. Deer horn picks were used to hack the ore from the dolomite. There is also another prehistoric mine at Canges di Ouis, near Mieres and which is very similar to Aramo.

Sinai

Timna Valley was first mentioned by Petherick in 1861 as a possible site of ancient smelting and was partly explored by Musil in 1902, Frank in 1934 and Glueck in 1935. Professor Beno Rothenberg (1972) made an exhaustive investigation between 1959 and 1964 with the primary objective of discovering the site of King Solomon's mines and this work together with his later studies there in the 1970s has added a vast amount to existing knowledge of prehistoric and ancient mining in the Middle East. In fact there is an area of 72 km² containing remains of copper working extending from the fourth millennium to late Roman times. Included in these are large scale mines operated by expeditions from Egypt under the Pharoahs from the fourteenth to the thirteenth century BC. Shafts and gallery mines date back on the basis of pottery finds to the Early Bronze Age.

In 1976 an Early Bronze Age mine dating back to 3000 BC was found in white sandstone, which was rich in malachite, with some azurite, cuprite and chalcocite. This was a large low cavern, the floor of which was strewn with copper ore and remains of stone tools some of which were round and square hammers drilled through to take shafts. Over 100 m of tunnels were cleared. Narrow shafts had been driven upwards according to the location of tool marks on the walls. These shafts were unsuitable for transport or access and it was suggested that they were used solely for ventilation and illumination.

An Eneolithic furnace of the fourth millennium BC was found on a hilltop. A large stone was moved and underneath was a mixture of burnt sand and slag fragments beneath which was a pit filled with burnt material containing 2·5% copper along with more slag. The furnace was bowl shaped, 25–30 cm deep and lined with a wall of compact sandstone, the width of the furnace being only 45 cm. At the bottom were burnt grey remains of siliceous material. A working surface in the vicinity had scattered debris of slag, charcoal, flint tools and pottery sherds which helped to date the furnace. This find provided valuable evidence of actual smelting of copper in Eneolithic times.

The smelting furnaces were mostly holes in the ground and later ones were made with stones of sandstone since the granite which is present on the site would have disintegrated with the heat. The flux used to secure reduction was iron oxide and the slag contained iron silicate and 50–60% of metallic copper. In very primitive furnaces there was no iron in the copper and after heating at 1300 °C for 8 h, the copper went through the slag and took iron with it. Conversely the later or Roman copper contained over 10% iron. No bellows were found, but they must have been used. During the Early Bronze Age in Sinai the first fortified cities were built and were accompanied by an enormous increase in metallurgical processing. At another site on a ridge a long Neolithic level containing azurite was found.

During the investigations in the 1970s a large workshop yard was found and what were originally thought to be cisterns were actually preparation pits. Crucibles were found along with wood ash. Tools consisted of crushing and grinding stones including stone hammers for preparation. Many metal mining tools were also discovered during the excavation of the site. Three different types of Iron Age pottery are thought not to represent three separate sites, but three different peoples settling and working in the vicinity. The big Eneolithic bowl furnace must have required at least four or even six bellows in the upper part of the furnace. The many copper and bronze objects found indicate some casting and probably some of these were goddess figures cast in moulds and given to the temple which had been found in 1969.

A site known as Timna Circle was found, but there was no habitation here, only a workshop with slag heaps. There was a wall with towers around and these were probably for defence. Aerial photography has disclosed tracks made by men going to and fro between the site and the mines in the sandstone cliffs 3·5 km away.

Russia and Poland

In East European Russia there are three sources of copper, i.e. in the Urals, in sandstone west of the Urals and in the region north of the Turkish border which lies between the Caspian and Black Seas and is known as Transcaucasia. There is native copper in the Caucasus as well as copper ores, but there is no tin in any of the three areas mentioned. The richest deposits of tin are to be found in Siberia and the Altai Mountains.

Sulimirski (1970) refers to traces of ancient mining in several areas of the Caucasus, South East Ukraine and the Urals. He mentions wide artificial caves on the steep bank of the river Kama and its tributaries which have been dug out in the search for ores. Some ancient mines have been uncovered at Magnitogorsk consisting of ancient shafts up to 20 m deep and galleries up to 210 m in length. Copper was smelted on the spot close to the mines or outcrops. There have been finds of slag, moulds, crucibles, pestles and hammers. If these mines were prehistoric the shafts were unusually deep and the galleries longer than so far known for such workings. Sulimirski suggests that oriental prospectors came from Troy II by sea to the mouth of the river Kuban and travelled by that river to the highland. A copper ore mine was found further east in the Altai Mountains near Ust Kan 2000 m above sea level. Among the finds were perforated stone hammer axes and wedges plus wooden tools, leather straps, elk hides and other equipment. These were apparently preserved in deep frozen ground for a few thousand years. It has been supposed that prospectors initiated this venture from the Caucasus. Siberia is rich in prehistoric copper mines.

There was some controversy in the 1950s and 1960s concerning the use of native copper and copper alloys for artefacts in Transcaucasia in the Eneolithic. Native copper, being too soft for weaponry and tools, it is logical to assume that the alternative would have been sought after. Caucasus is rich in lead, arsenic and copper and alloys could have been copper/tin or copper/arsenic or even copper/lead. Any tin used would have been obtained from the South Urals. Tuadze and Sakvarelidze (1959) state that native copper was used in Georgia in the Eneolithic. Silimkhanov (1964), however, disputes this and gives results of analyses of native copper from Azerbaijan, Armenia and Georgia which are at variance with the analyses of the earliest artifacts. Of 35 copper axes from Central Europe, dating from 2400 to 2000 BC, only seven were of native copper. It appears that alloys, such as copper/arsenic as indicated earlier, were used in Transcaucasia as early as the Eneolithic, but not native copper, which, however, could have been reserved for non-military objects.

Two principal Lengyel sites in Poland have yielded distinct traces of copper working. In the south at Zløta there were signs of copper casting dating to *c.* 2400 BC and in the north at Brzesc Kujawski there was evidence of hammering of copper tools and the preparation of semi finished objects in the form of bars and ingots according to Jazdzewski (1965).

8
Iron and Other Materials

In the prehistoric world after copper, tin and their alloy bronze, iron became gradually the most important basic metal at least for industrial use. Today it is, without doubt, the most important and has been in Europe since the Iron Age i.e. *c* 750 BC.

Iron

The metal in the form of oxides, sulphides etc. is a constituent of many rock types and next to aluminium, is possibly the most common in the earth's crust, amounting to approximately 4·5%. In the mid 1970s the total known world production of iron ore was 765 million t, of which the Soviet Union produced 203 million t, the USA 82 million t and Australia 62 million t. A very large proportion of the total production is worked by quarrying or the opencast method. The significant factor is therefore the problem concerning the reason why early man did not exploit such outcrops of iron ore earlier than he is supposed to have done. However, it must be remembered that even by opencast methods, iron is being exploited today at very great depths with the help of high capacity modern equipment and methods, a typical example being the giant excavations for taconite, a low grade iron ore, in the Mesabi Range in Minnesota, USA. Another factor is the comparative low iron content of many of the ores being worked today which could have created serious difficulties for primitive man. In Britain the rich Cumberland haematites are almost worked out whereas there are considerable reserves of lower quality Jurassic ores, Carboniferous siderite ores, etc. remaining. Mikami (1944) gives a very useful summary of the proved and potential reserves of iron in the world and these are shown, for the Western world, in Fig. 93 which is adapted from his map.

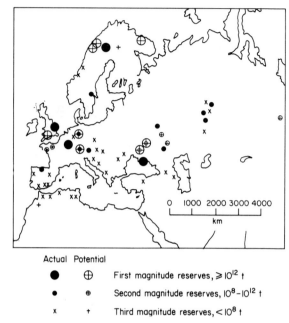

Actual Potential

●   ⊕   First magnitude reserves, $\geqslant 10^{12}$ t

•   ⊕   Second magnitude reserves, $10^8 - 10^{12}$ t

x   +   Third magnitude reserves, $< 10^8$ t

Fig. 93. Iron ore reserves. Acknowledgements to H. M. Mikami and Economic Geology, Minnesota, USA.

History of the Use of Iron

Lack of archaeological evidence and the difficulties of recognizing metal derived by man from the ores, led to some people, in the nineteenth Century, to presume that the so-called Iron Age preceded the Bronze Age. Gowland (1902), for example, appears to support this view and quoted Percy (1873), who said specifically that the Iron Age was earlier than the Bronze Age since it is easy to extract malleable iron direct from the ore. It was possible to reduce completely a block of red or brown haematite by heating it for a few hours well surrounded by charcoal and to forge it at red heat into a bar of iron. Some early authors referred to the numerous iron remains found in association with Bronze and Late Stone Age relics. The fact that iron rusts easily, when exposed to oxygen, does not help the argument. Iron objects have survived for nearly 3000 years, so under conditions of suitable burial, could remain in comparative reasonable condition for a further 2000 years or more. There will continue to be some element of controversy even today, especially if some new archaeological find reveals pre-Iron Age artefacts made from iron ore. As Rickard (1932) points out, the archaeological study of the subject has been confused by failure to distinguish between man-made and heaven-sent iron.

The Iron Age was a term given to one of the three ages and marked the major use of iron as distinct from that of meteoric iron. Woolley found iron at Ur dating from 3000 BC and Wainwright (1936) beads of iron at Gergah, south of Cairo, dating from 3500 BC. Both these were of high nickel meteoric iron about which more will be said later. The Iron Age actually commenced with the so-called Hallstatt C1 phase in Europe in c. 750 BC, but the Hittites had iron in the fifteenth century BC. The Anatolian Hittites came to power in c. 1800 BC and developed the use of iron. Until their collapse and that of Mycenae in 1200 BC, such iron was in great demand, especially by the Egyptians as a minor trade commodity. Their collapse led to a greater diffusion of the knowledge of iron and this reached Greece in c. 1100 BC, Italy in c.900 BC and northern Europe in about 750–700 BC (Hallstatt C1). Evidence from the Celts is available.

Although, as already indicated, iron was not in major use in Europe until the Iron Age, there is sporadic evidence of its use before this date. For example an iron chisel was found alongside a timber trackway in Holland dating from 1200–1000 BC. Decorations on Swedish bronzes were made by iron tools. The periods prior and up to the Iron Age are:

Reinecke D	1250–1200 BC	
Hallstatt A1	1200–1100 BC	
Hallstatt A2	1100–1000 BC	Late Bronze Age
Hallstatt B1	1000–900 BC	
Hallstatt B2	900–750 BC	
Hallstatt C1	750–	Iron Age

All the early iron was of the wrought type and being scarce and expensive, was reserved for jewellery and decoration during the early stages of its use and being more precious than gold, the use of flint, stone and bronze tools and weaponry continued. Although iron was plentiful in Egypt, Petrie (1900) points out that there was no industrial use of iron there before c. 800 BC.

Despite the scarcity of copper it is surprising that iron took a long time to replace bronze with its superior cutting edge for tools and weapons and the more abundant resources. There has been some consideration of the reason why eventually the use of bronze declined and iron increased in the so-called Iron Age. Probably there was an increasing difficulty in obtaining tin and disruption of trade routes resulted which can possibly be established by future archaeological excavations and analysis of articles made of bronze and iron

Types of Iron and Iron Ore

The first iron known to man was meteoric iron and is the purest form of iron in the native state. One of the earliest references to it occurs in the Sumerian texts of Mesopotamia when it was known as an-bar or "fire from heaven". It is highly possible that primitive man, however, often made use of it without knowing its origin.

The British Museum has 289 meteorites dating from 1875 to 1914. Some of the largest examples have been found in Greenland, i.e. at Bacubiri, weighing 50 tons, Ahnighito 36·5 tons and Chupaderos 15·5 tons. Wainwright (1936) mentions that meteorites can be split up into three classes, i.e. (a) large as in the examples already given, (b) average size varying from dust to the size of a man's head and (c) a mixture of iron and stone.

It was once thought that artifacts made from meteoric iron had been forged from iron derived from mined ore. No ore of iron contains the high amount of nickel, common to meteorites, which can vary from 5 to 26% and this is one means of identification of artefacts made from meteoritic iron. Secondly it is extremely malleable and pieces can be hammered or chiselled off the parent block. The Descabridora meteorite of Mexico, according to Friend (1926), weighs 575 kg and has a gap 9 cm long in which is wedged a copper chisel left by some primitive workman. The high content of nickel not only increases malleability, but helps to reduce rusting. Of the known 275 tons in museums, 94·4% is malleable. Europeans travelling in the Arctic region as late as 1771 and 1818 found Eskimos using implements made from meteoritic iron, it being the only source of iron available to them. When Spaniards invaded Mexico they were surprised to find some of the Aztec chiefs having many knives and daggers made of iron, although there were no signs of smelting furnaces. According to Rickard (1941), when asked where the iron originated the Aztecs pointed to the sky. It was found that they could easily detach pieces of the metal from a meteorite.

Meteoric iron is the only free type of iron, all other types must be obtained from the ores by mining or quarrying. The chief types of iron ores are:

Haematite: sesquioxide of iron Fe_2O_3. This has a black to red colour and contains 70% of iron. It occurs in nodular masses known as "kidney ore" or as earthy masses of red ochre.

Magnetite: double oxide of iron $FeO \cdot Fe_2O_3$ or Fe_3O_4. This is black and is a rich ore giving 72·4% of iron. Unfortunately it is becoming rare.

Limonite: a hydrated form of haematite $2Fe_2O_3 \cdot 3H_2O$. It contains 60%

iron and is brown, fibrous or earthy. It is formed by a weathering process as bog iron concretions.

Siderite: carbonate of iron $FeCO_3$ or chalybite or spathic ore. It contains $48\cdot3\%$ of iron and can vary in colour from yellow, red, brown to black. It occurs as a bedded ironstone deposit in the Coal Measures of the Carboniferous and also in the Jurassic limestones of Northamptonshire, Lincolnshire and Yorkshire.

Iron pyrites: iron sulphide FeS_2. This ore is known colloquially as "fool's gold" and is of little practical value owing to smelting difficulties.

Marcasite: disulphide of iron FeS_2. It occurs in the chalk of the South Downs including the cliffs from Dover to Folkestone.

All iron ores have a primary igneous source, occurring either as solidification of magma or being deposited from solutions on beds of lakes, sea or swamp during oolitic rock sedimentation.

Sources of Iron in Prehistory

It has been shown that there is evidence of the existence of a vast number of prehistoric silex mines both of the openpit and shaft types, far less evidence of copper mines, but quite appreciable when compared to those of iron and the remaining minerals to be considered later. The explanation for the differences in the numbers of silex, copper and iron mines varies for each group. Silex was plentiful and was mined in all parts of the world. With the discovery of copper and later iron its importance as a useful commodity declined and, at least in the developed countries, lost much of its industrial or commercial value. Therefore old workings and deposits remained, undestroyed by more modern excavations, for posterity to investigate. Copper on the other hand was scarce and occurrence of it limited to only a few countries of the world. Scarcity led to the exploitation of most known sources and in the process often the destruction of prehistoric mines. When no longer used for tools and weaponry copper, tin and the alloy bronze found other applications and even today are in great demand, their scarcity inflating market prices. When iron is considered the position is relatively unique. Reserves of deposits of iron were and still are vast in most countries of the world. The metal is still increasing in industrial importance despite the advent of today's plastics, lighter metals etc. Deposits of low grade oxidized ores are being increasingly worked and outcrops and shallow ores are being exhausted. Prehistoric man after his apprenticeship with meteoric iron turned his attention to the shallow ores and worked them. He had no need to sink shafts, but merely to dig out the ore wherever it was visible. Any possible surface iron mines would have been destroyed by later workings. Consequently evidence of prehistoric iron mining is virtually non-existent. However by identifying smelting sites and the discarded slag, studying the geology of an area and carrying out spectographic analyses of the iron and other metals in prehistoric tools and weapons, it is possible to estimate with a fair degree of reliability the area from which the ore was extracted.

Although there is a dearth of knowledge concerning the existence of actual iron ore mines of Iron Age date or earlier, there are extensive references to mines of Roman age or later, but many of these as in other contexts are not wholly reliable. Forbes (1964) lists mines which were supposed to have been worked during the Iron Age such as Bibracte and Come Chandron in Nievre, France, Polish mines such as Dahern in Pomerania and Siedlemin near Posen, Lutmersin and Muelhausen in the Harz district of West Germany, Tarxdorf in East German Silesia, Petros in Greece and Rudia in Czechoslovakian Moravia. He also includes Sana of North Bosnia in Yugoslavia which according to Forbes worked well into the Middle Ages. Siedlemin mine is also reputed to have continued working well into Roman times.

Britain

There is no doubt that extraction of iron from the ores, even if only in a crude manner, was in operation well before the Roman Conquest of Britain. It is recorded by classical authors, e.g. Caesar, how the invaders from Gaul were surprised to find the Britons armed with iron weapons. Caesar wrote in Bello Galleo VII 23 concerning the skill of the miners. There is also some mention of the ineffectiveness of the soft iron swords of the Britons against the bronze swords of the Romans. The former are reported to have bent easily when struck whereas the invaders' swords remained straight.

The British Isles are rich in iron today although many of the better qualities have been worked out. One of the most important sources of iron in prehistoric times was the Weald in Sussex. In fact it has been claimed by Straker (1931) that iron was smelted here as early as neolithic times. The beds comprising the geological formations of the Weald are:

Chalk	Upper Cretaceous	
Upper Greensand		
Gault		Marine Deposition
Lower Greensand	Lower Cretaceous	
Weald Clay		
Hastings Beds		Fresh Water Deposition

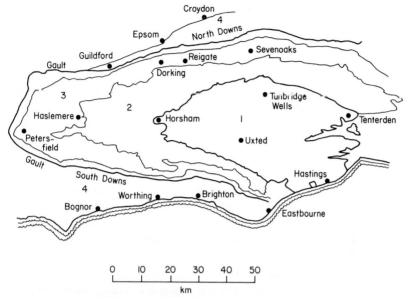

Fig. 94. Simplified sketch map of the Weald.

The actual so called Wealdon Beds comprise the Weald Clay and Hastings Beds whereas the Chalk in the north and south of the area constitute the escarpments of the North and South Downs respectively. This is shown in Fig. 16 and Fig. 94 is a sketch map of the Weald of Sussex and part of Kent.

Most of the carbonate iron ores come from the Weald Clay i.e. the lower beds of the Wadhurst Clay and the middle beds of the Hastings Sands, although Straker mentions the existence of ferruginous veins in other beds. In the Weald Clay beds there is much evidence of old mine pits, but none of occupation. It is here that the Romans soon after their successful invasion are reputed to have continued and expanded the existing ironworks. In the lower Greensand there is a brown siliceous ironstone called "carrstone", but there is no evidence of it having been smelted.

The actual smelting process necessitated excessive consumption of charcoal. The iron is long exhausted, but working originally declined owing to scarcity of wood arising from the destruction of the forests.

Numerous mine pits have been found at Crowhurst Park near Battle in Sussex. These are represented by large depressions up to ten metres in depth. They are supposed by three authors, Wilson (1955) and Straker and Lucas (1938) to be British-Romano. The Weald area probably represents what were the nearest iron deposits to London and in fact no iron ore has been found within a 50 mile radius of London, east, west or north. There might have been ores, but they could have been exhausted in prehistoric times.

Early Iron Age sites have been found on the Chilterns in Buckinghamshire at Chinnor, Bledlow and Ellesborough. Associated with these sites were smooth grits, burnt flints and iron slag. The nearest ore is in the Lias Marlstone, near Fawler, about 27 miles away. All the sites are quite near the Upper Icknield Way and the Ridgeway (Richardson and Young 1951).

It does appear, as Clark (1952) points out, that iron slag remnants found on any Iron Age settlement site indicate proximity to a source of iron ore. For example, there is close agreement between Hallstatt settlement habitats and the iron deposits in France. Early Iron Age settlers in Hampshire made use of the nodular marcasite found in the local chalk. All Cannings Cross, in Wiltshire, yielded slag and iron ore, some of it partly calcined, which was available some ten miles away on the Lower Greensand near Seend. It is possible, according to Fell (1936) that the Hunsbury Hill Iron Age fort in Northamptonshire was chosen in proximity to the siderite deposits which it actually overlies. Ironstone working at the end of the nineteenth century not only disclosed the camps, but destroyed some of the evidence. Archaeological excavation revealed 300 pits of various sizes from 1·5 m to 3 m in diameter and averaging 2 m deep. Rarely did the pits penetrate the ironstone. One pit contained a crouched skeleton. Others were possibly huts, or even storage pits or possibly pits for refuse. It was assumed that the Iron Age settlers could not have worked the ironstone yet a considerable amount of slag was found.

There is iron in the copper deposits of Alderley Edge in Cheshire and this was worked extensively by the Romans, but Sagui (1933) mentions lack of evidence of earlier working.

Roeder (1901) points out that there were large ironworks and mines at Coleford in the Forest of Dean in Roman times. Fox and Hyde (1939) suggest that early iron working was practised by a few families in the Forest of Dean, in c. 500 BC, and this would appear to be a reasonable hypothesis. Here the ore is more easily worked than say the ore in the Wealdon Beds, and, according to Fox and Hyde could have been worked fully by folk who had no more appliances than would enable them to go down 5–7 m. The authors found objects to which they gave a tentative date of 700–400 BC. In this area the deposits occur in the Carboniferous Limestone and Drybrook Sandstone which form an outcrop running

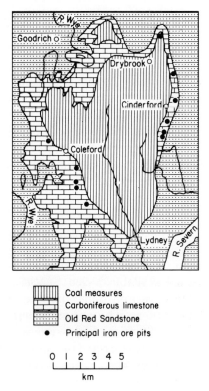

Coal measures
Carboniferous limestone
Old Red Sandstone
● Principal iron ore pits

0 1 2 3 4 5
km

Fig. 95. Geology of the Forest of Dean. 1 Wodhurst clay, Hastings beds, 2 Weald clay, 3 Lower Greensand, 4 Chalk. Acknowledgements to the Antiquaries Journal.

approximately north–south underlying the coal measures which outcrop in the neighbourhood of Coleford (see Fig. 95).

The massive industry of the Roman invaders soon after AD 43 and which continued for four hundred years, has unfortunately destroyed any evidence of prehistoric iron ore mining, as well as that of any other possible extraction of other important ores.

Macalister (1949) mentions the existence of iron in several other localities in the British Isles, amongst them Ireland, but there are no records of any prehistoric iron mining elsewhere.

Scandinavia

Peasant culture developed in the Iron Age in some countries partly as a result of the recognition and working of bog ores. Such ores have been produced as a result of heavy rainfall in countries of Scandinavia especially in Norway. Even today such ores are being worked by peasant communities. Brøgger (1940) suggests that they were worked in prehistoric times only during slack periods in the farming year.

Bog ore is not as free from impurities as, for example, haematite which contains usually not more than 8% magnesia, alumina, silica and lime. Bog ore, such as limonite, may have up to 25%. In Jutland limonite bog ore has been mined prehistorically under Iron Age tumuli.

The formation of bog ore is a relatively simple process. It requires the action of rain water which accumulates in stagnant pools, hence the name bog. As soil builds up from the bottom compounds or iron oxides, which have been formed in the soil, are precipitated as lumps of limonite in an earthy brown form.

Hungary

Hungary is one of the few countries from which details of actual prehistoric iron mines are available. Velem St Vid in western Hungary, quoted as the earliest known iron mine, dates apparently from Early Hallstatt times, i.e. 1100–800 BC. The iron ore, siderite, was worked with a 12 m diameter pit to a depth of 6 m. At this site excavators consider that a shaft 70 m deep must have existed at some time. The finds of antimony–bronze ingots have been dated, according to Bromehead (1940), to late Bronze Age times.

In 1951 a dolomite quarry near Lovas village on the shores of Lake Balaton exposed prehistoric bones. Earlier, in 1950, quarrymen had dug into a large cavity 5–6 m in diameter and 5 m deep filled with a crumbly red material finer in grain than the dolomite gravel. Meszaros and Vertes (1953) found a nest like red streak 1 m deep and 1·2 m wide under a layer of humus 50–60 cm deep. The pit eventually proved to be 20 m² in area. Sixty-one bone implements were found and seven antler tool fragments. There was also sporadic charcoal. A large wedge, apparently used for levering, was worn smooth. A spear point was shaped like a laurel leaf. The working was in red limonite of Early Upper Palaeolithic age, hence the term "paint mine". An ulna tool was burnt on one side and on the other ornamentation of a ladder pattern said by Vertes and his fellow author to be the first drawing by Palaeolithic man to be discovered in Hungary. There was evidence for firesetting, because the fires had been made in narrow places so these would not have been used for any other purpose. According to the excavators the paint was worked by the Szeleta cultures and dated, according to them, as 80 000 ± 5000 BC. Figure 96 shows a section through one of the excavated pits.

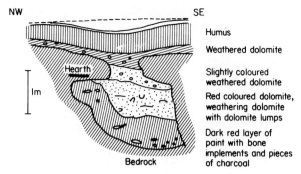

Fig. 96. Lovas paint mine-section through southern shaft of Pit No. 2. Acknowledgements to Acta Archaeologica, Budapest.

Other Localities

Red ochre has been used for decoration at least since Mousterian times, e.g. La Ferassie in France. It was used for cave paintings by Upper Palaeolithic man and in graves and in Neolithic times it was used for the decoration of pottery. It is still used by primitive man for body painting.

In Egypt there is much iron ore. Hawkes and Woolley (1963) presume that the industry began as a man made by-product of the refining of the gold gravels of Nubia having more than 6·5% iron. Half the residue in the pan after washing of the gold was magnetite. In West Sinai geological survey operations revealed heaps of excellent haematite at mouths of Egyptian copper mines according to Bromehead (1940).

Anatolia is rich in iron ores and these are normally easy to smelt. There were prehistoric mines in the Taurus Mountains, but they are now no longer visible. Speight (1948) suggests that such mines probably supplied Chaldea and Assyria.

Wertime (1964) examined the ancient mining area of Yazd in Iran and found a "bear" of iron 1 m in diameter issuing from a modernized lead smelter.

Villanovians and later the Etruscans were drawn to the ores of Tuscany in Italy and also those of Elba. Classical writers, such as Aristotle of the third century BC, have referred to the iron found on Elba. Actually iron was first known in Italy towards the close of the twelfth century BC. Sagui (1933) found on Mount Valerio in Tuscany cassiterite associated with iron ores and at Mount Rombola a peculiar ore which looked like clay ironstone, but also contained lead, tin and occasionally arsenic.

Haematite is said to have been mined in Poland during the Mesolithic period.

Boshier and Beaumont (1972) of the Anglo-American Corporation group have reported that haematite was mined in Southern Africa before 4000 BC and there are records of later mining here, but they are geographically somewhat outside the scope of the present book.

Metallic Iron Production

Like copper, but unlike silex, the extracted material must be treated to obtain the basic element for use in manufacture. Far more attention has been paid to studies of the processes of producing iron from the ore as used by early man than to prehistoric iron mining. As a result there are as many theories concerning the methods used by prehistoric man as for copper processing already considered. Most of the prehistoric processes continued to be used, with minor exceptions, until the Middle Ages. In fact in Europe there was little development until after about 600 BC. The Romans, however, used crude methods to obtain steel, but crucible steel was not really developed until the eleventh century AD.

Basically prehistoric man broke up the ore into a suitable size and heated it with charcoal producing a slag which was extracted from the furnace. The slag became molten and could be run off, the iron remaining in a spongy mass at the bottom of the furnace. The degree of success depended primarily on the temperature attained in the furnace which was in turn governed by the efficiency of the induced or forced draught used. Unfortunately a very large proportion of the iron remained behind in the slag, and later societies have reheated this to extract some of the iron which could have been as high in content as 60% of the slag.

The iron obtained by the early method is known as "bloomery" iron obtained in a "bloomery". The soft spongy mass was beat into shape with a hammer. Temperature is critical and although the iron can be reduced to a pasty mass at 800–900 °C, it requires a minimum temperature of 1535°C to achieve complete fusion and Hawkes and Woolley (1963) state that such a condition was not achieved until the fourteenth century AD.

Cleere (1972) mentions three basic types of furnace which are also those categorized by Coghlan (1956) as follows:

(a) a simple bowl furnace
(b) a domed or pot furnace
(c) a shaft furnace

The first metallurgists used the bowl furnace or a simple hole in the ground of hemispherical shape varying in diameter from 30 cm to 1·5 m and lined with clay. The hole was filled with charcoal and ore and formed a heap on the surface, the whole then probably being covered with turf, leaving a hole which was necessary for the escape of the gases. Some method of applying a forced draught was necessary and bellows were probably used. The two chief drawbacks were, (1) lack of provision for tapping off the slag and (2) no means of recharging the furnace. After each smelt it was necessary to dismantle the furnace in order to obtain the very limited quantity of bloomery iron. The slag settled at the bottom and consisted of silica and some iron oxide which solidified. The bloom iron

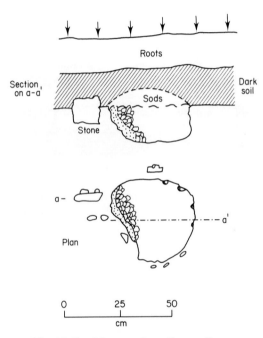

Fig. 97. Bowl furnace from Kestor, Devon.

remained as a spongy mass above the slag. Cleere estimates that production would be less than 1 kg with a furnace diameter of 30 cm consequently the open top furnace has been suggested so enabling additional charging to be carried out, but heat insulation and restriction of oxygen access to the reaction zone are essential. Figure 97 shows a type of bowl furnace.

The domed furnace has a circular hearth and with a domed housing built upwards and having a central opening. Stieren (1935) describes two types, one free standing and the other let into a hillside, remains of both having been found near Siegen in Westphalia. For this type of furnace, the construction of which is shown in Fig. 98, the draught could have been forced, or induced, by bellows. Stieren says that by positioning the furnace on a hillside and facing the prevailing wind, the draught would be sufficient to smelt the iron ore. Cleere however, as does Tylecote (1962), disputes this and considers that the draught would have been inadequate. The advantages of the domed furnace are that additional

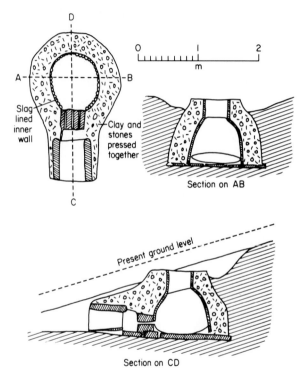

Fig. 98. Dome furnace E25 at Engsbachtel, Germany. Acknowledgements to A. Stieren and Romisch Germanische Kommission, Frankfurt.

charging can be carried out and there is also protection for the reaction zone by the clay and stone lining so a greater heat application can be obtained. There are numerous examples of this type of furnace having been used in western Europe, for example at Aalbuch in Württemberg and the one near Siegen described by Stieren. This type was also used during Roman times, and earlier during the La Tène phase of the Iron Age.

Normally the ore was prepared to the size of a walnut. Charcoal in western Europe generally came from beech and oak, which Stieren claims is the best for iron production. At 1100°C the first reduction took place and reduction continued above this temperature. A slag was produced which deprived the iron of further reduction. Smelting fluid and slag were produced in the bottom of the furnace and the cake of spongy bloom iron which had to be removed. In modern blast furnaces the iron flows easily. The higher the temperature reached the greater was the amount of carbon left in the crystallized iron. When a furnace had ended its useful life the stones etc. were removed and used to build a new one elsewhere.

The shaft furnace was merely an improved form of domed furnace with a cylindrical structure hence the term shaft. It appears to have been used mostly in the Roman period and later.

Gowland (1902) states that the first furnaces in the Mediterranean area were in the East Pyrenees or North West Italy.

Throughout the period of Hittite rule, according to Gurney (1976), in Anatolia iron was a precious metal as elsewhere in the Middle East, and smelting requiring the use of high temperatures was not understood. Iron was accordingly reserved for special items which were mostly in the luxury class.

Bromehead (1940) mentions iron furnaces with two blast pipes at Velem in West Hungary, of Early Halstatt date, 1100–800 BC. Siderite was the ore used and was reduced by roasting with charcoal leaving a solid bloom of iron which was then wrought into tools

In Denmark, i.e. in Jutland, carbonized peat was used for heating the furnaces owing to the shortage of timber. However, peat has been virtually rejected by authorities, according to Crawford (1966), as a metallurgical fuel owing to its high sulphur and the difficulty in obtaining it.

The carbon from the charcoal in the finished product was at first accidental, but in time the ancient blacksmith learned to control the amount of carbon.

The addition of limestone to furnaces was an innovation which came much later than the Iron Age. Limestone ($CaCO_3$), when added in suitable amounts, lowers the melting point by about 50°C which is insignificant, but in large amounts has the reverse effect. However, the slag contains more lime and less iron oxide. Prehistoric man had no knowledge of the use of limestone as a flux.

A fuller description of the process used in early ironmaking can be found elsewhere (Tylecote 1962).

Gold

Gold is the most exquisite of all things . . . Whoever posses gold can acquire
all that he desires in this world. Truly, for gold can he gain entrance for his
soul into paradise.

Christopher Columbus

It is quite possible that the first metal used by prehistoric man was gold,
although evidence on this is still lacking. Its uses would normally have
been restricted to those areas within easy reach of deposits and also
reserved for the manufacture of special luxury items.

The first gold was probably obtained from stream beds as early as the
sixth millenium BC. It would even have been possible for Palaeolithic
man to have obtained gold, but whether he used it is open to question.
One salient feature about gold is that it is generally found in the native
state and so treatment by primitive man would have been less difficult
than for other metals. The breakdown of quartz rocks causes the dust to
be washed down by stream action and deposited and hence the term
alluvial or placer gold. Gold also occurs in the form of nuggets and
exceptionally these may weigh up to 150 lb each. Purity is the primary
property of gold although it generally contains up to 12% silver and very
rarely less than 85% pure gold with very minute traces of silicon oxide
and compounds of iron. The melting point is 1063°C which would not
have been difficult for primitive man to achieve when preparing objects
of gold. Easily worked gold deposits were available for early man in
Cornwall, Scotland, Wales, Greece and Spain to mention only a few
countries where significant deposits were known. As with iron, many
prehistoric workings could have been destroyed by Roman and later
mining. Forbes (1964) mentions actual gold mines working during Iron
Age times such as Karaco and Verspatak in Transylvania, Mraçaj in
Bosnia and Siphnos in the Aegean area. He suggests that Karaco was
worked through Roman times Mraçaj and Verespatak possibly into the
medieval period.

Anatolia in the Early Bronze Age produced much gold especially from
the Taurus Mountains and from the beds of rivers in the Amanus
Mountains. Hawkes and Woolley (1963) consider that these sources were
probably exhausted in the Late Bronze Age. In the rich tombs of Alaca
Hüyük a jug made from gold was found along with many rich gold
ornaments. Even, however, iron was several times more valuable than
gold. Many gold ornaments were made in ancient Egypt and
Mesopotamia, but the source of the metal used is still an open question.

Speight (1948) suggests mines in Libya, or in North Persia and different parts of Asia Minor. It is possible that Central Asia provided gold. Gold was, however, probably once worked in Egypt at shallow depths. Around 2000 BC Egyptian prospectors found gold at Coptes near Luxor. There is probably no trace of gold in Egypt today. Prospectors looked for gold between 1899 and 1920 without any success.

Greece had very valuable gold workings during the Bronze Age, the gold from the mines having 8–25% of silver. The metal appears to have become rarer in the later Iron Age and local placers are now abandoned.

Alexander (1972) mentions the three river basins of the Vrbas, Bosna and Drina which are purported to have provided sites for the working of gold, silver, iron and copper deposits during the pre-Roman Iron Age in Yugoslavia. The two chief commodities were exported and so contributed suddenly to an increase in wealth.

There have been many finds of gold ornaments in Ireland and various gold sources have been suggested mostly as Briggs (1973) points out, located outside the country. This prompted Briggs and co-workers to investigate possible sources of gold within Ireland.

There is no major source of gold in Ireland and only the ore in the Wicklow area has been worked on a commercial scale in recent times. However, gold is known to be present in scattered areas in small amounts. Reeves (1971) summarizes the known locations as follows:

Placer gold

(1) Slieve an Orra, Co. Antrim
(2) The Moyala River, Co. Derry
(3) River Dodder, Co. Dublin
(4) Greystones Beach, Co. Wicklow
(5) The Gold Mines River Area, Co. Wicklow (this is the only known commercial source in recent times)
(6) Brea, Co. Wicklow

Gold *in situ*

(7) Clontibrit, Co. Monaghan (the stibnite here is reported to be gold bearing)
(8) Kilcrohane, Co. Cork
(9) Carrigacat, Co. Cork
(10) Avoca Head, Co. Wicklow (the gold here is found in the copper lode gossan)
(11) Bray Head, Co. Wicklow (here there are auriferous quartz veins in Cambrian quartzites)
(12) Croghan, Kinshelagh, Co. Wicklow

At Croghan the gold is located in volcanic rocks at an alteration zone with mineralized Silurian shales. This represents the best known source and here there is a system of valleys radiating from a hill so named. All traces of workings disappeared, according to Macalister (1949) in 1798. This area was probably overlooked by prehistoric man who washed the gold from the gravels of nearby streams.

Most of the prehistoric gold ornaments belong to the Bronze Age c. 2000 BC onwards. Reeves states that the "Annals of the Four Masters" mentions gold having been discovered in Ireland by Tighearmass MacFollaigh, in 1600 BC. MacFollaigh was one of the first Milesian kings. Location of the ore was not given, but the Annals go on to suggest smelting in the forests east of the River Liffey, between the present towns of Bray and Wicklow. Reeves gives Leinster as including a possible mining area.

In Wales, near Pumsaint in Carmarthenshire, there are remains of opencast trenching and adits which extend half a mile along the hillside to the north of the Cothi valley. These represent the Dolaucothi Roman gold mines described by Lewis and Jones (1969). The workings are flooded and dangerous and have never been examined by trained observers. As with many Roman mines the mineral was probably worked during the pre-Roman Iron Age, the prehistoric evidence, if any, having been destroyed by the highly developed Roman workings.

Sir Lindsay Scott (1951) gives a list of 18 possible sites from which gold could have been worked in the second millennium BC in Scotland. The author states that the principal sources were streams running down from the Leadhills, Briggs et al. (1973) considers the Sutherland Goldfield of Kildonan as being perhaps the best known and richest deposit in Britain and possibly worked by hand panning

There is no evidence of prehistoric gold mining in Spain, a country rich in the ores of other metals. However, gold was worked first by the Beaker people from rivers and this continued through the Bronze Age.

Silver and Lead

Unlike its fellow noble metal, gold, silver does not occur in a native state except at depth. There is no silver found in river gravels or sand and at depth it generally occurs in thin filaments and never in lumps or nuggets.

It was some time before prehistoric man discovered silver and probably only noticed it when extracting lead from the ore galena, or lead sulphide, which contains not only lead, but silver. In fact it was not until the Bronze Age in Europe that man discovered silver and even in the La Tène period north of the Alps it was rare.

Lead even appears to have been discovered before tin. There are several reasons for this since galena has a silvery colour, dark lustre and high density (7·5). Furthermore it melts at less than 800°C. Lead is very abundant in the form of the ore, galena. In Britain lead ores occur in North Wales, the Mendips, Derbyshire and North East England mostly in Carboniferous Limestone. In Ireland silver and lead are found in sufficient quantities in galena to repay the labour of extraction and treatment. Lead has been common since the fifth and fourth millennia BC. Later it was used as a flux to facilitate separation of iron from its ores. Lead may have been smelted even earlier than copper. It is possible that early man worked the lead ores of Derbyshire where they appeared at the surface, but any such workings would have been destroyed by Roman and medieval mines.

In Spain there were small quantities of lead at El Arger and El Officio and lead was worked in Sardinia in the Late Bronze Age. In Italy it was exploited by the Etruscans and their successors. The galena at the Bottino mines in Italy contained 0·32–0·56% silver and 75–80% lead, but apparently was never worked before the time of the Etruscans. According to Sagui (1924) work continued until the Middle Ages when it was stopped and resumed from 1829 to 1883 and restarted again in 1918.

Despite the rich deposits of lead in the temperate zone of Europe, in England, France, Germany and Yugoslavia its use was rare until the Late Bronze Age. It was used for weights, however, by the lake villagers of Switzerland and for the same purpose in Mesopotamia. At Uruk and Ur it was found in copper alloys. No pre-Roman lead mines have so far been discovered in Wales.

In Troy I, in Anatolia, dating from 3000 to 2500 BC shapeless lumps of lead ore were found and in Troy II pure silver, so silver was extracted from lead ores as early as 2500 BC. In Troy II also figurines of lead were discovered by Schliemann and in Troy III a wheel made of lead. There is an abundance of lead in Anatolia and it is possible that supplies came from Ida in Mysia on the Mt Olympus range and ancient workings are known at Hodsha Geruish (Balia) north-east of Mt Ida, at Karie Sennluk near Broussa and the Olympic Range. There are also ore deposits near modern Diarbekhrr in South Armenia, on the upper reaches of the Tigris and Keban on the Euphrates.

Forbes (1964) gives a list of lead and silver mines purported to have been worked in the Iron Age:

Batigna	silver and lead	Tuscany
Cartagena	silver and lead	S.E. Spain
Siphnos	silver and lead	Aegean
Campiglia Marittma	silver	Tuscany
Cassandra	silver	Macedonia
Markirch	silver	Rhine, France
Masse Marittma	silver	Tuscany
Bottino	lead	Tuscany
Laurium	silver and lead	Attica

The evidence, however, for attributing some of these mines to the Iron Age is very scanty.

Lead is relatively easy to smelt and it is quite feasible to assume that prehistoric man dropped a piece of galena on to an ordinary camp fire and noticed the reaction. Galena is a sulphide so it must first be roasted. However, whereas copper sulphides require a separate roasting operation that is not necessary with galena. The ore is partly roasted to the oxide, PbO, and then a reaction is started with the remainder of the galena, PbS, to give lead, the sulphur being driven off. The lead can then be recovered at the bottom of the fire.

Tylecote (1962) carried out an experiment on the smelting of galena under primitive conditions. He used a fire of dried sticks in a brick built square brazier, spaces being left in the upper part, but the bottom part was closed except for a single bottom opening. From 3 lb of Weardale galena he obtained 0·8 oz of metallic lead, the rest of the charge remaining as unaltered galena and yellow slag. Resmelting of the slag was carried out in the same furnace and 8 oz of lead plus about 2·5 lb of slag was obtained.

It has been mentioned that silver is rare in nature and is only found free in thin leaves at depth. When it did appear in this pure form at the surface it was converted to silver chloride by the action of chlorine in solution as sodium chloride in rain water and in this state is not easily recognized. The silver in galena must be melted and cannot be fashioned. Consequently it would have been some time before prehistoric man discovered that small quantities of silver could be extracted from the lead sulphide ore. The amount of silver per ton of lead varies considerably, for example, in England it is only 20 oz per ton whereas at Karahissarin it is as high as 600 oz per ton, according to Gowland (1903). Tylecote (1962) is of the opinion that silver was extracted from the copper ores of Devon and Cornwall in pre-Roman times. A good example of a more recent silver mine working deep natural silver, i.e. at Hilderston near

Linlithgow, is described by Aitken (1893), but this is dated from about AD 1600. In 1860 and 1870 an attempt was made to reopen the mine, but this was finally abandoned in 1873.

No silver has been found on Palaeolithic, Mesolithic or Neolithic sites. Simple objects are to be found dating back to the Bronze Age, but even these become rare in the Early Iron Age.

In Britain no Bronze Age articles of silver have been found. This is rather surprising when the amount of galena ore in these islands is taken into account. Even in the Iron Age objects are rare. In the late Celtic era the smelting of galena was carried out in a simple hole in the ground similar to the early iron bowl furnace. In Scotland silver was not used until Roman times or possibly Viking according to Gowland (1917).

A bracelet found in Spain contained 92·64% silver and 5·82% copper. There is much silver chloride in veins in this country.

Early silver was often in the form of electrum, i.e. gold and silver. A rod of electrum from Ilios in Egypt was found to contain 33·4% silver. Electrum was mostly reserved for decoration and is a whitish alloy being used in pre-Roman times because of the difficulty in separating gold and silver. It could be made to look like gold by dissolving silver superficially in acid. Tylecote gives analyses of gold objects amongst which are several to which the description electrum could be applied. For example, torcs and rings from a Snettisham hoard dating from the first century BC have principally the following analyses:

	Au	Ag	Cu
Long terminal torc	28·3	43·6	27·0
Ring	29·2	44·4	25·3
Ring terminal torc	58·1	38·3	2·9

Salt

The actual mining of salt dates back to the second millennium BC at Halle in Thuringia, but the date of the discovery of salt boiling is unknown.

In Britain Swinnerton (1932) found abundant debris of broken dishes on sites of Red Mounds on the Lincolnshire coast in 1932. Earlier in Essex, there had been discovery of evidence of brine having been poured on to heated bars of clay and the salt collected after evaporation. As long ago as 1850 pulverized or reddened brick coloured clay was found at Ingoldmells Point in Lincolnshire. There was also charcoal and fragments of pottery. Many sites have since been found and there is evidence of a large scale Iron Age salt boiling industry in Lincolnshire. Sites were up to 20 m in diameter. Brine was evaporated in shallow dishes of the type discovered by Swinnerton, over a fire and these were grouped for convenience during boiling operations. The pots used were typically Iron Age with rounded shoulders and simple barrel shaped or had flattened rims and were made from local clay and chopped grass or hay. The fabric was dark brown with a black core and pitted surfaces, according to Baker (1960).

There was an increasing demand in the Iron Age for salt owing to the development of settled agriculture and a change from a pronounced meat diet to that of plant food. This continued right into the first century AD. Baker points out that in prehistoric times Lincolnshire was isolated from the south of England and the people there were consequently isolated from more advanced methods such as the firebar system of Essex and elsewhere, so continued to use pots or crucibles. The industry of Lincolnshire was so large that enough salt could have been produced to supply the whole of the Midlands. So important was the method that actual salt mining was superseded for a long time. Other important sites of salt boiling were Dorset (Farrar 1964), the Biscay Coast, Halle on Saale (Riehm 1961), Leiden, La Panne, Morbihan and the Black Sea coast of the Caucasus.

Andrée (1922) mentions the abrupt termination of the Hallstatt salt mine workings and the discovery in 1890 of the remains of a settlement in the Dammbergwiese, near Hallstatt, which practised salt boiling. This site, dating from the La Tène period, i.e. from 500 BC, had wooden buildings and occupied 3000 m². Evidence of salt boiling included masses of burnt limestone 50–60 pieces of which were found in houses. These represented stones which had been heated to evaporate the brine which was later poured over them. Aigner (1911) was of the opinion that the settlement was Neolithic, i.e. before the salt mining era, but later he based his theory on iron found in the settlement and concluded that the site was at least 3330 years old. This would give a date of 1400 BC or within the D period of the Bronze Age (1400–1200 BC), whereas Andrée says that the site dates from the La Tène period of the late Iron Age.

Salt Mining

Salt in the form of rock salt, NaCl, occurs in many Triassic rocks in Central Europe and nearer home in Cheshire. When pure it is colourless or white, but small quantities of an impurity may tint it yellow, red or blue etc. It crystallizes in cubes, but also occurs in granular masses and in fibrous aggregates. In some areas rock salt occurs with gypsum and anhydrite, but these two minerals were never extracted for use in prehistoric times.

Rock salt was probably mined in the Saale Valley, at Reichenhall in Upper Bavaria, at Magdeburg, Halle in Thuringia and Margentheim in Württemberg. It was certainly worked at Hallstatt in the Salzkammergut, at Dürnberg near Hallein, in Salzburg and at Kouloe in South Caucasia.

In Austria old workings are numerous in the Alps alongside those of copper mines already discussed. Openings into the mountain sides have been closed or destroyed by modern workings for gypsum, salt clay and rock salt. However, many old workings have been intersected by new galleries and so preserved at depth.

At Hallstatt inclined adits or so ·called inclined shafts were driven into the mountain sides at 25°–60° to the horizontal until they intersected the rock salt deposit when galleries were then driven in the salt in various directions. The salt was then extracted as far as possible from large chambers opening off the galleries up to 12 m in length and 1 m high. The depth of working was from 70 m to 350 m from the surface. Some prehistoric workings have been found at a distance of over 390 m from the adit portals as disclosed by the more recent Maria Theresa gallery (see Fig. 99).

Although timbering was necessary, Bromehead (1940) says that falls of rock would not have constituted a hazard as the climate was drier than today. The art of timbering and boarding over the roof was very

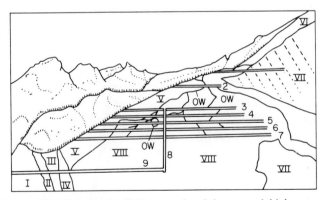

Fig. 99. Cross section through the Hallstratt salt mining area. 1 high water gallery, 2 Ferdinand gallery, 3 Kath. Theresa gallery, 4 Leopold gallery, 5 Josef gallery, 6 Christie gallery, 7 Marie Therese gallery, 8 Shaft or staple pit, 9 Kaiser Franz Josef gallery. I Tabular limestone, II limestone, III sandstone, IV bituminous limestone, V leached salt rocks, VI debris, VII basalt (melaphyre), VIII salt containing rocks. OW prehistoric salt workings.

advanced and was probably developed from experience gained by copper miners at Mitterberg. The timber used was larch.

The rock salt was worked with bronze picks with the aid of wood or stone hammers. Picks are shown in Fig. 100 and wooden shovels, as in Fig. 101, were used to fill leather sacks 95 cm long and 46 cm wide. These were carried out of the mine when full with the help of leather chest straps. The hammers had red beech shafts.

Some form of ventilation at the working distance mentioned would have been necessary, i.e. in the form of intake and return airways. An alternative would have been to use a central partition of skins or boarding in adits and galleries. Even with natural ventilation one, or a combination of both methods would have been necessary. Evidence of the method used has not been found, which is not surprising. In the copper mines inlets and outlets were necessary in the same circuit to allow fire setting to be used. Andrée (1922) mentions the wafting of sheets of leather to induce a current of air! Even in modern shallow gypsum mines in Britain with intakes, returns and fan ventilation traces of methane gas have been detected so necessitating the use of safety lamps. It is highly likely that gas was present at times in the Hallstatt salt mines and wafting would constitute a danger especially as naked lights were the only sources of illumination known. Even during the present century wafting and naked lights in gassy coal mines were in use in Britain before both were prohibited by legislation.

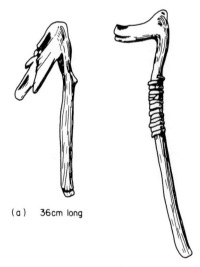

(a)   36cm long

(b)   42 cm long

Fig. 100. Picks from Dürrnberg near Hallein.

Fig. 101. Wooden shovels from Dürrnberg near Hallein (after Andrée). Handle 27 cm long, 4 cm wide, shovel 12 cm wide, 20 cm long.

Lighting was by the use of pine wood spells, thousands of which have been found at Dürnberg. At Hallstatt torches were stuck in staves 1 m long held by two rings of lime bark.

Other finds included the skeleton of a miner who had been killed by a roof fall and a maple wood platter, probably used for the preparation of a miner's meal. There were various relics of articles of dress worn by the miners such as leather shoes and caps, the atmospheric environment assisting in the preservation of such items.

In the Triassic rocks there are large deposits of very hard anhydrite (calcium sulphate) which must be extracted today with the aid of explosives. In Britain anhydrite, which appears to be soft and easily forms a mud when wet, causes heavy wear on modern drill bits. In prehistoric mines the anhydrite was carefully avoided when the rock salt was being extracted. In Austria even in present day rock salt mines 10 percussive drill bits are used per eight hour shift. On this basis the number of bronze picks used by the prehistoric miner must have been colossal, but several workers state that there is no evidence of the existence of foundries for the recasting of bronze tools (Forbes 1964.)

Barth (1973) has made a close survey of the finds from the Hallstatt salt mines and has divided the working area into two groups, i.e. North and East. Unfortunately some of the articles and evidence cover single items

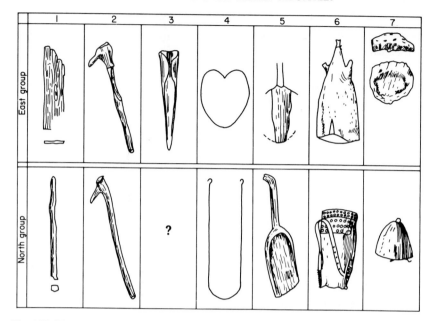

Fig. 102. Finds from two groups of the Hallstatt salt mines. Acknowledgements to F. E. Barth and the Anthropologische Gesellschaft in Vienna.

which might not be fully representative. However, Barth is able to show clearly a differentiation between quality of various articles which are shown in Fig. 102. These consist of lighting spells, tool shafts, working tools, scratches on working surfaces, shovels, transport materials and head coverings.

Lighting spells. At Hallstatt these are of two kinds; four edged spells 5–8 mm thick and wide as well as flat spells 1–3 mm thick and up to 50 mm wide. The East Group had flat spells with only sporadic finds of the four edged type, which was universal in the North Group.

Shaft tools. The East Group had short thick shafts which in the upper third part were distinctly reduced in width. There was a large club shaped head and strongly conical characteristic shaft. The North Group shafts had long thin handles with small cylindrical heads and wide parallel sided shafts.

Working tools. The sample from the East Group was part of a bronze pick, but the type of shaft can be envisaged. Probably the North Group had used other types, but these have not been found.

Scratches. Marks on the walls of the Hallstatt mines were of diverse form, the East Group having heart shaped scratches, but those of the North

Group consisted of elongated U shapes and were not easily definable. *Shovels.* Ten shovels have been found those of the East Group being oar shaped and not of uniform leaf outline, whereas those of the North Group were large in size and of clear assymmetrical cross section and leaf shaped. The East Group was marked by the absence of a handle, but the North Group has either short thin round handles or bent as shown in Figs 101 and 102.

Transport materials. The East Group had carrying bags of simple form without carrying straps and made from the skins of animals, the neck being tied off and the foreleg skins serving as handles for carrying. The North Group bags were more sophisticated, being sewn up from cowhide and stiffened with wood with a complicated carrying handle.

Head coverings. Flat berets of felt were most common in the East Group, four complete examples and three fragments being found. In addition there were conical and wedged shaped hats with hairy insides. The North Group had single conical head coverings consisting of three triangular pieces sewn together. At the joint was a wide strap of leather; the ends being cut tassel-like and hanging down both sides, presumably for tying under the chin.

According to Hoffman and Morton (1928), the wooden shovels which were found were used solely for the removal of salt powder and small pieces of salt. Such wooden shovels would have had an extremely short life when used for the shovelling of rock. These two authors also mention the evidence for porridge, barley, sourbeans, apples and cherries being part of the diet of the salt miners and also the use of wood for the building of log huts.

An analysis of the findings of Barth would on first impression indicate that the North Group was later and much more developed than the East Group. Adaptation and practibility appears to be the keynote of the finds from the East Group whereas those of the North Group are more sophisticated, better finished and so required more effort in manufacture. Yet Barth remarks that it is technically more difficult to prepare the wide flat spells of the East Group, who also had adits approaching the more level ones. The working tool of the East Group, the "lappenpickel" is in the inventory of the Late Bronze Age Urnfield culture and has been found with associated burials. This would date the East Group between 1250 and 700 BC.

Some archaeologists have suggested that the rock salt mines could have been worked by the Neolithic peoples and cite the evidence of finds of serpentine and granite hammers and deer horn picks. However, Kyrle (1913) strongly disputes this assertion despite the finds. Andrée (1922) comments that mining did not start until the Middle Bronze Age, 1600–900 BC at least in Austria. Baker (1960) gives a date of 1400 BC. Koulpe was probably worked much earlier possible c. 2000 BC. The production at Hallstatt was interrupted by the invasion of the Celts in c. 400 BC. As mentioned earlier salt mining ended suddenly in the Early Iron Age and the boiling of salt and evaporation of brine from mine sumps took over.

There is not yet any valid reason to indicate whether a seasonal work force, as conceived by Kromer (1959), and virtually all male, or whether there was a highly specialized full time mining community which is the most common view and supported by Barth and Hodson (1976). These two authors are of the opinion that further work on the finds from the Hallstatt cemetery are a key to the study of the relationship between technological, commercial and social change which took place at the dawn of European history.

According to Filip, Hallstatt was, during the period of that name, an important trading centre and had a high level of culture. Prosperity was principally due to the working of salt and long distance trade in that commodity. Such trade was with Italy in the south and north to Bohemia. The transit station from Hallstatt and Hallein Dürenberg was today's Linz on the Danube according to Filip (1960), which also traded in graphite from the Ceské Budejovice Basin.

Other Materials

During his mining exploitations prehistoric man must have encountered many other rocks, minerals, ores, coal etc. without realizing their potential. For example, he ignored wolframite, nickel, cobalt, zinc blende and certain ores of lead. Zinc in fact was not recognized in Europe until AD 1509 and nickel was not isolated from its ore until AD 1751.

At Velem St Vid in Hungary opencast mining of copper and antimony continued right through the Iron Age to provide metals for the making of antimony bronze. According to Eaton and McKerrell (1976), alloys of copper with lead, antimony and zinc were wholly absent during both the Early and Middle Bronze Ages in the Near East. Alloys of 1–5% arsenic and copper are "arsenical copper alloys" whereas tin–bronzes have more than 5% tin. From 3000 BC to 2000 BC tin–bronze appears to be absent or scarce in Egypt, Palestine, Crete and mainland Greece, but about 25·5% of the alloys used in Iran, Central Anatolia, Troad and the Cyclades are tin–bronze. The remainder appear to be arsenical copper alloys. In the Middle Bronze Age, i.e. 2200–1600 BC in the Near East, tin bronzes increase, but arsenical copper is still in greater use. Eaton and McKerrell use these facts to support their opinion that arsenic was mined and used earlier than tin in the Near East for alloying. Arsenic would have been easily worked as it occurs often in association with copper. It is widely distributed, the chief ores being realgar (AsSO), orpiment (As_2S_3) and mispickel or arsenical pyrites $(FeAs_2FeS_2)$.

Many softer ores were mined primarily for their uses as pigment, the principal ones being:

yellow and red	—	iron (haematite)
black	—	mangenese oxide

At Lascaux in France earthy iron oxide lumps had been cut into pencils of various colours ranging from reddish brown to straw.

green	—	malachite or chrysocolla
white	—	kaolin or china clay
vermilion	—	cinnabar or mercury sulphide
yellow	—	orpiment or arsenical sulphide
blue	—	lapis lazuli
purple	—	azurite

Lapis lazuli was obtained from the mines of Badakshan, but it is dubious whether it was used as a pigment. It has been found at Sialk in present day Iran.

Pre-Roman cinnabar mines existed at Avala in North Serbia and at Goruacchina in Tuscany and worked by the Vinça people at Suplja Stena in Yugoslavia according to Childe (1957).

Semi Precious Stones

Man, or to be strictly correct, woman has always attached great importance to self-adornment and later decoration of purses, handbags etc. and in the case of males, swords and knives. Long before the discovery of metals prehistoric man looked for "magical" stones, for very early in prehistory gems and semi precious stones were valued, not merely on aesthetic grounds, but for their presumed magical properties. Lapis lazuli beads were worn for hundreds of years by prehistoric man. They were also used as objects of trade and barter and many writers speak of caravan loads of semi precious stones travelling overland from the Orient to cater for the needs of the Near East and the Balkans.

European prehistoric man searched stream gravels and residues for semi precious stones. He also mined some gems such as turquoise in 3200 BC, for the Egyptians loved ornaments and favoured vivid colours in contrast. He fashioned into the most effective jewels deep blue lapis lazuli, red carnelian and light blue turquoise. The ancient turquoise mines are Wadi Maghara and Serabit El Khadam in carboniferous sandstone.

Palaeolithic man knew nothing about metals, but between 100 000 and 7000 BC he used over 14 varieties of semi precious stones. Some idea of when such stones were first used is given by the following taken from a paper by Ball (1929):

Chalcedony	
Quartz	100 000–75 000 BC
Jasper	
Serpentine	75 000–40 000 BC
Obsidian	
Pyrite	
Steatite	50 000–25 000 BC
Amber	
Jadeite	c. 22 000 BC
Calcite	
Amethyst	
Fluorspar	20 000–16 000 BC
Agate	
Jet	
Nephrite	
Chloromelamite	20 000 7000 BC
Sillimanite	7000–4000 BC
Turqoise	7000–2200 BC
Haematite	c. 6400 BC or earlier
Alabaster	c. 3500 BC
Carnelian	
Lapis lazuli	
Smoky quartz	3300–2700 BC
Chrysacolla	
Garnet	2000–1000 BC
Malachite	1780–1203 BC
White felspar	3500–3000 BC
Onyx	3200–3000 BC
Callainite	c. 2500 BC
Emerald	2200–1800 BC

Lapis lazuli, as well as being mined at Badakshan in North East Afghanistan, was also obtained from Lake Baikal in Siberia. In the Hermitage Museum at Leningrad are vases carved from lapis lazuli and measuring 1·25 m across.

Jade in the form of jadeite has already been mentioned as a material for tools and weaponry. It was also used for ornamental purposes as it still is today. As stated by Smith (1965), large numbers of jade axes have been found in Europe, i.e. in Brittany, France, Germany, Belgium, Switzerland, Italy and Yugoslavia. In Italy jade is found in Piedmont in form of boulders and pebbles of jadeite, in or near the bed of the River Po. Tshumi (1949) has listed six jadeite sources in Switzerland and a few in Piedmont.

Coal

It is rather surprising that there is little evidence of one of today's most important fossil fuels having been used in prehistoric times. One possible reason is that there was always an abundance of wood.

Coal outcrops widely in most industrial countries in Europe as well as in Britain. The "black rock" must have been seen by prehistoric man and it would be surprising indeed if he had not put some on a camp fire. It is, as has been seen, a well known fact that he heated rocks, copper, tin, lead and iron so why not coal? If he had he would have discovered a superior alternative to wood and charcoal and one, which at least in the Forest of Dean, South Wales, the Midlands and north of England, was easily recognized, easily worked and in great supply. Unfortunately at least in Britain, there is yet little evidence of the intentional use of coal as a fuel by prehistoric man.

At Landek, on the left bank of the Oder at Ostrava Petrkovice in Czechoslovakia, the Brno Archaeological Institute carried out in the 1950s extensive investigations into the possible use of coal in the Palaeolithic settlement there. The site is on carboniferous sandstone and, according to Klima (1956), is one of the most important Palaeolithic sites in Silesia. Evidence for three huts was found and these were oval in shape having two hearths on the longitudinal axis of each making six in all. The hearths had been dispersed by solifluxion leaving particles of coal and coke in ash layers. In the ash, which was greyish black and 2·5 cm thick, were fragments of animal bones and mammoth ivory particles. The hearths were bowl shaped hollows in the ground. Numerous small lumps of haematite were also found and these had been baked to accelerate their decomposition into forms suitable for use as red pigment. A statuette carved in haematite was also found. This Gravettian site, over 30 000 years old, is situated near the outcrop of the Ostrava coal seams, according to Demek and Miroslav (1971), and it is presumed that the settlers dug out coal and used it as a source of heat. According to Klima coal was also used for the making of ornaments at Kesserloch and Kniegrotte.

Three settlement sites were excavated by Bren (1955) in the mining district of Kladno-Rakovnik. Here was found extensive evidence for the manufacture of bracelets of sapropelite, which is a form of lignite or brown coal. Bracelets were found in many stages of manufacture from rough pieces of sapropelite to half completed discs and the completed article. The tools used in manufacture were also found. In many La Tène graves in Czechoslovakia such bracelets have been found on actual skeletons.

Webster (1955) mentions the deliberate use of coal as a burning agent in a Bronze Age cremation burial in South Wales. This appears to be the only mention of such use of coal by prehistoric man in Britain. Webster also refers to coal cinders being found in the late Palaeolithic site in Czechoslovakia, already mentioned, but he is of the opinion that these were the result of forest fires on a coal outcrop. It appears more likely that the theory put forward by Klima, based on the available evidence, is the more realistic.

If extraction and burning of coal appears to be a rarity in prehistoric times this is certainly not true of the Roman occupation of Britain. It is from this period that the first major evidence of the utilization of coal is available. The Romans appear to have used coal only where wood from forests was scarce and where peat was either absent or difficult to dig. Probably they outcropped coal seams irrespective of quality, to a shallow depth. Prehistoric man, like the Romans, would have found the coal to be greatly oxidized being near to the basset edge, but it would have been reasonably satisfactory on open fires where smoke production was not a serious drawback. For steel making of course ordinary bituminous coal would not have been entirely satisfactory.

Webster suggests that the Romans confined their use of coal to those sites near the outcrops. This is certainly not true if cognisance is taken of the evidence of coal usage in Wiltshire and Buckinghamshire. Several Wiltshire sites such as Knook at Nuthills, Rushall Stanton St, Quentins, Silbury Hill and Stockton where Cunnington (1930, 1933) suggest that the coal found on these sites came from as far afield as Somerset and South Wales.

Coal would appear to have been worked at Benwell near Newcastle upon Tyne by the Romans, a large quantity having been found in one of the guardrooms at Housesteads on the Wall. At Baydon in Hampshire coal is thought to have been used by the Romans for smelting.

These references to Roman exploitation and use of coal do not directly concern prehistory. They are mentioned to illustrate the relative ease, compared to copper and other metals, of working shallow deposits of the valuable commodity coal. It is extremely likely that Iron Age man at least, and probably his predecessors in Britain did also take advantage of the immense reserves of fossil fuel. Evidence of actual prehistoric coal mining is unlikely to be found at least in Britain. All the known outcrops of coal have been surveyed or worked through the ages of history and many are still being worked by the National Coal Board today. It is, however, possible that some habitation sites of prehistoric age in Britain will be found which will provide some evidence of coal utilization if not of actual coal extraction.

So we arrive at the end of our survey of prehistoric mining and its closely related industries, having considered flint, copper and its alloys, iron and other materials. Chronologically we finish with the Roman invasion and occupation of western Europe, the dawn of the written record so far as Europe is concerned. The development of ancient mining and later medieval and more recent mining is another story.

9
Rocks and Mineral Properties

It is probably true to say that prehistoric man, through the millennia up to the dawn of history, extracted from the earth most of the minerals and rocks which are worked today, where these were at or near the surface and so were easily recognizable. So far, with a few important exceptions, attention has in previous chapters been directed mainly to sources of materials and methods of extraction. To complete the picture it might be useful to cover in a little more detail the elementary properties and classification of those materials which have been mentioned, omitting the more important ores of copper and iron which have been covered more appropriately in Chs 7 and 8.

Rocks

Basically all the materials worked by prehistoric man can be covered by the classification of igneous, sedimentary and metamorphic rocks the various minerals worked being constituent elements of these rocks.

Igneous rocks are those which have been formed directly from lavas emanating from volcanic activity. They in turn can be classified according to their grain or constituent mineral size as volcanic, hyperbyssal and plutonic; or according to chemical composition as acid, intermediate, basic or ultrabasic examples of which are given in Table 3.

The primary minerals forming igneous rocks are quartz, the felspars, micas, amphiboles, pyroxenes and olivines. Secondary minerals are the alteration products of these minerals such as serpentine, talc, kaolinite, calcite, dolomite, hydrated silicates of alumina, zeolites, chlorites etc.

Rocks which contain more than 66% silica, and up to 75% generally, are termed acid igneous rocks and have muscovite micas, some biotite, a predominance of quartz, the amphibole hornblende, the acid or orthoclase falspars which predominate over the plagioclase or basic

234

TABLE 3: Classification of igneous rocks

	Acid	Intermediate	Basic	Ultrabasic
	Si 66%		Si 52%	
Volcanic	Obsidian	Trachyte	Basalt	Linburgite
Hyperbyssal	Quartz Porphyry	Felspar Porphyry	Dolerite	
Plutonic	Granite	Syenite	Gabbro	Peridotite

felspars and other minor minerals. Intermediate rocks have between 52 and 66% silica and have some biotite mica, less quartz than in the acid rocks, plagioclase or soda lime felspars and the amphibole hornblende with some pyroxene content such as augite in the less acid varieties. Ferrous minerals are also present. The basic rocks have less than 52% silica and contain no quartz, but plagioclase felspars, olivine in the more basic varieties and pyroxene minerals such as augite, ferrous minerals are often abundant. Ultrabasic rocks contain essentially lime minerals with no felspar. What distinguishes amphiboles from pyroxenes is the 124° or lozenge shaped cleavage of the former as in hornblende from the 87° or octagonal cleavage of the latter.

The grain size indicates the relative rate of cooling. Fine grained rocks such as volcanic, have cooled from the lava rapidly on the surface. Hyperbyssal rocks have cooled at a moderate rate as the lava has flowed into the stratification and produced dykes, sills etc. The plutonic rocks are recognizable by their large grains and present evidence of relative slow cooling at depth. Generally it can be said that reduction in silica and increase in soda lime and lime minerals from acid to basic and ultrabasic igneous rocks results in a pronounced increase in specific gravity the basic rocks being heavier per unit volume than the acid varieties.

Acid Igneous Rocks

The finest grained igneous rocks are the volcanic types such as pitchstone, obsidian, rhyolite and dacite. They have a relatively low specific gravity (2·5–2·6). Rhyolite is pale and only contains a few crystals as does obsidian whereas pitchstone is more crystalline due to its longer cooling time. It is found in the Malvern Hills, Shropshire and the Lake District. Such rocks are often given the general description of extrusive to differentiate between them and those formed at depth.

Hyperbyssal rocks of the acid variety include quartz porphyry and felsite. They are moderately fine grained and have porphyritic crystals of quartz and orthoclase felspar, the accessory minerals being biotite and hornblende.

Plutonic acid rocks are granite and grano-diorite. Granite, the most important and common plutonic rock, is large grained and contains chiefly quartz, felspar and mica. The dark mineral which is predominant gives the granite its true name such as biotite granite, augite or hornblende granite. The specific gravity is usually 2·6–2·8.

All the acid rocks mentioned contain over 66% silica and so are products of acid magmas. Thus such rocks are not found where volcanic activity has produced alkaline magmas. This explains the scarcity of obsidian in some volcanic districts although even with acid magmas a slower rate of cooling for some reason may produce pitchstone which owing to its crystalline structure was unsuitable for the tools required by prehistoric man. Arran pitchstone is very well known.

Intermediate Igneous Rocks

These contain 52–66% silica and typical examples of volcanic varieties are trachyte and andesite. Trachyte is pale grey or sometimes purplish and fine grained. The specific gravity is 2·6–2·8. Epidiorite is an amphibole rock containing hornblende as essential mineral with albite, quartz, iron ores, garnets etc. as accessories. It is generally hard and massive although it was used by prehistoric man for axe manufacture (Group I of the South Western Committee classification).

Hyperbyssal rocks in this case are felspar porpyry and microdiorite. The plutonic rocks are syenite and chlorite.

Basic Igneous Rocks

These are all low in silica, i.e. less than 52% and the chief volcanic example is basalt. This has a high specific gravity 2·9–3·0. There are various varieties such as tephrite, limburgite, which can also be ultrabasic, leucite etc. It is black in colour. Neolithic axes have been made from this rock. Hyperbyssal rocks include dolerite, quartz dolerite and olivine dolerite. Dolerite is usually dark grey or black and sometimes greenish. The plutonic rocks are gabbro, diorite and norite. These are hard and massive and have a high crushing strength. They are black and white or grey and very coarsely crystalline. They are common in the Scottish Highlands, Anglesey, NW. Ireland, Pembroke, the Lake District and Leicestershire (Charnwood Forest).

Volcanic tuff is a general term and rocks bearing this description can be found in the acid or basic forms depending on the type of lava from which they were formed. Another general term or field name is greenstone. This is a basic rock with dolerite texture which has been altered by contact chiefly in dykes. It is a hard stone and was useful for the manufacture of axes in prehistoric times.

Sedimentary Rocks

These rocks constitute the other class of rock which, as the name indicates, has been formed from sediments as distinct from igneous magmas. These rocks can be split into various types depending on the mode of formation and type of sediment, i.e. mechanical, chemical and organic.

Sedimentary rocks formed by mechanical action may be arenaceous or sandy such as for example sandstones or conglomerates or argillaceous clays and shales.

Rocks formed by chemical action include carbonates such as limestones, chlorides, e.g. rock salt and gypsum, a sulphate.

Organically formed rocks are very important economically and may be calcareous, such as limestones, carbonaceous as in the case of coal, ferruginous, i.e. ironstones or siliceous as flints and cherts.

Many of the sandstones and limestones are excellent building stones as they are comparatively easy to work and shape, but were not used as such much before Roman times.

Flint and chert were two of the most important materials used in prehistoric times. The principal difference between the two is that flint is found in beds of chalk whereas chert might be found in rocks other than chalk such as sandstone, marl or limestone.

There are several theories relating to the formation of flint and there is still some considerable doubt regarding the origin of this siliceous material. It is believed by some that sponges extracted silica from sea water and that this was eventually dissolved out by the action of the rain water. One theory is that the silica was deposited as gelatinous lumps on the sea bed as the chalk was being formed. Another theory, which is the most popular, is that the rain water percolated through the chalk after uplift of the land and sea recession, the silica being removed and deposited as flint elsewhere in the chalk.

Flint contains about 98% pure silica and varies in colour probably according to the chemical composition of the streams during deposition. In the pure state flint is jet black, but there are brown varieties as at Grand Pressigny, pink flints in Egypt and other coloured varieties from blue, violet to various shades of red. Normally the flint is covered with a white cortex. The main qualities of flint are its durability and its special conchoidal fracture which renders it ideal for shaping. It has a specific gravity of 1·4–1·45 and occurs as nodules or slabs in the chalk.

The ferruginous varieties of organically formed rocks include the hydrated oxide of iron, limonite and the carbonate chalybite.

The chief carbonaceous rock is coal and this occurs in seams, being the fossilized remains of organic matter. Primarily it is formed from wood, which decays and becomes buried. The next stage is peat which is dug out near the surface for fuel. Further decay and consolidation produces lignite or brown coal and then sub-bituminous coal. The ordinary black type of coal is termed bituminous and the final stage in the formation of coal is anthracite. Throughout these changes, as a result of increasing pressure during burial, there is a loss of volatile constituents and an increase in the carbon content:

	% carbon	% volatiles
Peat	57	40·5
Lignite	70	29·6
Sub-bituminous	80	19·0
Bituminous	85	12·5
Anthracite	94	5·0

Cannel coal does not fit into any of these categories being a lustreless coal with a conchoidal fracture. Sometimes known as sapropelic coal or "candle coal" it burns with a very bright flame.

In the Upper Lias of the Jurassic system in Yorkshire jet is found. It is a black bituminous coal which is easily carved or cut and readily polished. It has been used in prehistoric times especially for bead making.

Rock salt or halite ($NaCl$) is often found in the newer rocks, such as Red Marl, in the Stassfurt deposits of Germany, Cheshire, Austria etc. It is marked especially by its cubic crystallization. When pure it is colourless or white, but impurities can tint it yellow, pink or blue. It is often found in the same formations as gypsum or hydrated sulphate of lime ($CaSO_4 \cdot 2H_2O$) and with anhydrite ($CaSO_4$). Rock salt was mined as indicated in Ch. 8, by prehistoric man in Austria in Hallstatt times, but gypsum and anhydrite were generally ignored.

Metamorphic Rocks

Rocks classified under this term are those igneous or sedimentary rocks which have been altered, along with their mineral constituents by either regional metamorphism resulting from pressure inherent in the process of mountain building or by heat or thermal metamorphism. The latter effect results from contact with igneous intrusions at the lava stage.

Examples of metamorphic rocks include gneiss, schist, slate, marble, quartzite and phyllite. These are the most common. Gneiss may be ortho-gneiss resulting from the metamorphism of an igneous rock such as granite or para-gneiss from similar action on a sedimentary rock such as sandstone. The appearance is foliated with micaceous layers sandwiched between granitic textures. The density is 2·55–3·0. There are various forms of gneiss depending on the dominant constituent such as pyroxene gneiss, hornblende gneiss etc.

Schist is a similar rock to gneiss, but has often a very wavy foliation or is very contorted. It is very soft and is easily cut. Slate is a very fine grained rock formed from shales or clay under pressure with the result that the cleavage becomes slaty and easily separated. Phyllite is a dark green or greyish rock similar to slate, but producing thinner and weaker leaves than slate. Gneisses, schists and slates are very common in areas of mountain uplift or building such as in the Highlands of Scotland, North Wales and the Lake District of England.

Quartzite is formed from sandstone of high quartz content under pressure. It is very hard, abrasive and compact.

Marble is of varying colour depending on the action of solutions in the dolomitic or calcitic limestone from which it has been formed under pressure. It may be white, in its purest form, green, blue, black, red etc. It is massive and granular, but is easily cut and worked. Lacking silica it is fairly non-abrasive.

Not only are igneous and sedimentary rocks changed visually by metamorphism, but constituent minerals are changed at the same time by the action. New minerals are formed especially by contact with thermal agencies such as that resulting from igneous activity. Thus in limestone, which has been metamorphosed, we have epidote, idocrase, spinel, tremolite, diopside and wollastonite. In clays and such sediments there is chlorite, sericite, garnet, stauralite etc. In basic rocks olivine is changed to serpentine, but new minerals are not often found in metamorphosed acid igneous rocks.

Ores

The ores of copper and iron are referred to in Chs 7 and 8 respectively.

Gold

This was probably one of the earliest metals to be extracted partly as a result of its striking appearance. It is a heavy metal having a density of 19·3. The chief source of gold is the native variety. It occurs in gold bearing quartz veins, but is only a minor constituent of the igneous rocks. The rare ores of gold are calverite, krennerite, petzite and sylvanite.

Silver

Silver is rare in the native state and is mostly derived from the ore of lead, galena. In tetrahedrite silver may replace copper. Rare ores of silver are argentite, embolite, kerargite, polybasite and stephanite. The density is 10·5. Lead is easy to work and is soft durable and malleable. It has a density of 11·33. Galena is the most important ore of lead and was possibly worked by prehistoric man, but evidence is lacking. Lead is rare in the native state. Other ores of lead are cerussite (lead carbonate), anglesite (lead sulphate) and pyromorphite (lead chlorophosphate).

Arsenic

This occurs in sulphate rocks as realgar (70%) and orpiment (61%). Another ore is mispickel (46%) or arsenical pyrites and is fairly common. It also occurs in the native state. Allied with copper in prehistoric times it was used to make arsenic/copper alloys.

Mercury

This is the only metal which is liquid at ordinary temperatures. It has a specific gravity of 13·6. Many authors have mentioned its use by prehistoric man, i.e. near Vinça in Yugoslavia, cinnabar (mercury sulphide) being the ore. Prehistoric man probably used cinnabar as a pigment. It occurs amongst other places in southern Spain, Austria, Italy and Turkey. It has a density of 8·0–8·2.

The Gems and Semi Precious Stones

Finally the group of semi precious stones which has been of interest throughout prehistory and historical times right up to the present day is worthy of mention. Many of the gems have their origin in silica or in the purest form of this element, quartz. Quartz is a colourless form of SiO_2 when pure and when fully transparent is known as rock crystal. It is a constituent of all igneous rocks in varying amounts as already mentioned, except in the case of the very basic rocks. When crypto as opposed to pure crystalline form, it is chalcedony which can occur in stalictic masses and has a splintery to uneven fracture. In its hydrated form quartz becomes opal ($SiO_2 + H_2O$) whose colour may be blue, yellow or milky white. Other varieties of quartz are:

Smoky quartz	brown or yellow
Cairngorm	brown or yellow
Jasper	opaque red with iron oxide
Carnelian	red
Sard	brownish red
Plasma	leak green
Chrysophase	apple green
Rose quartz	pink
Tiger's eye	golden yellow
Milky quartz	white and translucent
Amethyst	violet
Onyx	banded form of chalcedony

These silica derivatives represent the most common semi precious stones simply because silica, after oxygen, is the most common element in the earth's crust.

Other gemstones are:

Emerald which is known as beryl and is beryllium silicate ($Be_3Al_2 (SiO_4)$) and is found in pegmatites, mica schists often in very large crystals.

Topaz is a fluorsilicate of alumina (AlF_2) SiO_4 and is found often with tin ores. It is the result of action by fluoric acid on granite, schist or gneiss.

Lapis lazuli or lazurite is a mineral of rich bluish colour and is an aggregate of hauyne, diopside amphibole mica and pyrites. ($3(NaAlSiO_4) Na_2S$). In prehistory its chief source is believed to be the mines of Afghanistan.

Serpentine is a hydrated silicate of magnesia and iron ($Mg_6(OH)_6 (Si_4O_{11})$ H_2O). It is a dull green in colour often with red and yellow markings from contact with iron oxide. It is an alteration product of olivine.

Steatite is also known as talc or soapstone and is a hydrated silicate of magnesia ($H_2O MgO_4 SiO_2$). It is pale green or sometimes colourless, but is very greasy and soft. It is formed from magnesian minerals by alteration in igneous and metamorphic rocks.

Calcite is a common veinstone and an important constituent of limestone, chalk and other calcareous rocks. It is a soft mineral and has a density of 2·7. It is a carbonate of lime ($CaCO_3$). It is colourless when pure, but may be white, brown, red or yellow.

Turquoise is a hydrated basic phosphate of alumina ($Al_2(OH)_3PO_4H_2O$) and occurs in veins and nodules in igneous rocks. It may be colourless or even peacock blue and is opaque. Its density is 2·7.

Alabaster is a form of granular gypsum or hydrated sulphate of lime $(CaSO_4 \cdot 2H_2O)$. It may be tinted or white, but normally it is colourless. *Garnet* occurs in igneous rocks as a silicate of aluminium, iron, chromium, magnesium and manganese. Such igneous rocks may be granite, aplite, andesite, trachyte etc. but may also be found in gneiss. Its density is 3·4–4·4.

Jade constitutes one of the toughest stones in existence and is found in two forms, jadeite and nephrite. *Jadeite* or chloromelanite is a sodium aluminium silicate $(NaAl\ (Si_2O_6))$. It is a pyroxene and has a specific gravity of 3·3. Its lustre is greasy and is green in colour, but may be brilliantly coloured, such as in greens, bright apple or emerald. The apple green colour is often due to the presence of chromium. It is normally found in river beds, but has been mined in quarries and underground. *Nephrite* is slightly less heavy than jadeite and has a specific gravity of 2·9–3·1. It is a calcium magnesium silicate $(CaMg(Si_2O_6))$ and is green or brown, but sometimes of sober green, resulting not from chromium, but iron oxide. Nephrite has been excavated in large sizes at Jordanstal, Germany.

Amber Although this cannot be classed strictly as a mineral, it was very important in prehistory being traded over long distances (the so-called Amber Route) from Scandinavia and the Mediterranean coast. It is actually a mineral resin and is used today as a gem. Its chief constituent is carbon $(CH_4 + nCH_2)$ and has a wide variation in properties both chemical and physical.

Hardness

Hardness of natural materials, especially those mentioned, is very difficult to define precisely, but is nevertheless a most important property together with density particularly during the process of archaeological excavation. One of the simplest hardness tests on homogeneous materials, such as the normal minerals, can be made with the Moh's scale of hardness. This lists arbitrarily minerals in the order of their increasing hardnesses in a relative sense, i.e. (1) talc, (2) gypsum, (3) calcite (4) fluor, (5) apatite, (6) felspar, (7) quartz, (8) topaz, (9) sapphire or corundum and (10) diamond. Each of these minerals may be scratched by the next higher one in the scale. (1) and (2) can be scratched by the finger nail, (3), (4) and (5) by a steel point such as an ordinary pocket knife while (6) requires a hard steel point such as a file, (7) scratches glass, (8) scratches hard steel while (9) can only be scratched or marked by a diamond. Some of the hardest materials made by man such as tungsten carbide can scratch (9). This scale depends on a variety of properties such as silica content, compactness and toughness, but if not the most accurate is the simplest readily available means of identification of hardness in the field.

Some of the Moh hardness values of the materials mentioned in this chapter can be identified from the scale, but a more complete list is as follows:

Agate	6·5–6·7
Alabaster	2·0
Amber	2·0–2·5
Amethyst	7·0
Anhydrite	3·0–4·0
Arsenic	3·0–4·0
Augite	6·0
Azurite	3·5–4·0
Beryl	7·5–8·0
Biotite	2·5–3·0
Calcite	3·0
Cassiterite	6·0–7·0
Chalcocite	2·5–3·0
Chalcopyrite	3·5–4·0
Chalybite	4·0–4·5
Chert	7·0
Chromite	5·5
Chrysoberyl	8·5
Chrysocolla	2·0–4·0
Cinnabar	2·0–2·5
Coal	2·0–2·5
Cuprite	3·5–4·0
Diopside	5·0–6·0
Enargite	3·5
Epidote	6·0–7·0
Felspar	6·0
Flint	7·0
Fluorspar	4·0
Galena	2·5
Garnet	6·0–7·0
Gypsum	2·0
Haematite	6·5
Hauyne	5·5–6·0
Hornblende	5·0–6·0
Iron pyrites	6·0–6·5
Jadeite	6·5–7·0
Jasper	6·5–7·0
Kaolin	1·0

Lapis lazuli	5·5
Lead	1·5
Leucite	5·5–6·0
Limonite	4·0–5·5
Magnetite	5·5
Malachite	3·5–4·0
Marcasite	6·0–6·5
Mispickel	5·5–6·0
Muscovite	2·0–2·5
Native copper	2·5–3·0
Native gold	2·5–3·0
Native iron	4·0–5·0
Native silver	2·5–3·0
Nephrite	5·5–6·0
Obsidian	5·0–5·5
Olivine	6·5–7·0
Opal	6·0
Orpiment	1·5–2·0
Pitchblende	4·0–6·0
Quartz	7·0
Realgar	3·5–3·6
Rock salt	2·5
Rose quartz	7·0
Sapphire	9·0
Serpentine	3·0–4·0
Siderite	4·0–4·5
Sillimanite	6·5–7·0
Smoky Quartz	7·0
Spinel	8·0
Staurolite	7·0–7·5
Talc	1·0
Tetrahedrite	3·0–4·0
Topaz	8·0
Tourmaline	7·5
Travertine	3·0
Turquoise	6·0
Zircon	7·5

This chapter has treated the chief igneous, sedimentary and metamorphic rocks, the ores and gemstones. An attempt has been made to give a little more detail concerning the materials already mentioned in the earlier chapters and which have been mined or quarried by prehistoric man. On the other hand it is not claimed that the coverage is exhaustive nor can it be in a book of this nature. Rather this chapter can be regarded as an appendix for quick reference.

Appendix One
Reference Summary of Sites

Site[a]	Location	Type[b]	Material	Age[c]	Date[d]	Page
Aalborg	Denmark	bell pits and adits	flint	N	c. 1800	97
Acigol	Turkey	unconfirmed	obsidian	?	?	109
Aibunar	Bulgaria	u/g, s and g	copper	E	c. 4000	189
Alderley Edge	Britain	u/g, s and g	copper	BA	?	171
Avala	Yugoslavia	unconfirmed	cinnabar	N	?	229
Avennes	Belgium	pits and g	flint	N	?	78
Ballygalley Hill	N. Ireland	opencast	flint	N	?	64
Beer Head	Britain	depressions	flint	UP-N	?	65
Bingol	Turkey	unconfirmed	obsidian	?	?	109
Bjerre	Denmark	pits and s	flint	N	c. 1800	100
Blackpatch	Britain	u/g, s and g	flint	N	c. 3140	44
Bow Hill	Britain	unconfirmed	flint	N	?	48
Braives	Belgium	pit	flint	N	?	78
Brioverien	France	quarry	epidiorite	N	?	122
Buchan Ness	Britain	quarries	flint	?	?	64
Carnon	Britain	surface	tin	BA	c. 2000	173
Chale Ghar	Iran	adits	copper	BA	c. 3200	192
Champignolles	France	u/g, s and pits	flint	N	?	80
Church Hill	Britain	u/g, s and g	flint	N	c. 3390	40
Ciftlik	Turkey	unconfirmed	obsidian	?	?	109
Cissbury	Britain	u/g, s and g	flint	N	c. 2770	35
Dolaucothi	Britain	unconfirmed	gold	pre-R	?	218
Durrington	Britain	trenches	flint	N	?	62
Easton Down	Britain	pits	flint	N-BA	c. 2530	49
East Horsley	Britain	pit	flint	N	?	64
Erevan	Russia	unconfirmed	obsidian	?	?	109
Ergani Maden	Turkey	unconfirmed	copper	?	c. 7000	134
Findsbury	Britain	quarry	flint	P	?	65
Gallerup	Sweden	pits	flint	N-IA	?	96
Giali	Turkey	unconfirmed	obsidian	?	?	109

Site	Location	Type	Material	Age	Date	Page
Graig Llwdd	Britain	unconfirmed	micro-diorite	N	?	116
Grand Pressigny	France	quarry	chert	?	?	79
Great Langdale	Britain	scree	volcanic tuff	N	c. 2600	116
Grimes Graves	Britain	u/g, s and g	flint	N	c. 2300–1300	53
Hallstatt	Austria	u/g, adits	salt	BA-	c. 1400	223
Harrow Hill	Britain	u/g, s and g	flint	N	c. 2980	37
Hov	Denmark	pits, u/g, s and g	flint	N	c. 1800	97
Huelva	Spain	unconfirmed	copper	BA	?	194
Karabajir	Bulgaria	trenches, s and g	copper	?	?	190
Kars	Russia	unconfirmed	obsidian	?	?	109
Kervalot	France	quarry	horn-blendite	N	?	122
Kleinkems	W. Germany	adits	jasper	N	c. 2000	92
Koulpe	Austria	adits	salt	BA	c. 2000	228
Kozlu	Turkey	u/g, adits and g	copper	BA	c. 2800	191
Krzemionki	Poland	u/g, s and g	chert	N	?	102
Kvarnby	Sweden	pits	flint	N-IA	c. 2900	96
La Flénu	Belgium	trenches	flint	N	?	78
La Vigne du Cade	France	u/g, s and g	flint	N	?	84
Laghe Morad	Iran	adits	copper	BA	c. 3000	192
Landek	Czecho-slovakia	opencast	coal	P	c. 32 000	231
Lavant Caves	Britain	galleries	flint	N	c. 3000	47
Liddington	Britain	unconfirmed	flint	?	?	63
Lipari	Italy	unconfirmed	obsidian	?	?	109
Lovas	Hungary	pit	limonite (paint)	P	c. 80 000	210
Löwenberg	Switzerland	quarry	chert	N	c. 3000	103
Lumbres	France	adits	flint	?	?	85
Magyororsdomb	Hungary	bell pits and X cuts	chert	N	c. 2600	106
Martins Clump	Britain	pits	flint	N	?	62
Massingham	Britain	pits	flint	N	?	62
Mauer	Austria	u/g, s and g	chert	N	c. 4000	103
Mayen	W. Germany	quarry	basalt	N-	?	122
Mazorayeh	Iran	adits	copper	BA	c. 3000	192
Meefe	Belgium	pits and g	flint	?	?	78
Mieres de Milagro	Spain	u/g and s	copper	?	?	196
Milos	Greece	unconfirmed	obsidian	?	?	109
Mitterberg	Austria	adits	copper	BA	c. 2000–1000	180
Monte Tabuto	Italy	adits and g	chert	E	?	100

Site	Location	Type	Material	Age	Date	Page
Mount Gabriel	Ireland	adits	copper	BA	c. 1500	174
Mur de Barrez	France	u/g, s and g	flint	N	?	81
Mynydd Rhiw	Britain	quarry	dolerite	N	?	119
Nemrut Däg	Turkey	unconfirmed	obsidian	N	?	109
Obourg	Belgium	trenches	flint	N	?	76
Orme's Head	Britain	unconfirmed	copper	pre-R	?	171
Oronsko	Poland	pits	flint or chert	N	?	101
Pantellaria	Italy	unconfirmed	obsidian	?	?	109
Peppard	Britain	openpits	flint	?	?	51
Petit Morin	France	u/g, s and g	flint	N	?	83
Petite Garenne	France	openpit	flint	?	?	84
Pipstone Hill	Britain	pits and adits	flint	?	?	65
Plouguin	France	quarry	sillimanite	N	?	122
Prescelly	Britain	unconfirmed	dolerite	?	?	116
Purbeck	Britain	unconfirmed	shale	N	?	124
Regensberg	W. Germany	unconfirmed	flint	?	?	95
Ringland	Britain	pits	flint	?	?	63
Rocio	Portugal	u/g, s and g	flint	N	?	100
Rudna Glava	Yugoslavia	shafts	copper	E	c. 4000	187
St Gertrude	Holland	u/g, s and g	flint	N	c. 3000	87
Sardinia	Italy	unconfirmed	obsidian	?	?	109
Saspow	Poland	pits	flint	N	c. 3000	102
Sélédin	France	quarry	dolerite	N	c. 3800–2000	119
Sinai	Egypt	u/g, s and g	copper	BA	c. 1100	197
Spiennes	Belgium	u/g, s and g	flint	N	c. 3400–1700	68
Stoke Down	Britain	pits	flint	N	c. 3000	46
Strépy	Belgium	trenches and g	flint	?	?	77
Supla Stena	Yugoslavia	unconfirmed	cinnabar	N	?	229
Tata	Hungary	quarry	chert	N	c. 1860	105
Trevebulliagh	N. Ireland	unconfirmed	porcellanite	?	?	116
Tokaj	Hungary	unconfirmed	obsidian	?	?	111
Tolmere Pond	Britain	depressions	flint	?	?	83
Talmessi	Iran	unconfirmed	copper	?	c. 5500	155
Tullstorp	Sweden	pits	flint	N-IA	?	96
Veaux	France	quarry and pits	chert	N	?	85
Velim St Vid	Hungary	opencast	iron	BA	c. 1000	210
Vert la Gravelle	France	adits	flint	N	?	83
Viehofen	Austria	shafts	copper	BA	?	178
Villevenard	France	pits	flint	?	?	84
Windover Hill	Britain	pits?	flint	N	c. 3500–2500	48

a Only sites or sources mentioned in the text are included in the above table

b Where no site investigation has been carried out and there is no surface evidence of prehistoric working the site or source is classified as unconfirmed. u/g = underground, s = shaft and g = gallery.

[c] Age is denoted as P = Palaeolithic, N = Neolithic, E = Eneolithic, BA = Bronze Age, IA = Iron Age and pre-R = pre-Roman.

[d] Actual available radiocarbon dates are given in the text. Here only very approximate dates are used and derived from radiocarbon dates or are general estimates. Comparatively few radiocarbon dates for mine or quarry sites are available. In most cases either there is little information to use or wide estimates would be useless, so question marks appear in the table. Dates, where given, are in calendar years BC.

Appendix Two
Methods of Dating

Without some estimate or determination of date, be it relative or absolute, all forms of archaeological excavation constitute to a certain extent a waste of time and effort. One object is to assign the site or related culture to a period in prehistory or if possible to determine a reasonable age for the site. Without dating further work on exposing structures or artefacts, human remains etc. becomes pointless and arbitrary. This fact is no more obvious than with prehistoric mining sites. In this sphere there is likely to be a paucity of finds apart from the geometry of the excavation. Without some tiny piece of chronological evidence a hole in the ground could be assumed to be of any date within a span of several or maybe tens of thousands of years back from the present day. So we look for datable material, for evidence which will narrow the range of dates and for any clues which help to assign a relative date to the site.

Methods of dating can be relative or absolute. Only a few in both categories are strictly applicable to mining sites, but are worth mentioning for the sake of completeness. This survey is of course not intended to be complete and the reader who is not at all conversant with any of the methods outlined below is advised to consult one or more of the references given at the end.

Relative Methods

These include estimation of the effects of glacial action such as change in sea level of the Pleistocene. Variation in levels of the shore line such as raised beaches may be useful in dating occupation by prehistoric man. Allied to this is the formation of river terraces by rivers cutting deep into their beds. Soil examinations can enable the observer to estimate whether one soil level is appreciably older or younger than another and the type of soil can be used to determine the climate in existence at the time of occupation. Fluorine and nitrogen analyses of soils will indicate whether human activity has taken place in previous times or whether burials have taken place. Careful examination and analyses of sediments taken from various levels of excavation enable ascertainment of relative age, i.e. that a lower bed is older than an upper bed. Remnants of artefacts of known age or cultural period contained in individual beds of sediments are very useful in this respect. With filled in mine shafts it is worth remembering that lower beds may be newer than the upper ones if the material constituting the debris is from a newer shaft in the course of excavation. Pollen analysis enables type of vegetation growing at the time to be determined and sites can be placed in order of relative age. If the absolute date is known for one of the sites then pollen analysis is useful for fixing the date of other sites. Recognition of remnants and small pieces of artefacts, pottery, animal and human bones etc. is of course within the sphere of a trained person who has the knowledge of the dates when such materials were used, customs of burial practised or animals were domesticated.

Sedimentation, pollen analysis and identification of finds are examples of relative dating which can be used in excavation of prehistoric mining sites and indeed were the only ones available before the introduction of radiocarbon methods. It is when these can be related to absolute dates that they are really invaluable.

Absolute Methods

There are many absolute dating methods. Some are special to a particular material or time scale or to a stage in prehistoric evolution and only a few as in the case of the relative methods, are applicable to the investigation of mining sites. Whereas most of the methods of relative dating, especially the ones requiring close observation, fall within the scope of the trained archaeologist practically all the absolute methods have to be performed by specialists, as not only do they require expertise in a particular field, but are very time consuming.

Absolute dating methods include:

(1) astronomical
(2) dendrochronology
(3) deep sea cores
(4) fission track
(5) obsidian dating
(6) potassium argon
(7) radiocarbon

(8)   thermoluminescence
(9)   varves

Astronomical Methods

These are no longer so important with the advent of more precise methods capable of surveying a wider field with more accuracy. However, some importance was once attached to the study of climates based on changes in the earth's orbit. Such fluctuations involving ecliptic obliquity have a cycle of 40 000 years and similar changes can be noted in the study of varves, tree rings and deep sea cores. Sun spot cycles and radiation are also affected.

Dendrochronology

Basically the method involves the study of rings formed in trees during growth. Originally it was used to study growth changes as a result of climatic fluctuations, but later as a form of dating wood relics in a semi-absolute manner. Normally growth produces one concentric ring per annum the thickness of ring decreasing with age, but narrow rings are produced during dry periods when wet and so the climate influences growth.

Cross dating is an absolute method. For example tree ring width on a piece of wood of unknown age can be related to those of similar widths on a tree of known age. It is possible to have two or more cross checks as references, e.g a relic of known age between that of the old one to be dated and the young tree. However, it is possible to date a good specimen without a cross reference when climatic fluctuations are known to have been minimal. The best type of wood to date is pine, such as that from the bristle cone pine, whereas larch, beech and oak are difficult owing to the nature of the tree rings formed and the effect of climatic fluctuations. In practice a full cross section is preferable for examination as opposed to cores or radial sampling.

Deep Sea Cores

With this method it is possible to obtain a record of the changes in temperature of the shallow waters of the oceans during the Pleistocene. Usually cores taken of the sedimentation of the sea bed up to 5 cm in diameter and maybe 20–25 m long. Cores if in good condition can give a record of the strata back from the present to one million years.

Fission Track

Whereas the radiocarbon method is limited to age assessment up to 70 000 years and the potassium argon method to between 70 000 and three million years, fission track can be used over 20 years to 1000 million years. However, it is limited to use on crystalline or glassy materials. The theory is that ^{238}U impurities produce very fine damage tracks in the material. The submicroscopic damage marks can be counted and their density gives an indication of the age of the specimen under test. Although the method gives an indication of the age within limits, it is more suitable for geological specimens, but it does find an application on manufactured glass objects of age from three to 300 years.

Obsidian Dating

This is a specialized method being restricted to that important volcanic rock used by prehistoric man, namely obsidian. As previously indicated it was in great demand for the manufacture of tools, vases etc. As soon as this rock is exposed it is subject to hydration and a layer is formed whose thickness increases with age since exposure. It may be exposed during tooling, mining or quarrying. Although obsidian, flint, chert, jasper etc. are subject to patination with exposure only obsidian displays hydration weathering.

Basically the method involves the measurement of the hydration layers which may be a few tenths to 20 μm in thickness. From $D = kt^2$ where D is the thickness of the hydration layer in μm, k a constant and t the time since exposure in years, the last named can be calculated. In California, $D = kt^{\frac{3}{4}}$ is used. For calibration a sample obsidian of known age is required. k is influenced by locality and chemical composition.

Potassium Argon Dating

This is a method applicable to materials older than can be dated by the radiocarbon method, i.e. to millions of years. Potassium occupies 2·8% by weight of the earth's crust and is thus one of the most abundant elements. ^{40}K has a half life of $1·30 \pm 0·04 \times 10^9$ years and so compares with the age of the earth. ^{40}K decays to ^{40}A and the latter can be measured more easily than most other elements. The samples must be melted to extract the gases and these are purified. The quantities are then measured by isotopic analysis with a mass spectrometer.

The method was first used at Olduvai Gorge in Africa for the dating of fossil hominoids 12–14 million years old.

Radiocarbon Dating

Some reference has already been made to this method in Ch. 6. Despite its imperfections and these are many, it is still the best available tool for the absolute dating of suitable relics up to an age of 60 000 years.

About 60–70 years ago it was found that our planet was being bombarded by subatomic particles having high energy properties. This is termed cosmic radiation. Contact with the earth's atmosphere sets free neutrons which transmute nitrogen in the air into radioactive ^{14}C and is absorbed by plants and other living matter. ^{14}C behaves in the same way as ordinary carbon ^{12}C. As living matter decays radiocarbon is lost to the atmosphere and in 5000 years, the early accepted half life, half has decayed. The amount of ^{14}C set up in the atmosphere over a given time balances the loss sustained in the same time by radioactive decay. Thus $\frac{carbon\ ^{14}}{carbon\ ^{12}}$ is constant in the atmosphere. As a body decays, no more ^{14}C is taken up $\frac{^{14}C}{^{12}C}$ decreases and the process is to measure the actual decrease. The original ratio is known so the new ratio gives the fraction remaining and based on the known half life of the isotope the absolute age can be determined. There is a statistically determined error given as $+$ or $-$, shown $\pm$ with the date. Not all the radiocarbon actually disappears, but the remainder is small. For example a determined date of 3500 ± 60 does not mean that the actual date lies between 3440 and 3560, but that there is 68% chance that the date is within 60 years of 3500 and 95% with twice the standard error, i.e. 120 years.

There is a wide variety of materials which can be dated by the radiocarbon method, but all must have been organic living matter or derived from it. Charcoal is one of the best since it is almost pure carbon. Any age determined for charcoal of course is the age of the tree when it was felled which could well have been centuries before being burnt in, say, a prehistoric mine. Other materials which can be dated are dry wood, seeds (if carbonized), bones and sea shells. At one time it was necessary to use a large sample of the specimen, but now many laboratories can obtain results with quite small supplies. The specimen is first crushed, cleaned and dried and then burned to give carbon dioxide, which is passed into lime water where calcium carbonate is precipitated. This is dissolved in acid when carbon dioxide is again liberated. By burning magnesium in the gas it is finally reduced to pure carbon. The sooty carbon is then spread on to a counter the disintegrated ^{14}C atoms being recorded automatically. The solid carbon counter has now been replaced by a gas counter and usually carbon dioxide or acetylene is used for counting. Oxalic acid is the modern standard used for comparison.

There are a few problems and assumptions to be made. One is that it is limited to c. 60 000 years as after this age little radiocarbon remains. Contamination by newer materials is a serious drawback as for example newer peaty soils mixed with old charcoal, and streams flowing over coal outcrops.

The assumptions to be made are basic to the method. For example it has to be assumed that radiocarbon decay is constant with time and is not related to change in temperature of the atmosphere or burial. Furthermore it must be assumed that ^{14}C in the atmosphere has always been constant, that there has been no change in cosmic activity and that ^{14}C in all living bodies was constant at any given time. Large scale burning of coal and oil releases ^{14}C free carbon dioxide into the atmosphere. There must have been no contamination since death. The half life must have been determined accurately. Libby, when he developed the method, used a value of half life of 5568 years. This has now been revised to 5730 ± 40 years therefore the earlier dates obtained require recalibration on the basis of the revised half life, i.e. corrected date BP (before present) $= 1\cdot03 \times ^{14}C$ date BP.

In 1960 some doubt was being expressed about the assumption that the amount of ^{14}C in the atmosphere and the proportion in living matter has been constant over 40 000 years. Hans E. Suess at the University of San Diego showed by counting the annual tree rings of the long living old bristle cone pine tree and cross dating with wood of known age, that there had been major fluctuations. Tree ring dates agreed with ^{14}C dates back to AD 650 and down to 1200 or possibly 1500 BC there were slight discrepancies. However, dates earlier than 1200 BC had to be corrected by an increasing amount. For example a radiocarbon date of 2000 BC is too young according to the dates deduced by Suess and should be 2500 BC and a ^{14}C date of 4000 BC should be 4850 BC. One serious disadvantage of the theory of Suess is that the correction curve which he drew fluctuates or kinks appreciably and therefore when used for recalibration of old ^{14}C dates it is possible to read off two or more alternative corrected dates corresponding to the old date.

Thermoluminescence

This is a very complex method of dating ceramics, pottery, sherds and in certain cases rocks. Thus it fills a gap amongst the many methods of dating at present available. The most useful, the radiocarbon method, cannot of course be used for the dating of pottery. Sherds often represent the majority of finds on prehistoric sites and unless they can be dated are virtually useless.

Pottery and ceramics have the property of storing energy by trapping electrons. This energy is released when the material of the pot is heated to a high temperature when the visible light emitted can be measured. At the same time such materials have radioactive impurities such as thorium and uranium in a few parts per million. The susceptibility of the sample to the production of luminescence by an artificial known source is measured. Thus there are basically three measurements. By combining these the absolute age can be determined. The error has been stated to be $\pm 3\%$.

Varves

This is a method developed in Sweden in the late nineteenth century by de Geer. It is used in connection with the dating of Pleistocene sediments and all those formed under pre-glacial conditions. Retreating ice deposits coarse material first which is lighter in colour and fine grained later this being darker. This in glacial areas is an annual phenomenon and the laminated sediments left behind are termed varves. De Geer found that by counting the number of varves, which may be a few millimetres to several centimetres wide, good agreement with ^{14}C dates for Sweden and the same later for Finland. Post-glacial Sweden was dated to 6923 BC and Finland 8100 BC. One difficulty as with dendrochronology is the formation of more than one feature per annum.

The preceding summary is not intended to be a complete coverage, but only to provide background material and to highlight the significant features of methods which might be useful for dating certain aspects of prehistoric mining sites of any age. For fuller treatment of the subject the references given here should be consulted.

References

Brothwell, D. and Higgs, E. (1969). "Science in Archaeology." Thames and Hudson, London.
Deevey, E. S., Jr. (1961). In "Old World Archaeology." 196–200.

Renfrew, C. (1961). *In* "Old World Archaeology." 201–209.
Renfrew, C. (1973). "Before Civilisation—the Radiocarbon Revolution." Penguin, Harmondsworth.
West, R. G. (1968). "Pleistocene Geology and Biology." Longman, London.

Other Reading

Atkinson, R. J. C. (1975). *Antiq. Survival* **49**, 175–177.
Bakker, J. A., Vogel, J. C. and Wiślański, T. (1969). *Helios, Berl.* **9**, 3–27.
Barker, H. (1958). *Antiq. Survival* **32**, 253–263.
Clark, R. M. (1975). *Antiq. Survival* **49**, 251–262.
Fergusson, G. J. (1958). *Nucleonics*, **13**, 18–23.
Pearson, G. W., Pilcher, J. R., Baillie, M. G. L. and Hillam, J. (1977). *Nature* **270**, 25–28.
Vogel, J. C. (1969). *S. Afr. Arch. Bull.* **24**. 83–87.
Waterbolk, H. T. (1971). *Proc. prehist. Soc.* **37**, 15–24.
Zeuner, A. F. E. (1970). "Dating the Past." Methuen, London.

References

Aigner, A. (1911). "Ein Kulturbild aus prähistorische Zeit." Munich.
Aitken, H. (1893). *Trans. Inst. Min. Eng.* **6**, 193–198.
Alexander, J. (1972). "Yugoslavia." Thames and Hudson, London.
Alexander, W. and Street, A. (1946). "Metals in the Service of Man." Pelican, Harmondsworth.
Allcroft, H. A. (1916). *Sussex archaeol. Coll.* **58**, 68–74.
Althin, C. A. G. (1951). "The Scanian Flint Mines," pp. 139–158. Medded Lunds University.
Andrée, J. (1922). "Bergbau in der Vorzeit." Kabisch, Leipzig.
Anon. (1932). *Ant. J.* **12**, 167.
Armstrong, A. L. (1936). *Proc. prehist. Soc.*, **2**, 215.
Ault, N. (1920). "Life in Ancient Britain.", p. 115. Longmans, London.
Baker, F. T. (1960). *J. Lincs. archit. Archaeol. Soc.* **8**, 26–34.
Ball, S. H. (1927). *Engng Min. J.* **128**, 483–485.
Ball, S. H. (1929). *Econ. Geol.* **26**, 681–738.
Barth, F. E. (1973). *Mitt. anthrop. Ges. Wien* **102**, 26–30.
Barth, F. E. and Hodson, F. R. (1976). *Ant. J.* **56**, 159–176.
Batemen, A. M. (1927). *Econ. Geol.* **22**, 570–614.
de Baye (1885). Review by C. Emile in *Matér. Hist. Prim. Nat. de l'Homme* **19**.
Becker, C. J. (1959). *Antiq.* **33**, 87–92.
Becker, C. J. (1976). *In* "Festschrift für Richard Pittioni" pp. 1–12. Franz Deuticke, Vienna.
Becker, C. J. (1977). *Reall. Germ. Alterstumkunde* **2**, 245–250.
Blance, B. (1961). *Antiq.* **35**, 192.
Booth, A. St J. and Stone, J. F. S. (1951). *Wilts. archaeol. nat. Hist. Mag.* **54**, 381–388.
Boshier, A. and Beaumont, P. (1972). *Optima* **22**(1), 1–12.
Boule, M. (1884). *Matér. Hist. Prim. Nat. de l'Homme* **18**, 65.
Boule, M. (1887). *Matér. Hist. Prim. Nat. de l'Homme* **21**, 5–21.
Bray, W. and Trump, D. (1973). "Dictionary of Archaeology." Penguin, Harmondsworth.
Bren, J. (1955). "Historia", 9A Acta. Musei, Prague.
Briart, A., Cornet, F. and de Houzeau, L. A. (1868). *Soc. Sci. Arts et Lettres de Hainaut.*

Briggs, C. S. (1976). *Brit. archaeol. Rep.* **33**.

Briggs, C. S., Brennan, J., and Freeman, C. (1973). *Bull. Hist. Met. Group* **7, 2**, 18–26.

Brøgger, A. W. (1940). *Antiq.* **14**, 163–181.

Bromehead, C. E. N. (1940). *Geogrl Mag. London.* **96(2)**, 113–120.

Brothwell, D. (1969). "Diet, Economy and Biological Change." Rep. Conf. on Econ. and Settlement in Neolithic and E.B.A. Britain and Europe. Leicester University Press, Leicester.

Brothwell, D. and Brothwell, P. (1969). "Food in Antiquity" p. 23. Thames and Hudson, London.

Brown, M. A. and Blin-Stoyle, A. E. (1959). *Proc. prehist. Soc.* **25**, 188–208.

Burleigh, R. (1975). Rep. of Second Int. Feuerstein Symposium, No. 3, pp. 89–91. Staringia, Maastricht.

Bush, J. J. and Fell, C. (1949). *Proc. prehist. Soc.* **15**, 1–20.

Butler, J. J. and Van der Waals, J. D. (1966). *Palaeohistoria* **12**, 41–139.

Case, H. J. (1966). *Palaeohistoria* **12**, 141–177.

Cernych, E. N. (1978). *Proc. prehist. Soc.* **44**, 203–217.

Charles, J. A. (1975). *Antiq.* **49**, 19–24.

Childe, V. G. (1930). "The Bronze Age." Cambridge University Press.

Childe, V. G. (1948). *Man* **133**, 120–122.

Childe, V. G. (1951). Review of Coghlan's "Notes on Prehistoric Metallurgy of Copper and Bronze in the Old World" Occ. Papers in Technology 4. *Antiq.* **25**.

Childe, V. G. (1954). "What Happened in History." Pitman, London.

Childe, V. G. (1957). "The Dawn of European Civilisation." Routledge and Kegan Paul, London.

Childe, V. G. (1963). "Social Evolution." Watts, London.

Childe, V. G. (1965). "Man Makes Himself." Watts, London.

Clark, G. and Piggott, S. (1933). *Antiq.* **7**, 166–183.

Clark, J. D. G. (1934). *Arch. J.* **91**, 56–57.

Clark, J. D. G. (1948). *Proc. prehist. Soc.* **14**, 219–232.

Clark, J. D. G. (1952). "Prehistoric Europe." Methuen, London.

Clark, J. D. G., Evans, E. E., Leese, H. G., Childe. V. G. and Grieves, W. F. (1937). *Proc. prehist. Soc.* **3**, 439–441.

Clarke, R. (1935). *Antiq.* **9**, 38–56.

Clarke, W. G. (1914). "Report on Grimes Graves." Lewis, London.

Clarke, W. G. (1915). *Proc. prehist. Soc.* **2**, 148–151.

Clason, A. T. (1971). *Hel.* **11**, 1.

Cleere, H. F. (1972). *Ant. J.* **52**, 8–23.

Clough, T. H. McK and Green, B. (1972). *Proc. prehist. Soc.* **38**, 108–155.

Coe, M. D. and Flannery, K. V. (1964). *Am. Antiq.* **30**, 43–49.

Coghlan, H. H. (1939). *Man* **39**, 92, 136.

Coghlan, H. H. (1942). *Ant. J.* **22**, 22–38.

Coghlan, H. H. (1951a). *Man.* **51**, no. 156, 90–93.

Coghlan, H. H. (1951b). Notes on Prehistory of Copper and Bronze in the Old World. Occ. Papers in Technology No. 4. Pitt Rivers Museum, Oxford.

Coghlan, H. H. (1956). Prehistoric and Early Iron in the Old World. Occ. Papers in Technology. No. 8. Pitt Rivers Museum, Oxford.

Coghlan, H. H. and Case, H. (1957). *Proc. prehist. Soc.* **23**, 91–123.

Cole, G. A. G. and Hallisey, T. (1924). "Handbook on the Geology of Ireland." Murby, London.

Cole, S. (1970). "The Neolithic Revolution." British Museum (Natural History).

Coleman, P. (1957). *Bull. r. Soc. belge* **16**, 247–249.

Collins, A. L. (1893). *Trans. Inst. Min. Eng.* **3**, 83–92.

Cook, W. H. and Killick, J. R. (1922). *Proc. prehist. Soc.* **4**, 133–154.

Courtin, J. (1957). *Bull. Soc. Etud. Scient. nat. Vau.*

Crawford, I. A. (1966). *Antiq.* **39**, 139–140.

Crawford, O. G. S. (1939). *Antiq.* **12**, 79–81.

Culican, W. (1966). "The First Merchant Venturers." Thames and Hudson. London.

Cummins, W. A. (1974). *Antiq.* **48**, 201–205.

Cunnington, M. E. (1930). *Wilts. archeol. nat. Hist. Mag.* **45**, 170.

Cunnington, M. E. (1933). *Antiq.* **7**, 89–90.

Curwen, C. (1928). *Sussex archaeol. Coll.* **69**, 95.

Curwen, E. and Curwen, C. (1923). *Sussex archaeol. Coll.* **67**, 102–138.

Curwen, E. and Curwen, E. C. (1927). *Sussex Notes and Queries* **1**, 168–170.

Curwen, E. C. (1929). *Sussex archaeol. Coll.* **70**, 33–85.

Curwen, E. C. (1934). *Sussex archaeol. Coll.* **75**, 137–170.

Curwen, E. C. (1954). "The Archaeology of Sussex." Methuen, London.

Davies, H. (1937). *Archaeol. J.* **93**, 200–219.

Davies, O. (1928). *Ann. Br. Sch. Ath.* **30**, 74–85.

Davies, O. (1932). *Nature, London.* **31**, 985–987.

Davies, O. (1935). "Roman Mines in Europe." Oxford University Press.

Davies, O. (1936). *Man* **36**, 92–93.

Davies, O. (1946). *Archaeol. Camb.* **99**, 57–63.

Davies, O. (1948). *Archaeol. Camb.* **100**, 61–66.

Dayton, J. E. (1971). *Wld Archaeol.* **3**, 49–70.

Deady, J. and Doran E. (1972). *J. Cork hist. archaeol. Soc.* **77**, 25–27.

Delibrias, G. and Le Roux, C. T. (1975). *Bull. Soc. préhist. fr.* **72**, 78–82.

Demek, J. and Miroslav, S. (1971). "Geography of Czechoslovakia", pp. 213–215. Academia, Prague.

Desch, C. H. (1927). *Discovery* **8**, 342.

Dyer, J. F. (1973). "Southern England." Faber and Faber, London.

Dyer, J. F. and Hales A. J. (1961). *Rec. Bucks.* **17**, 49–61,

Eaton, E. R. and McKerrell, H. (1976). *Wld archaeol.* **8**, 169–191.

Engelen, F. H. G. (1969). *Der Anschnitt Bochum* **21**, 15–22.

Evans, E. D., Smith, I. F. and Wallis, F. S. (1972). *Proc. prehist. Soc.* **38**, 235–275.

Evans, J. D. (1971). *Proc. prehist. Soc.* **37**, 95–117.

Evans, J. G. (1969). "Environment of Early Farming Communities in

Britain." Rep. Conf. on Econ. and Settlement in Neolithic and E. B. A, Britain and Europe. Leicester University Press.

Evans, J. G. (1975). "The Environment of Early Man in the British Isles", p. 128. Elek, London.

Farror, R. A. H. (1964). *Proc. Dorset nat. Hist. archaeol. Soc.* **84**, 137–144.

Fell, C. I. (1936). *Archaeol. J.* **93**, 57–100.

Filip, J. (1960). "Celtic Civilisation and its Heritage." New Horizons, Prague.

Forbes, R. J. (1955). "Studies in Ancient Technology", Vol. 6. Brill, Leyden.

Forbes, R. J. (1964a). "Studies in Ancient Technology", Vol. 7. Brill, Leyden.

Forbes, R. J. (1964b). "Studies in Ancient Technology", Vol. 8. Brill, Leyden.

Fox, C. (1932). *Proc. prehist. Soc.* **7**, 154.

Fox, C. and Hyde, H. A. (1939). *Ant. J.* **19**, 369–404.

Friend, N. J. (1926). "Iron in Antiquity." Griffin, London.

Fülöp, J. (1973). *Acta archaeol.* **25**, 3–35.

Gabel, C. (1957). *Antiq.* **31**, 90–92.

Galley, A. (1971). *Germania* **49**, 223.

Giles, D. J. and Kuijpers, E. P. (1974). *Science* **56**.

Glenn, T. A. (1935). *Archaeol Camb.* **90**, 189–218.

Gomme, G. L. (1884). *Norfolk Archaeol.* **9**, 65.

Goodman, C. H., Frost, M., Curwen, C. and Curwen, E. C. (1922). *Sussex archaeol. Coll.* **65**, 69.

Gowland, W. (1902). *Archaeologia* **56**, **II**, 267–322.

Gowland, W. (1903). *Archaeologia* **57**, **II**, 359–422.

Gowland, W. (1917). *Archaeologia* **69**, 121–160.

Grieves, T. A. P. (1975). *Proc. prehist. Soc.* **41**, 153–166.

Grinsell, L. V. (1958). "The Archaeology of Wessex." Methuen, London.

Gurney, O. R. (1976). "The Hittites." Penguin, Harmondsworth.

Hamal-Nandrin, J. and Servais, J. (1923). *Rev. anthrop.* **33**, 344.

Hammond, N. (1978). "The Times." London, 1st June.

Harrison, R. J. (1974). *Antiq.* **48**, 99–109.

Hawkes, C. F. C. (1940)." The Prehistoric Foundations of Europe", pp. 138–140. Methuen, London.

Hawkes, J. (1934a). *Antiq.* **8**, 24–42.

Hawkes, J. (1934b). *Proc. prehist. Soc.* **7**, 379.

Hawkes, J. (1973). "A Guide to the Prehistoric and Roman Monuments in England and Wales." Sphere, London.

Hawkes, J. and Wooley, Sir L. (1963). "History of Mankind", Vol. 1. Allen and Unwin, London.

Hencken, H. O'N. (1932). "The Archaeology of Cornwall and Scilly." Methuen, London.

Herity, M. and Eogan, C. (1977). "Ireland in Prehistory." Routledge and Kegan Paul, London.

Hoffman, E. and Morton, F. (1928). *Wien prähist. Z. Vienna.* **15**, 82–101.

Holleyman, G. (1937a). *Sussex Archaeol. Coll.* **78**, 230–252.

Holleyman, G. (1937b). *J. R. anthrop. Inst.* **78**, 237.

Holzer, H. F. (1971). *Archaeol Aust.* **49**, 1–22.

Hörter, F., Michels, F. X. and Röder, J. (1950) Part I, Jahrbuch für Geschichte und Kultur des Mittelrheins und seiner Nachbargebiete, Year 2 & 3, pp. 1–32. Raiffeisendruckerei, Neuwied am Rhein.

Houlder, C. H. (1961). *Proc. prehist. Soc.* **27**, 108–143.

Humphreys, H. (1952). *Antiq.* **26**, 125–134.

Jackson, J. S. (1968). *Archaeol. Aust.* **43**, 92–114.

Jahn, M. (1956). Ablangungen der sächsischen Akademie der Wissenschaften zu Leipzig. Akademie, Berlin. **48**, 5–40.

Jahn, M. (1960). Der älteste Bergbau in Europa. Akademie-Leipzig, Berlin, 1–62.

Jazdzewski, K. (1965). Poland. Thames and Hudson, London.

Jovanovic, B. (1971). *Rep. Anthrop. Institut. Belgrade* **9**, 103–119.

Jovanovic, B. (1976). *Der Anschnitt.* **5**, 150–157.

Jovanovic, B. and Ottaway, B. S. (1976). *Antiq.* **49**, 194–113.

Jukes, J. B. (1861). *In* Kinahan (1861) "Note on the Mines of the South West of Cork", pp. 27–28.

Keiller, A., Piggott, S. and Wallis, F. S. (1941). *Proc. prehist. Soc.* **7**, 50–72.

Kellaway, C. A. (1971). *Nature* **223**, 30–35.

Kinahan, G. H. (1861). Explanatory Memoir of the Geol. Survey of Ireland to One-Inch Sheets 200–205 and part of 199.

Kinahan, G. H. (1885). *J. R. geol. Soc. Ireland* **8**, 1–514.

Kirnbauer, F. (1958). *Archaeol. Aust.* **3**, 51–54.

Klima, B. (1956). *Antiq.* **30**, 98–101.

Kopper, J. S. and Rosello-Bordoy, G. (1974). *J. field Archaeol.* **1**, 161–170.

Kromer, K. (1959). "Das Graberfeld von Hallstatt." Sansoni, Florence.

Kyrle, G. (1913). *Jb. Altertum*, **3**.

Kyrle, G. (1918). *Oster. Kunstop.* **17**, part 1.

de Laet S. J. (1958). "The Low Countries." Thames and Hudson, London.

Lanting, J. N., Mook, W. S. and Van den Waals, (1973). *Hel.* **13**, 38–58.

Law, W. (1927). *Sussex Notes and Queries* **1**, 222–224.

Layard, N. F. (1925). *Proc. prehist. Soc.* **5**, 34–35.

Lease, H. G., Clark, J. G. D., Evans, E. E., Childe, V. G. and Grieves, W. F. (1938). *Proc. prehist. Soc.* **4**, 317.

Lech, J. (1975). Rep. Second Int. Symp. on Flint. Staringia, Maastricht.

Le Roux, C. T. (1971). *Antiq.* **45**, 283–286.

Le Roux, C. T. (1973). Report of the 98th Congress of the Natural Society of Savoy St. Etienne, pp. 9–20.

Lewis, P. R. and Jones, G. D. B. (1969). *Ant. J.* **49**, 244–272.

Lloyd, S. (1967). "Early Highland Peoples of Anatolia." Thames and Hudson, London.

de Loë, Baron. (1928). "Belgique Ancien", Vol. 1. Ages de la Pierre, Brussels.

Lottin, M. le Dr (1884). *Matér. Hist. Prim. Nat. de l'Homme* **18**, 3rd Series, 505–506.

Lüning, J. (1972). *Prähist. Z.* **47**, 145–173.

Macalister, R. A. S. (1949). "The Archaeology of Ireland." Methuen, London.

MacAlpine Woods, G. A. (1929). *Proc., Devon archaeol. Expl. Soc.* **1**, 10–14.

MacAlpine Woods, R. and MacAlpine Woods, G. (1933). *Proc. Devon archaeol. Expl. Soc.* **2**, 28–39.
MacAlpine Woods, R. and MacAlpine Woods, G. (1948). *Proc. Devon archaeol. Expl. Soc.* **3**, 44–50.
Mahr, A. (1937). *Proc. prehist. Soc.* **3**, 261.
Manning, C. R. (1855). *Norfolk Archaeol.* **4**, 356.
Manning, C. R. (1872). *Norfolk Archaeol.* **7**, 173–174.
Mazcek, M., Preuschen, E. and Pittioni, R. (1952). *Archaeol. Aust.* **10**, 61–70.
Mazcek, M., Preuschen, E. and Pittioni, R. (1964). *Archaeol. Aust.* **35**, 98–110.
Meier-Arendt, W. (1975). "Die Steinzeit in Köln." Römisch-Germanisches Museum, Köln.
Mellaart, J. (1960). *Antiq.* **31**, 270–278.
Mellaart, J. (1975). "The Neolithic of the Near East." Thames and Hudson, London.
Mercer, R. (1976). Grimes Graves-an interim statement. Rep. on Settlement and Economy in 3rd: and 2nd. Millenia B.C. *Br. archaeol. Rep.* **33**, 101–112.
Meszaros, Cy. and Vertes, L. (1953). *Acta. Archaeol.* **5**, 1–34.
Mikami, H. M. (1944). *Econ. Geol.* **39**, 1–24.
Much, M. (1878). *Mitt. ZentKommn scheiz. Landesk.* **14**.
Much, M. (1879). *Mitt. ZentKommn scheiz. Landesk.* **5**.
Muhly, J. D. and Wertime, T. A. (1973). *Wld. Archaeol.* **5**, 111–122.
de Munck, M. E. (1886). *Bull. Soc. Anthrop. Brux.* **5**.
Nandris, J. (1975). *Bull Inst. Archaeol.* **3**, 7 1–94.
Norfolk Norwich Nat. Soc. Trans. (1859). **5**, 250.
Norfolk Archaeol. (1946). **29**, 13.
North, F. J. (1962). "Mining for Metals in Wales." National Museum of Cardiff.
Oates, J. (1973). *Proc. prehist. Soc.* **39**, 147–181.
Passmore, A. D. (1942). *Wilts. archaeol. nat. Hist. Mag.* **49**, 118–119.
Peake, A. E. (1913a). *Archaeol J.* **70**, 33–68.
Peake, A. E. (1913b). *Proc. prehist. Soc. East Anglia.* **6**, 404.
Peake, A. E. (1914). "Grimes Graves Excavations." Prehist Soc. East Anglia. Lewis, London.
Percy, I. (1873). "Metallurgy of Iron and Steel." Murray, London.
Petrie, Sir F. (1900). "Researches in Sinai." Murray, London.
Peyrolles, D. and Peyrolles, R. (1959). *Bull. Soc. prehist. fr.* **56**, 525–531.
Phillips, P. (1975). "Early Farmers of West Mediterranean Europe." Hutchinson, London.
Piesse, C. L. (1927). *Discovery, London* **8**, 342.
Piggott, S. (1954). "The Neolithic Cultures of the British Isles." Cambridge University Press.
Piggott, S. (1955). Proc. prehist. Soc. **21**. 96–101.
Piggott, S. (1973). "Ancient Europe." Edinburgh University Press.
Pittioni, R. (1950). *Ann. Rep. Inst. Archaeol. London.* 40–41.
Pittioni, R. (1954). Urgeschichte des österreichen Raumes. Franz Deutsche. Vienna.
Pittioni, R. (1957). *Archaeol. Aust.* **1**, 264–278.

Pliny. Natural History. Book 23.
Plowright, C. B. and Wade, A. G. (1859). *Norfolk Norwich Soc. Trans.*, **250**.
Prevost, R. (1959). *Bull. Soc. prehist. fr.* **56**, 161–162.
Proc. prehist. Soc. (1937). **3**, 440–441.
Proc. prehist. Soc. (1938). **4**, 317.
Proc. prehist. Soc. (1958) **24**, 218.
Pull, J. R. (1932). Flint Mines of Blackpatch. Williams and Norgate, London.
Pull, J. R. (1933). *Sussex County Mag.* **7**, 801–814.
Pull, J. R. (1953). *Sussex County Mag.* **27**, 15–21.
Ramin, J. (1977). "La Technique Miniere et Metallurgie des Anciens." Latomus, Brussels.
Reed, T. T. (1934). *Am. J. Archaeol.* **38**, 383.
Reeves, T. J. (1971). *Bull. geol. Surv. Ireland.* **1**, 73–85.
Reid, C. (1918). *Man* **18**, 9–11.
Reisch, L. (1974). "Materialhafte zur Bayrischen Vorgeschichte", p. 29. Michael Lossleben, Kallminz.
Renfrew, C. (1967). *Antiq.* **41**, 276–287.
Renfrew, C. (1969). *Proc. prehist. Soc.* **35**, 12–47.
Renfrew, C. (1973). "Before Civilisation." Jonathan Cape, London.
Renfrew, C. (1978). *Antiq.* **52**, 199–203.
Renfrew, C., Dixon, J. E. and Cann, J. R. (1966). *Proc. prehist. Soc.* **32**, 30–72.
Richardson, K. M. and Young, A. (1951). *Ant. J.* **31**, 132–148.
Rickard, T. A. (1932). "Man and Metals", Vol. 1. McGraw Hill, London.
Rickard, T. A. (1941). *J. R. Anthrop. Inst.* **71**, 55–66.
Riehm, K. (1961). *Antiq.* **35**, 181–191.
Ritchie P. R. (1968). *In* Studies in Ancient Europe" (Ed. Coles and Simpson) pp. 117–136. Leicester University Press.
Rodden, R. J. (1962). *Proc. prehist. Soc.* **28**, 267–288.
Röder, J. (1955). *Antiq.* **29**, 68–76.
Roeder, C. (1901). *Trans. Lancs. Cheshire antiq. Soc.* **19**, 77–118.
Rothenberg, B. (1972). "Timna." Thames and Hudson, London.
Rutot, M. A. (1921). *Ant. J.* **1**, 54–55.
Ruttkay, E. (1970). *Mitt. anthrop. Ges. Wien.* **100**, 70–79.
Sagui, C. L. (1924). *Econ. Geol.* **19**, 542–549.
Sagui, C. L. (1928). *Econ. Geol.* **23**, 671–680.
Sagui, C. L. (1930). *Econ. Geol.* **25**, 65–86.
Sagui, C. L. (1933). *Econ. Geol.* **28**, 20–40.
de Saint-Venant, M. J. (1900). Congress-international d'Anthropologie Compte-rendu 12 Paris.
Sanders, H. W. (1910). *Archaeologia* **12**, 101–124.
Sangmeister, E. (1966). *Palaeohistoria,* **12**, 395–407.
Savory, H. V. (1968). "Spain and Portugal." Prager, New York.
Schild, R. (1976). *Sci. Am.* **234**, 98–99.
Schmid, E. (1952). *Der Anschnitt* **4**, 4–13.
Schmid, E. (1960). *Der Anschnitt.* **12**, 3–11.
Schmid, E. (1963). *Der Anschnitt.* **15**, 10–21.

Schmid, E. (1972). Records of Paris Symposium on "The Origins of Homo Sapiens". Unesco, Paris.

Schmid, E. (1975). 2nd Int. Symposium on Flint. Staringia, Maastricht.

Schwantes, G. (1932). *Germania.* **16**, 177–185.

Scollar, I. (1955). *Antiq.* **29**, 159–160.

Scollar, I. (1957). *Antiq.* **31**, 100–103.

Scollar, I. (1959). *Proc. prehist. Soc.* **25**, 56.

Scott, L. (1950). *Proc. prehist. Soc.* **17**, 40.

Scott, L. (1951). *Proc. prehist. Soc.* **17**, 16–82.

Selimkhanov, I. R. (1964). *Proc. prehist. Soc.* **30**, 66–79.

Sheets, P. D. (1975). *Am. Antiq.* **40**, 98–106.

Shepherd, R. (1970). Proc of Symposium on Strata Control in Roadways. Inst. Min. Eng.

Sieveking, G. G., Longworth, I. H., Hughes, M. J., Clark, A. J. and Millett, A. A. (1973). *Proc. prehist. Soc.* **39**, 182–218.

Simpson, D. D. A. (1971). Proc. Conf. on Economy and Settlement in Neolithic and E. B. A., Britain and Europe. 131–152.

Smith, C. W. (1965). *Proc. prehist. Soc.* **31**, 25–33.

Smith, E. (1911). "The Ancient Egyptians", p. 10, Harper, London. 10.

Smith, R. A. (1911). *Archaeologia* **63**, 109–158.

Speight, W. L. (1948). *Min. J. Wash.* **12**, 595–596.

Spielmann, P. E. (1926). *Nature, London* **18**, 411.

Stayt, H. A. (1931). "The Bavenda", p. 6. Oxford University Press.

Stenberger, M. (1962). "Sweden." Thames and Hudson, London.

Stieren, A. (1935). *Germania,* **19**, 12–20.

Stone, J. F. S. (1933). *Wilts. archaeol. nat. Hist. Mag.* **45**, 330–365.

Stone, J. F. S. (1934). *Wilts. archaeol. nat. Hist. Mag.* **46**, 225–242.

Stone, J. F. S. (1937). *Wilts. archaeol. nat. Hist. Mag.* **47**, 68.

Stone, J. F. S. (1958). "Wessex before the Celts" pp. 42–43. Thames and Hudson, London.

Stone, J. F. S. and Wallis F. S. (1947). *Proc. prehist. Soc.* **13**, 47–53.

Straker, E. (1931). "Wealdon Iron." Bell, London.

Straker, E. and Lucas, B. H. (1938). *Sussex archaeol. Coll.* **79**, 224–232.

Sulimirski, T. (1970). "Prehistoric Russia." Baker, London.

Swinnerton, H. H. (1932). *Ant. J.* **12**, 239–253.

Thomas, N. (1976). "Guide to Prehistoric England." Batsford, London.

Thompson, F. C. (1958). **Man 58**, 1–7.

Todd, K. R. U. (1949). *Surrey Archaeol. Coll.* **51**, 142–143.

Toms, H. S. (1928). The Flint Mine Problem. Sussex County Herald for 3, 11 and 18 August and 1 September 1928.

Tringham R. (1971). "Hunters, Fishers and Farmers of East Europe, 6000–3000 BC" Hutchinson, London.

Triphook, T. D. (1865a). *J. geol. Soc. Dublin* **6**, 44–47.

Triphook, T. D. (1865b). *J. geol. Soc. Dublin* **6**, 218–226.

Tshumi, O. (1949). *Urgeschichte der Schweiz.* **6**, 610–611.

Tuadze, F. and Sakvarelidze, T. (1959). "T. Bronze drevnei gruzii." Izd. Ak. Nank. Gruz. Tbilisi, Russia.

Tylecote, R. F. (1962). "Metallurgy in Archaeology" Arnold, London.

Tylecote, R. F. (1970). *Antiq.* **44**, 19–25.

Van de Breek, J. H. M. (1956–9). *Palaeohistoria* **5–7**, 7–18.

Verheyleweghen, J. (1962). *Hel.* **2**, 193–214.

Verheyleweghen, J. (1966). *Palaeohistoria* **12**, 529–558.

Vertes, L. (1964). *Acta Archaeol.* **16**, 187–215.

Wade, A. G. (1922). *Proc. prehist. Soc. East Anglia* **4**, 82–91.

Wainwright, G. A. (1936). *Antiq.* **10**, 5–24.

Wainwright, G. A. (1944). *Antiq.* **18**, 57–64.

Wainwright, G. J. and Longworth, I. H. (1971). Report on Research Committee of Soc. Antiq. London. No. 29.

Waterbolk, A. T. and Butler, J. J. (1965). *Hel.* **5**, 227–251.

Webster, G. (1955). *Ant. J.* **35**, 199–216.

Wertime, T. A. (1964). *Science* **146**, 1257–1267.

Willert, H. (1951). *Bergb.-Rudsch.* **3**, 268–275.

Wilson, A. E. (1955). *Sussex archaeol. Coll.* **93**, 59–74.

Wilson, A. J. (1977). *Engng Mining J.* **178**, 12, 68–73.

Worth, R. N. (1874). *Archaeol. J.* **31**, 53–60.

Zschocke, K. and Preuschen, E. (1932). *In* "Materealien zur Urgeschichte Österreichs." Vienna Museum, Vienna.

Zschocke, K., Preuschen, E. and Pittioni, R. (1934). *Mitt. anthrop.* **64**, 327.

Index